Climate Change: Impacts on UK Forests

Edited by Mark Broadmeadow

Edinburgh: Forestry Commission

ICF

INSTITUTE OF
CHARTERED
FORESTERS

Applications for reproduction of any part of this Bulletin should be addressed to:
HMSO, Licensing Division, St Clements House, 2–16 Colegate, Norwich NR3 1BQ.

First published in 2002 by the Forestry Commission, 231 Corstorphine Road, Edinburgh EH12 7AT.

ISBN 0 85538 554 5

BROADMEADOW, MARK, S.J. ed. (2002)
Climate change: impacts on UK forests
Forestry Commission Bulletin 125
Forestry Commission, Edinburgh. i–xii + 1–198pp.

FDC 111.83:(410)

Keywords: climate change; elevated CO_2; entomology; forestry; forest management; modelling; pathology; phenology; species suitability; stability; water use; wind.

Printed in the United Kingdom
on Robert Horne Hello Matt

FCBU125/PPD(ECD/KMA)/LTHPT-2500/FEB02

Acknowledgements

I am indebted to the many colleagues within Forest Research who diligently refereed the papers presented in this Bulletin, but particularly to Andy Moffat. I would also like to thank the Institute of Chartered Foresters for organising the meeting in April 2000, from which this publication was born. The Bulletin could not have been produced without the hard and timely work of Kirstie Adamson and Elaine Dick of Policy and Practice Division, and the overseeing hand of Helen McKay. Thanks are also due to the many individuals and organisations who have made data and photographs available; they are acknowledged in the individual chapters. My final thanks must go to Jenny Claridge, for keeping me in line and ensuring the high quality of the text.

Unless otherwise credited, photographs are from FORESTLIFE Picture Library 0131 334 0303 and Forest Research Photo Library.

Contents

Foreword   v

Summary   vii
Résumé   viii
Zusammenfassung   ix
Crynodeb   x

List of Contributors   xi

Section one: Background

1.   Global climate change: setting the context   1
2.   The changing climate of the UK: now and in the future   9

Section two: Climate change impacts

3.   Climate change and damage to trees caused by extremes of temperature   29
4.   Climate change impacts: storms   41
5.   Implications of climate change: soil and water   53
6.   Climate change and the seasonality of woodland flora and fauna   69
7.   Effects of climate change on fungal diseases of trees   83
8.   Climate change: implications for forest insect pests   99
9.   Impacts of increased CO_2 concentrations on tree growth and function   119
10.   Impacts of climate change on forest growth   141

Section three: Predictions and responses

11.   Modelling the future climatic suitability of plantation forest tree species   151
12.   Impacts on the distribution of plant species found in native beech woodland   169
13.   Challenges ahead: how should the forestry sector respond?   181

Appendix one: ICF Position Statement On Climate Change   191

Foreword

'As we start this new century we know that, unless everyone fights to counteract the worst effects of climate change, people all over the world face more frequent severe weather conditions, rising sea levels and devastating floods, together with their growing economic and human costs.'

The Rt Hon John Prescott MP, Deputy Prime Minister
(UK Climate Change Programme Consultation, 2000)

In April 2000, the Institute of Chartered Foresters and the Forestry Commission jointly organised a highly successful Conference *Trees and Climate Change*. The Conference brought together leading experts in policy, science and technology to address a forestry audience on the implications of climate change for trees and woodlands and on the importance of forests to the global carbon cycle. A selection of papers presented to the Conference are reproduced, appropriately updated, in the Bulletin.

I was fortunate in being able to attend the conference in my capacities both as the current President of the Institute of Chartered Foresters and as Head of the Forestry Commission's Policy and Practice Division with responsibilities for advising on forestry policy in relation to climate change.

Since April 2000, there have been many important developments in our understanding of climate change and in UK and international policy. In November 2000 the Parties to the UN Framework Convention on Climate Change held their 6th Conference of the Parties in the Hague, aimed at resolving some of the outstanding issues in the Kyoto Protocol, which they had signed in 1997. Although the Conference in the Hague failed to reach agreement, the substantial progress made there led to the successful Conferences in Bonn in July 2001 and Marrakech in October/November 2001. The UK took a leading role in developing the packages of measures that tied together these complicated negotiations, and UK scientists and negotiators will undoubtedly continue to be heavily involved in the international drive to achieve mitigation of climate change.

The UK is among the very few countries to have produced a comprehensive domestic strategy for climate change. This was published as *Climate Change – The UK Programme* in November 2000 to coincide with the Hague Conference. The UK Programme sets out the measures we will take as part of the international effort to mitigate climate change and how we will prepare to adapt to any changes that may occur. The Forestry Commission and the Northern Ireland Forest Service were involved in producing the UK Programme. We and our colleagues in Northern Ireland will continue to be involved at UK and country level in developing policy and in briefing our UK negotiators on forestry issues as they follow up the success of the Marrakech conference.

Trees and woodlands hold an important place in the debate on climate change. Not only do they play a role in locking up carbon and as a source of renewable energy and construction material, but they are themselves also vulnerable to environmental change. Practising foresters and arborists are key players in our national efforts to achieve sustainable development. They are used to thinking long-term and dealing with uncertainty. I hope this Bulletin will help set the context for them to continue to manage our trees, woodlands and forests in a changing environment.

Tim Rollinson

President
Institute of Chartered Foresters
February 2002

Summary

It is now widely accepted that mankind's activities are having a discernible effect on the global climate, and these changes will impact upon the functioning of many of the planet's natural systems. Climate change will have a variety of direct and indirect effects on forests and, thus, will have implications for forest management. This Bulletin presents current thinking on how climate change predictions for the UK may affect tree growth, health and productivity, and also how they may impact upon the functioning of forest ecosystems. The Bulletin covers the potential impacts of climate change on UK forestry but not the role that forestry may play in mitigating climate change through carbon sequestration and fossil fuel substitution.

Climate scenarios for the UK, based on results downscaled to a 10 km grid from the Hadley Centre global climate model, HADCM2, are presented. The direct impacts of these climate change scenarios on forest growth and condition are then discussed – specifically the effects of changing temperature and water supply, and the increased incidence of storms. The predictions are made largely by comparison to past climate events which demonstrate the likely magnitude of any climate change impacts. The direct effects of rising atmospheric carbon dioxide concentrations are also presented, using examples from a range of long-term impact studies. The observed trends in forest yield indices are discussed in the light of both rising carbon dioxide levels and the fertilisation effect of anthropogenic nitrogen emissions and deposition. In addition to the observed rise in forest productivity resulting from changes to the climate and atmospheric composition, the functioning of forest ecosystems has also changed. This is demonstrated through the description of a number of examples where the phenology, or timing of specific events, has changed over the course of the past few decades, including a discussion of how climate change may impact upon the distribution of woodland flora and fauna. An assessment is also made of both the direct and indirect effects of tree pests and pathogens, including some of the current most damaging agents of forest decline, and a review of how some more exotic insects and diseases may become more prevalent in the future.

The response of the forestry sector in the UK must be made on the basis of robust predictions of the future effects of climate change, which, in turn, are reliant on validated models of forest growth and function. A number of modelling approaches are described, varying from simple empirical to some of the state-of-the-art mechanistic or physiological models, including predictions as to future growth and condition trends of UK forests. However, predictions are only as good as the scenarios they are based upon, and the range of climatic, edaphic and biological factors that are considered. The limits to our ability to predict the future of our forests are discussed in detail. Nevertheless, forestry policy is being formulated in the light of current knowledge of the most likely effects of global warming, and, out of necessity, will be subject to revision as we gain in our understanding of the impacts and consequences of climate change through continuing research.

Résumé

On accepte désormais généralement que les activités humaines ont un effet discernable sur le climat mondial, et que ces changements auront des incidences sur le fonctionnement d'un grand nombre des systèmes naturels de la planète. Le changement climatique exercera une variété d'effets directs et indirects sur les forêts et aura donc des implications au niveau de la gestion forestière. Ce bulletin présente les opinions actuelles sur la façon dont, selon les prédictions les plus récentes, le changement climatique au Royaume-Uni pourrait influer sur la croissance des arbres, leur santé et leur productivité, en même temps que d'avoir des incidences sur le fonctionnement des écosystèmes forestiers. Ce bulletin couvre les répercussions que pourrait avoir le changement climatique sur la foresterie au Royaume-Uni, mais n'aborde pas le rôle que la foresterie pourrait jouer pour atténuer le changement climatique grâce à la séquestration du carbone et au remplacement des combustibles fossiles.

Des scénarios climatiques récents élaborés pour le Royaume-Uni et basés sur des résultats du modèle climatique mondial du Hadley Centre, HADCM2, réduits à l'échelle d'une grille de 10 km, sont présentés. Les incidences directes qu'auraient ces scénarios de changement climatique sur la croissance de la forêt et son état sont ensuite discutées — particulièrement les effets des changements de température et d'alimentation en eau, et la fréquence accrue des tempêtes. Ces prédictions sont faites dans une large mesure par comparaison avec des phénomènes climatiques passés démontrant l'ampleur probable de toute répercussion causée par le changement climatique. Les effets directs des concentrations croissantes de gaz carbonique dans l'atmosphère sont aussi présentés, en utilisant des exemples provenant d'une variété d'études réalisées sur leurs incidences à long terme. Les tendances ayant été observées dans les indices de rendement forestier sont discutées à la lumière des niveaux croissants de gaz carbonique et de l'effet fertilisant des émissions et du dépôt de nitrogène anthropiques. Outre cette augmentation observée de la productivité de la forêt résultant des changements du climat et de la composition atmosphérique, le fonctionnement des écosystèmes forestiers a aussi changé. Ce qui se trouve démontré par la description d'un certain nombre d'exemples pour lesquels la phénologie, ou chronologie des phénomènes spécifiques, a changé au cours des dernières décennies; les répercussions que pourraient avoir les changements climatiques sur la répartition de la faune et de la flore forestières sont aussi discutées. Une évaluation des effets directs et indirects des insectes nuisibles et agents pathogènes attaquant les arbres (dont certains des agents les plus nocifs du déclin forestier) se trouve aussi donnée, et l'on examine dans quelle mesure certains insectes et certaines maladies plus exotiques pourraient devenir plus répandus dans le futur.

La réponse du secteur forestier du Royaume-Uni doit se faire sur la base de prédictions solides sur les effets à venir du changement climatique, qui, à leur tour, dépendent de modèles fiables simulant la croissance et la fonction de la forêt. Le bulletin décrit un certain nombre d'approches de modélisation, allant du modèle empirique simple, aux modèles mécanistes ou physiologiques dernier cri, y compris les prédictions relatives aux tendances qui marqueront la croissance et l'état des forêts du Royaume-Uni dans le futur. Toutefois la justesse des prédictions est étroitement liée à celle des scénarios sur lesquels elles s'appuient, et à l'éventail des facteurs climatiques, édaphiques et biologiques considérés. Les limites restreignant notre capacité de prédire l'avenir de nos forêts se trouvent discutées en détail. Néanmoins, la politique forestière est formulée à la lumière des connaissances que nous avons actuellement des effets les plus probables du réchauffement planétaire, et, par nécessité, devra être révisée au fur et à mesure que nous verrons notre compréhension des incidences et des conséquences des changements climatiques s'améliorer grâce à des recherches continues.

Zusammenfassung

Es wird heutzutage allgemein akzeptiert, dass menschliche Aktivitäten einen wahrnehmbaren Einfluß auf das Weltklima haben und dass diese Veränderungen die Funktionen vieler natürlicher Systeme unseres Planeten beeinflussen werden. Eine Klimaänderung wird eine Vielzahl von direkten und indirekten Auswirkungen auf Wälder, und somit auch auf die Forstbewirtschaftung haben. Dieses Bulletin präsentiert die derzeitige Auffassung, wie sich die neuesten Vorhersagen zur Klimaänderung in Großbritannien auf Wachstum, Gesundheit und Produktivität der Baumbestände sowie die Funktion der Waldökosysteme auswirken könnten und es behandelt die möglichen Einflüsse einer Klimaänderung auf die Forstwirtschaft Großbritanniens. Es befaßt sich aber nicht mit der Rolle, die die Forstwirtschaft in Hinsicht auf eine Abschwächung der Klimaänderung spielen könnte, wie etwa durch dauerhafte Kohlenstoff-Fixierung und Ersatz fossiler Energieträger.

Es werden neue Klimaszenarien für Großbritannien vorgestellt, basierend auf Ergebnissen des Weltklimamodells (HADCM2) des Hadley Centres, die auf ein 10 km-Gitternetz bezogen wurden. Die direkten Einflüsse dieser Szenarien zur Klimaänderung auf Wachstum und Zustand der Wälder werden diskutiert – insbesondere die Wirkungen veränderter Temperaturen und einer veränderten Wasserversorgung, und die zunehmende Häufigkeit von Stürmen. Die Vorhersagen basieren größtenteils auf Vergleichen mit zurückliegenden Klimaereignissen, welche das wahrscheinliche Ausmaß möglicher Klimaänderungen deutlich machen. Weiterhin werden die direkten Auswirkungen ansteigender Kohlenstoffdioxidkonzentrationen in der Atmosphäre anhand einer Reihe von Langzeitstudien dargelegt. Die erkennbaren Trends in den verzeichneten Forsterträgen werden sowohl angesichts steigender Kohlenstoffdioxidwerte als auch unter Berücksichtigung des Düngungseffektes von anthropogenen Stickstoffimmissionen und –ablagerungen diskutiert. Neben der beobachteten Zunahme der Forstproduktivität aufgrund klimatischer und atmosphärischer Veränderungen hat sich auch die Funktion der Waldökosysteme verändert. Dies wird anhand einiger Beispiele dargestellt, bei denen sich die Phänologie oder der Zeitpunkt bestimmter Ereignisse im Laufe der letzten Jahrzehnte verändert hat. Es wird ebenfalls diskutiert, wie sich eine Klimaänderung auf die Verbreitung der Waldflora und –fauna auswirken könnte. Sowohl direkte als auch indirekte Einflüsse von Baumschädlingen und –krankheiten werden bewertet, einschließlich derjenigen Organismen, die zurzeit die schlimmsten Waldschäden verursachen. Auch einige im Moment eher seltenere, exotische Insekten und Krankheiten, die jedoch in Zukunft häufiger auftreten könnten, werden genannt.

Die Reaktion des Forstsektors in Großbritannien muss auf zuverlässigen Vorhersagen zu den Einflüssen von Klimaänderungen in der Zukunft beruhen, diese wiederum sollen sich auf überprüfte Modelle für Waldwuchs und –funktion gründen. Eine Reihe von Herangehensweisen zur Modellerstellung werden beschrieben. Sie reichen von einfachen, auf Erfahrung aufbauenden Modellen bis hin zu einigen modernen mechanistischen oder physiologischen Modellen und beinhalten Trendvorhersagen über Wachstum und Zustand britischer Wälder. Vorhersagen jedoch sind nur so gut wie die Daten, auf denen sie basieren, und das Spektrum von klimatischen, edaphischen und biologischen Faktoren, die sie betrachten. Die Grenzen unserer Fähigkeit, die Zukunft unserer Wälder vorherzusagen, werden im Detail diskutiert. Trotzdem wird Forstpolitik heute angesichts des derzeitigen Kenntnisstands über die Auswirkungen einer weltweiten Erwärmung gemacht, die am wahrscheinlichsten sind. Sie wird zwangsläufig überarbeitet werden müssen, wenn zukünftige Forschung unser Verständnis von Wirkungen und Konsequenzen einer Klimaänderung vergrößert.

Crynodeb

Derbynnir yn eang bellach bod gweithgareddau dynol ryw yn cael effaith ganfyddadwy ar hinsawdd y byd, a bydd y newidiadau hyn yn cael effaith ar weithrediad llawer o systemau naturiol y planed. Caiff newid hinsoddol amrywiaeth o effeithiau uniongyrchol ac anuniongyrchol ar goedwigoedd, ac felly bydd gan hyn oblygiadau am reolaeth goedwig. Mae'r Bwletin hwn yn cyflwyno'r syniadau cyfoes ar sut y gallai'r rhagddywediadau diweddaraf am newid hinsoddol effeithio ar dyfiant, iechyd a chynhyrchedd coed a hefyd sut y gallent effeithio ar weithrediad ecosystemau coedwigoedd. Mae'r Bwletin yn cynnwys effeithiau posibl newid hinsoddol ar goedwigaeth Prydain ond nid y rhan y gallai coedwigaeth ei chwarae wrth liniaru newid hinsoddol trwy ymneilltuo carbon ac amnewidiad tanwydd.

Cyflwynir yma rhagdybiadau hinsoddol am y DU, ar sail canlyniadau diweddar a leihawyd i grid 10 km o fodel hinsawdd y byd yr Hadley Centre, HADCM2. Yna trafodir effeithiau uniongyrchol y rhagdybiaethau newidiadau hinsoddol hyn ar dyfiant ac ansawdd coedwigoedd - yn benodol effeithiau newid mewn tymheredd a chyflenwad dŵr, ac amledd cynyddol stormydd. Gwneir y rhagdybiaethau i raddau helaeth trwy gymariaethau i ddigwyddiadau hinsoddol yn y gorffennol sydd yn arddangos maint tybiaethol unrhyw effeithiau newid hinsoddol. Cyflwynir hefyd effeithiau uniongyrchol y cynnydd yng nghrynhoad carbon diocsid yn yr awyr, gan ddefnyddio enghreifftiau o ystod o astudiaethau'r effeithiau hir gyfnod. Trafodir y tueddiadau a welwyd mewn mynegyddion cynnyrch coedwigoedd yng ngoleuni y codiad mewn lefelau carbon diocsid ac effeithiau ffrwythloni gollyngiadau a gwaddodiadau nitrogen anthropogenig. Ar ben y codiad a welwyd mewn cynhyrchedd coedwigoedd sydd yn ganlyniad newidiadau i'r hinsawdd a chyfansoddiad atmosfferig, mae gweithrediad ecosystemau coedwigoedd wedi newid hefyd. Dangosir hyn trwy ddisgrifiad nifer o enghreifftiau lle mae ffenoleg, neu amseriad digwyddiadau penodol, wedi newid dros y degawdau diweddaraf, gan gynnwys trafodaeth o sut y gall newid hinsoddol effeithio ar ddosbarthiad llystyfiant a chreaduriaid y coedwigoedd. Ceir asesiad hefyd o'r effeithiau uniongyrchol ac anuniongyrchol plâu a phathogenau coed, gan gynnwys rhai o'r ysgogwyr mwyaf andwyol dirywiad coedwig, ac arolwg o sut y gall rhai o'r trychfilod ac afiechydon mwy ecsotig fynd yn fwy mynych yn y dyfodol.

Rhaid i sector coedwigaeth y DU ymateb ar sail rhagdybiaethau cedyrn o effeithiau newid hinsoddol i'r dyfodol, sydd, yn eu tro yn dibynnu ar fodelau dilysiedig o dyfiant a gweithrediad coedwigoedd. Disgrifir nifer o agweddau modelu sydd yn amrywio o'r empirig syml hyd at fodelau mecanistig neu ffisiolegol diweddaraf, gan gynnwys rhagdybiaethau o dueddiadau tyfiant a chyflwr coedwigoedd y DU. Ond mae ansawdd y rhagdybiaeth yn dibynnu'n llwyr ar ansawdd y senarios y seilir nhw arnynt, ac ar yr ystod o ffactorau hinsoddol, edaffig a biolegol a ystyriwyd. Trafodir cyfyngiadau ein galluoedd i ragdybio dyfodol ein coedwigoedd yn fanwl. Serch hynny, llunir polisi coedwigaeth yng ngoleuni'r wybodaeth bresennol o effeithiau mwyaf tebygol cynhesiad byd-eang, ac o reidrwydd bydd yn agored i ddiwygiadau wrth i'n dealltwriaeth o effeithiau a chanlyniadau newid hinsoddol gynyddu trwy ymchwil barhaus.

List of contributors

Pam M. Berry
Environmental Change Institute,
University of Oxford,
1A Mansfield Road, Oxford, OX1 3SZ

Mark S.J. Broadmeadow
Environmental Research Branch,
Forest Research, Alice Holt Lodge,
Farnham, Surrey, GU10 4LH

Melvin G.R. Cannell
Centre for Ecology and Hydrology,
Bush Estate, Penicuik,
Midlothian, EH26 0QB

Terry P. Dawson
Environmental Change Institute,
University of Oxford,
1A Mansfield Road, Oxford, OX1 3SZ

Hugh Evans
Entomology Branch,
Forest Research, Alice Holt Lodge,
Farnham, Surrey, GU10 4LH

Barry A. Gardiner
Silviculture Branch,
Forest Research, Northern Research Station,
Roslin, Midlothian, EH25 9SY

John N. Gibbs
Pathology Branch,
Forest Research, Alice Holt Lodge,
Farnham, Surrey, GU10 4LH

Robin M.A. Gill
Woodland Ecology Branch,
Forest Research, Alice Holt Lodge,
Farnham, Surrey, GU10 4LH

Paula A. Harrison
Environmental Change Institute,
University of Oxford,
1A Mansfield Road, Oxford, OX1 3SZ

Steven J. Hendry
Pathology Branch,
Forest Research, Northern Research Station,
Roslin, Midlothian, EH25 9SY

Mike Hulme
Tyndall Centre for Climate Change Research,
School of Environmental Sciences,
University of East Anglia, Norwich, NR4 7TJ

David Lonsdale
Pathology Branch,
Forest Research, Alice Holt Lodge,
Farnham, Surrey, GU10 4LH

Tom R. Nisbet
Environmental Research Branch,
Forest Research, Alice Holt Lodge,
Farnham, Surrey, GU10 4LH

Richard G. Pearson
Environmental Change Institute,
University of Oxford,
1A Mansfield Road, Oxford, OX1 3SZ

Graham D. Pyatt
Woodland Ecology Branch,
Forest Research, Northern Research Station,
Roslin, Midlothian, EH25 9SY

Chris P. Quine
Woodland Ecology Branch, Forest Research,
Northern Research Station, Midlothian, EH25 9SY

Tim J. Randle
Mensuration Branch, Forest Research, Alice Holt
Lodge, Farnham, Surrey, GU10 4LH

Duncan Ray
Woodland Ecology Branch, Forest Research,
Northern Research Station, Midlothian, EH25 9SY

Derek B. Redfern
Pathology Branch, Forest Research, Northern
Research Station, Roslin, Midlothian, EH25 9SY

Tim Rollinson
Policy and Practice Division, Forestry Commission,
231 Corstorphine Road, Edinburgh, EH12 7AT

Institute of Chartered Foresters, 7A St Colme Street,
Edinburgh, EH3 6AA

Tim H. Sparks
Centre for Ecology and Hydrology,
Monks Wood, Abbots Ripton,
Huntingdon, Cambridgeshire PE28 2LS

Nigel A. Straw
Entomology Branch,
Forest Research, Alice Holt Lodge,
Farnham, Surrey, GU10 4LH

Alan D. Watts
Centre for Ecology and Hydrology,
Hill of Brathens,
Banchory, Aberdeenshire, AB31 4BY

Background

1. Global climate change: setting the context   1

2. The changing climate of the UK: now and in the future   9

1

Global Climate Change: Setting the Context

Forestry and climate

The association between climate and forestry has been a matter of discussion for many centuries with, for example, John Evelyn highlighting the importance of water, sun and temperature to the success of plantations in his treatise to the Royal Society in 1662[1]:

> '...Water in this action ... does not as we affirmed, operate to the full extent ... without the soil and temper of the climate co-operate' and 'This we find, that the hot and warmer regions produce the tallest and goodliest trees' and 'as is found in our American plantations, ... both since so much improved by felling and clearing these spacious shades and letting in the air and sun.'

These observations may seem outdated, but many of the modern approaches to forestry, including provenance selection and silvicultural management are based on the long-standing knowledge of the relationships between climate and forest productivity. It is therefore not surprising that there is great concern over the implications of a changing climate to the forestry industry, particularly since the species and provenances planted at present and in the recent past reflect the current climate. There are also a number of species important in ancient and semi-natural woodlands which are close to or at their climate limits, and thus conservation and biodiversity benefits may be threatened. Among the questions that need to be answered (and asked in some cases) are: Will the species and provenances currently planted survive under a changed climate? Will forest productivity change (for the better or worse)? Do management practices need to change? What are the consequences for habitat action plans? Are conservation and recreation benefits threatened? Can forestry play a significant role in counteracting climate change?

These questions are not easy to answer. Firstly, we do not know what a future climate will bring. Secondly, even if we could second-guess the *climate*, predicting the *weather* and, most importantly, the extreme events such as droughts and storms, is not possible. Finally, it is difficult to make integrated assessments of the impact of climate change on the complex processes and interactions present within forest ecosystems.

Climate change and forestry research

Much research undertaken by both the Forestry Commission and other research and academic institutions relates directly to the debate over the responses of forests to climate change. Numerous examples exist, but the following are some of the key research areas where a considerable body of relevant data already exists:

- provenance trials;
- yield modelling;
- site-yield research for Sitka spruce, Corsican pine, Douglas fir and for lowland forestry;
- investigations of climate related pathology, particularly drought and temperature;
- modelling of wind, storms and forest stability;
- species suitability and Ecological Site Classification modelling;
- studies of physiological responses to drought;
- research into the climate dependency of pathogen and insect pest outbreaks;
- assessments of the carbon balance of peatland after clear-fell and re-stocking;
- studies on the impact of rising atmospheric carbon dioxide concentrations;
- research into the improvement of genetic stock (particularly Sitka spruce);
- climate requirements for native species.

Forestry research in the UK is therefore in a strong position to apply the knowledge gained across this wide range of research areas to help answer the $64 000 question – 'How will UK forestry respond to climate change?' This Bulletin brings together many of these separate research programmes, in some cases drawing together the fruits of over fifty years research, and presents analyses of how forestry in the UK is likely to respond over the coming century. The majority of the information summarised in this Bulletin was presented at a conference in Glasgow in April 2000, while additional information available within Forest Research is also presented. The range of individual subject areas that are relevant to climate change indicates the importance of an integrated approach and, over the coming years, of providing robust predictions of the impacts of climate change on forestry.

What is climate change?

The relevance of climate change to our everyday lives has been growing over the last decade, and the evidence of global climate change is now stronger than ever[2]. In the past, a number of phrases have encompassed what we mean by *anthropogenically driven environmental change*. These terms have included *global warming*, the *greenhouse effect* and *climate change* itself. What we really mean, is how regional or local climate is affected by changes to the global climate as a result of man's emissions of greenhouse gases. In the UK, we have witnessed droughts, floods and storms over recent years, which may or may not be directly related to global climate change – whether or not these natural events do represent the first signs of climate change, the consensus view is that they represent the direction in which our climate is likely to move. To these climate driven impacts should also be added the consequences of some of mankind's other activities, including rising tropospheric ozone pollution, and enhanced atmospheric nitrogen deposition.

Is climate change inevitable?

Mankind can act to reduce the rate at which greenhouse gas concentrations are rising – both through reducing emissions of those gases such as carbon dioxide and methane, and through locking up the main culprit, carbon dioxide (sequestration). What is often not made clear is the immediacy that is required for any of these actions, as a result of the inertia that is present within the greenhouse gas balance of the atmosphere, and also within the global climate system: carbon dioxide concentrations will stabilise over 100–300 years; global temperature over a few centuries, and sea level rise, over several millennia[3]. Given that the global population is expected to double by about 2050, and that developing countries and countries in transition will have significantly higher power requirements over the coming decades, it is unlikely that global carbon emissions will peak in the near future, unless a low carbon economy is put in place through international negotiation and initiatives.

The Intergovernmental Panel on Climate Change has assessed a wide range of global economic development pathways for the planet, and developed a set of emissions scenarios for these[4]. For all six of the emissions scenarios, the implications are that atmospheric carbon dioxide concentrations rise sharply, reaching levels of between 540 and 970 ppm by the year 2100. The uncertainty in predictions of future greenhouse gas concentrations and thus global temperature rise is no reason for complacency – the key message is that climate change will become a fact of life, and its effects must be mitigated or adapted to.

The role of carbon sequestration

The role of carbon sequestration in limiting the rise in atmospheric carbon dioxide concentrations has been discussed widely. The successful management of carbon sinks can reduce the rate of carbon emissions into the atmosphere, and certainly, if these carbon stocks were lost to the atmosphere, the consequences would be extremely serious for global carbon balance. However, carbon sequestration is not an option in isolation. In the UK, carbon sequestration through sink management and afforestation can only act as one, probably small, element in our national commitment to reductions in global carbon emissions, since the carbon stocks of the UK forest estate are of the order of only one year's emissions. Furthermore, once woodland is mature, it is at best a very weak sink, and might be vulnerable to climate change itself, with the potential for large carbon emissions in the future. At a global scale, carbon emissions are currently approximately 6.5 [a]GtC yr^{-1}, and are predicted to peak at 10–20 GtC yr^{-1} over the next 50 years[2]. The global sequestration potential of the biosphere has been estimated as only 100 GtC over the next 50 years, thus highlighting that although important in the short-term, particularly for gaining time to implement low carbon technologies, sequestration projects can make little impact on the global carbon budget. An additional role that forests might play in carbon balance is through the potential for forest residues to provide wood-fuel for energy generation and substituting for fossil fuels.

The UK Climate Impacts Programme

An important national research and assessment programme was established in 1997 by the then UK Government, Department of the

---

[a]1 gigatonne is 10^{15}g, or one thousand million tonnes

Environment, entitled the UK Climate Impacts Programme (UKCIP). The primary aim of the Programme is to raise the profile of climate change awareness, and to facilitate both individual sector and integrated assessments of climate change impacts. To help focus resources at a local level, the programme has promoted a series of regional studies of climate change impacts[5,6], which for two regions, East Anglia and the North West have culminated in fully integrated assessments through the REGIS study[7]. Sectoral studies of the implications for climate change have also been undertaken, including impacts on UK nature conservation[8] and natural ecosystem responses[9] (see Chapter 12). However, the most important output from the programme has been the climate scenarios for the 2020s, 2050s and 2080s[10] which are described in detail in Chapter 2, and are either referred to, or used directly in the majority of the chapters in this Bulletin. Recently published socio-economic scenarios are also now available[11]. Although the work presented in this Bulletin (apart from Chapter 12) was not undertaken as part of the UK Climate Impacts Programme, where implications of climate change are described in terms of the climate scenarios, they are fully compatible with the other outputs from UKCIP.

Aims of the Bulletin

This Bulletin covers the direct impacts of global climate change on UK forestry, including an assessment of how interactions with other biotic and abiotic factors may affect these impacts. It does not cover subject areas such as carbon sequestration, fossil fuel substitution, or indeed, the global carbon cycle in detail. These are important areas in their own right, and would warrant their own treatment. However, as they have policy implications, they are discussed briefly, but the emphasis of the Bulletin is on the consequences of changes to the physical environment of forests. It may be argued that it is difficult to

separate physical from socio-economic impacts of climate change. Pressures from recreation and falling timber prices together with other constraints resulting from national policy and land-use change may alter the appearance of UK forestry to a greater extent than the predicted changes to our climate alone. However, a thorough evaluation of socio-economic issues relating to global climate change can only be undertaken if the direct impacts of climate change on forest growth and function are more fully understood – the *raison d'être* for this publication.

This Bulletin is intended to provide general information to forest managers and others involved in the forestry industry, explaining the scientific basis for the tentative recommendations that are made. It also provides a knowledge base in anticipation of recommendations and advice that may be given in the future. Its target audience is not restricted to the forestry industry, and because of the large range of subject areas covered, it will be of value to students and researchers who require a wide but detailed coverage of climate oriented forestry research.

Structure of the Bulletin

The Bulletin is presented as three sections. Firstly, an introductory section describes scenarios of how, it is thought, global warming will affect the climate of the UK (Chapter 2). This includes a discussion of the timeframe over which climate change is expected to progress and, most importantly, an indication of the areas of uncertainty and the magnitude of these potential errors. It is important to realise that scenarios are not forecasts, but that they represent a consensus view of the direction and likely scale of any changes. In the second section, the impacts of climate change on individual aspects of forest growth, condition and ecology are assessed. Each of the broad climatic drivers; temperature (Chapter 3), wind (Chapter 4) and rainfall and water balance

(Chapter 5) are dealt with in turn. Many of these predictions are made on the back of experience of climate extremes to date, using case studies. To these three drivers must be added a fourth environmental variable – carbon dioxide concentration – or, as described in the 1970s, the 'joker in the pack', referring to its 'beneficial' effect of preventing the next ice-age being forecast at that time[12]. Experience-based analysis cannot shed light on the impacts of rising carbon dioxide levels, but the results of experimental impact studies are described in Chapter 9. There is, however, evidence that forest growth rates have increased in recent years, and the relative contribution from a number of factors, including rising carbon dioxide concentrations are discussed in Chapter 10. The second section also provides assessments of how climate change may affect diseases and insect pests of forest trees (Chapters 7 and 8), and also, how climate warming could influence the activity and seasonality of forest fauna and flora (Chapter 6). The final section describes how predictions of the future of UK forests can be made using state-of-the-art models. As well as a general description of modelling approaches to forestry, specific examples are given of their application to species suitability for commercial forestry in the light of climate change (Chapter 11) and to wildlife and conservation value (Chapter 12). A discussion of the implications of these assessments for forestry policy is also given (Chapter 13). Detailed information is provided within each chapter, while key findings are presented for each, and summarised in the concluding chapter.

The reality of climate change research in a forestry context

Although some of the individual aspects of predicted climate change are relatively easy to identify – and indeed, each is dealt with as a single chapter in this Bulletin – it is the interactions between these single factors that makes the prediction of overall impacts of global climate change on UK forestry an all but impossible task. These potential interactions are evident in the example given in Figure 1.1, where a simplified flow diagram illustrates the network of inter-related factors influencing the overall effect of temperature change on forest productivity. In this example, changing temperature not only impacts directly on the form and function of the tree, but also on pests, pathogens and the environment itself, through its effects on water balance, litter turnover and nutrient availability. Furthermore, changes to the timing and abundance of food sources such as foliage and seeds will have consequences for insect, bird and mammal species. Any discussion of the effects of climate change on a forest (or any other ecosystem) should always include an awareness of potential interactions of this nature.

It is apparent that while a simplified picture of the impacts of climate change can be portrayed, it is unlikely that the individual effects will exist in isolation. The findings of climate change research are thus more difficult to interpret than might appear at first sight, and it is essential that careful thought be given to any advice offered, particularly with regard to unseen interactions.

Forest management, research and the future

By its very nature, forestry has long lead times for the effects of decision-making and forest management to be borne out. Decisions implemented now will have consequences for the current rotation, and as time progresses, it will become more important to act. The difficult task is to balance taking proactive decisions now with an uncertain future ahead, with the potential for acting too late, but being more certain of the effects of and necessity for those actions. It would be ideal to employ 'no regret' strategies at this stage, and some are

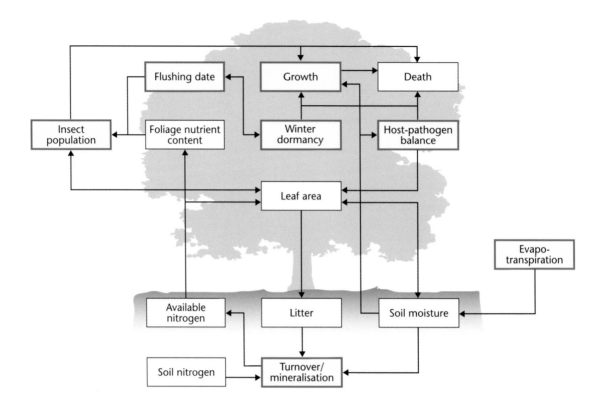

Figure 1.1 *Simplified flow diagram of the impact of temperature change (boxes with red outline) on forest ecosystem growth and function.*

available, particularly using best practice for current conditions and not taking risks. However, more detailed and targeted advice is needed now, and will become increasingly important as time progresses. Prescriptive advice cannot be given because of the uncertainties in the climate change predictions, the complex responses of forest ecosystems to them, and because of the difficulties of incorporating disease and insect driven damage and mortality within wider modelling frameworks. However, we are in a position where we can say what we think is likely to happen in general terms, and therefore there are conservative strategies that can be adopted. The Bulletin will provide UK forestry with an understanding of global climate change and how forests may respond to it. With a better understanding of the important issues,

informed decisions can be made now to protect the future of our forests.

Finally, it is clear that advice can only be developed and improved on the back of continuing research. This is essential so that new findings on the progress of climate change can be responded to, together with improvements in the range of uncertainties associated with climate change scenarios.

References

1. EVELYN, J. (1729). *Silva: or a discourse of forest-trees, and the propagation of timber in his majesty's dominions,* 5th edn. Walthoe and others, London.

2. IPCC (2001). *Climate change 2001: the scientific basis,* eds J.T. Houghton, Y. Ding, D.J. Griggs, M. Noguer, P.J. van der Linden and D. Xiaosu.

WG1 Report to the IPCC Third Assessment. Cambridge University Press, Cambridge.

3. IPCC (2001). *Climate change 2001: impacts, adaptations and vulnerability.* Summary for policymakers. Intergovernmental Panel on Climate Change. Cambridge University Press, Cambridge.

4. NAKICENOVIC, N., ALCAMO, J., DAVIS, G., DE VRIES, B., FENHANN, J., GAFFIN, S., GREGORY, K., GRUBLER, A., JUNG, T.Y., RAM, T.K., LA ROVERE, E.L., MICHAELIS, L., MORI, S., MORITA, T., PEPPER, W., PITCHER, H., PRICE, L., RAIHI, K., ROEHRL, A., ROGNER, H.-H., SANKOVSKI, A., SCHLESINGER, M., SHUKLA, P., SMITH, S., SWART, R., VAN ROOIJEN, S., VICTOR, N. and DADI, Z. (2000). *Emissions scenarios.* A special report of Working Group III of the Intergovernmental Panel on Climate Change. Cambridge University Press, Cambridge, UK and New York, NY, USA.

5. WADE, S., HOSSELL, J., HOUGH, M. and FENN, C., eds (1999). *The impacts of climate change in the South East.* Technical report. W.S. Atkins, Epsom.

6. NAW (2000). *Wales: changing climate, challenging choices: the impacts of climate change in Wales from 2000 to 2080.* Technical report. The National Assembly for Wales, Cardiff.

7. HOLMAN, I. and LOVELAND, P. (2001). *Regional climate impact studies in East Anglia and North West England.* Final report to MAFF, DETR and UKWIR. Soil Survey and Land Research Centre, Silsoe.

8. HOSSELL, J.E., BRIGGS, B. and HEPBURN, I.R. (2000). *Climate change and nature conservation: a review of the impact of climate change on UK species and habitat conservation policy.* HMSO, DETR and MAFF, London.

9. HARRISON, P.A., BERRY, P.M. and DAWSON, T. P. (2001). *MONARCH: modelling natural resources responses to climate change.* Final Report to Funding Partners. Environmental Change Institute, University of Oxford.

10. HULME, M. and JENKINS, G.J. (1998). *Climate change scenarios for the United Kingdom.* UKCIP Technical Report No.1. Climatic Research Unit, University of East Anglia, Norwich.

11. UKCIP (2001). *Thinking ahead: socio-economic scenarios for climate change impact assessment.* UK Climate Impacts Programme, Oxford..

12. GRIBBIN, J. (1978). *The climate threat.* Collins, Glasgow.

CHAPTER TWO   Mike Hulme

The Changing Climate of the UK: Now and in the Future

KEY FINDINGS

- There is convincing evidence that human activities, notably the burning of fossil coal, oil and gas for energy and changing land use, are altering the global climate.

- Analysis of historic climate data confirms that the UK climate has recently been warming at a rate of between 0.1ºC and 0.2ºC per decade; cold days are fewer, hot days are more frequent, and the growing season has lengthened. More of the annual precipitation falls in winter and less in summer, and more of the increased winter precipitation falls in heavier events.

- Future warming over the UK during the 21st century is likely to be in the range of 0.1ºC to 0.3ºC per decade, with more rapid warming in the southeast compared to the northwest. Warm years, such as 1997, will become increasingly frequent – for some scenarios by the 2080s, nearly all years will be warmer than 1997.

- Winters in the UK are likely to become wetter, summers perhaps a little drier. Summer soil moisture levels will decrease. Precipitation events, especially in the winter half-year, are likely to become more intense.

- There is rather mixed evidence for changes to the storm regime of the UK. Very severe winter gales may increase in number, as may summer gales, but the changes are not large and the conclusion is not robust.

- Climate warming will cause further rises in sea-level around the UK shoreline – by between 1 cm and 10 cm per decade over the next 100 years. Relative sea-level will increase the most in the areas where land is already sinking, for example the southeast, and will increase the least in the north and west. Extreme high water levels for many parts of the UK shoreline are likely to increase.

What is happening to global climate and why?

The changing global climate

Evidence for the warming of our planet over the past one hundred years is now overwhelming[1]. This is seen not only in climate observations, but also in physical and biological indicators of environmental change such as retreating glaciers, thinning of Arctic sea-ice and longer growing seasons. Scientists are also increasingly confident that many of the patterns associated with this warming suggest an anthropogenic influence on climate[2]. This raises the remarkable likelihood that over the next one hundred years we will fashion a climate on Earth that will be warmer than any that the human species has previously lived through. The rate of this change may be unprecedented in the history of our planet and may induce significant risks for human welfare and sustainability.

Recent work[3] has established the first reconstructions of Northern Hemisphere surface air temperature for the last millennium based on a combination of tree-ring, ice core, coral and historical documentary evidence (Figure 2.1). While the uncertainty of these series increases further back in time, the data indicate relatively cool centuries between 1600 and 1900, highlight the effect of large volcanic eruptions in cooling the planet in certain years (e.g. 1601), and clearly suggest that the observed twentieth century warming has been most unusual. The year 1998 was probably the warmest of the last millennium.

Instrumental climate data allow us to monitor more accurately the changing global-mean air temperature since 1856. These data show a global warming at the surface of between 0.4°C and 0.8°C, with the six warmest years all occurring in the last decade. For the majority of land areas the recent warming has been greater at night-time than during the day, partly reflecting increased cloudiness over land. Data series are much shorter for upper air temperatures (above 8 km), but radiosonde measurements taken since the 1960s suggest that the lower stratosphere has been *cooling* at a rate of about 0.5°C per decade.

Figure 2.1 *Record of Northern Hemisphere mean summer surface air temperature (1000AD to 1998AD) reconstructed using palaeo-data and expressed as deviations from the 1961–90 average of 20.5°C. The observed data are shown in black. [Source: Tim Osborn, CRU].*

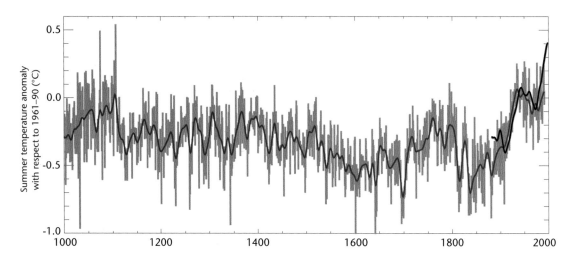

The human influence on climate

Why should the surface of the planet have warmed in such a way, while the lower stratosphere has cooled? Global climate can vary naturally, due both to what is called 'internal variability' within the climate system and to changes in external forcing unrelated to human activities – for example, changes in the sun's radiation and volcanic activity. Recent climate model simulations show that these natural causes of global temperature variability *cannot,* on their own, explain the observed surface warming[2]. When these simulations are repeated with rising historic concentrations of greenhouse gases and shifting distributions of sulphate aerosols, much better agreement between observed and modelled global patterns of temperature change is achieved. Although the precise contribution of human activities to global warming cannot yet be stated with confidence, it is clear that the planet would not be warming as rapidly if humans were not currently emitting about 6.5 billion tonnes of carbon into the global atmosphere each year. The Intergovernmental Panel on Climate Change (IPCC) concluded in its recent Third Assessment Report[4] that, '. . . *most of the warming observed over the last 50 years is likely to be attributable to human influence.*'

Possible future climates and sea-level rise

Given that humans are implicated in the cause of global warming, and recognising that the potential consequences of a rapidly warming climate for natural and human systems are large, it becomes important to estimate the possible range of future climates we will experience over future decades and centuries. Fundamental to this exercise are estimates of future greenhouse gas emissions – whether from energy, industrial or land-use sources. Of particular importance are estimates of future carbon dioxide (CO_2) emissions, the greenhouse gas that alone causes about 60–65% of the human-induced greenhouse effect. Recent calculations[4] suggest that, given the range of possible future emissions cited in the IPCC Special Report on Emissions Scenarios[5], the current 2001 CO_2 concentration of about 370 ppm would rise by 2100 to between 540 ppm and 970 ppm. These concentrations compare with concentrations before the industrial age of only about 280 ppm. Concentrations of other important greenhouse gases are also expected to continue rising, with changes in methane (-11 to +112%), nitrous oxide (+12 to +46%) and tropospheric ozone (-12 to +62%) predicted from the same set of emissions scenarios[5].

What effect will this growth in CO_2 and other greenhouse gas concentrations have on global climate? It depends largely on how sensitive the Earth's climate is to rising greenhouse gas concentrations. By combining a range of choices for the climate sensitivity[a] with the range of possible future emissions, a range of future changes in global temperature and sea-level can be calculated. The annual global-mean surface air temperature over the period 1961–90 was 14.0°C and this has already risen to 14.3°C during the 1990s. In the future, the planetary temperature reaches between 15.4°C and 19.8°C by 2100 according to the IPCC Third Assessment Report, representing rates of change of between 0.1°C and 0.5°C per decade. This compares to a global warming rate of 0.15°C per decade since the 1970s and a warming of about 0.05°C per decade since the late 19th century.

One of the most striking consequences of a warming climate will be the rise in global-mean sea-level. Observed sea-level has risen by between 10 and 25 cm over the last century, reaching its highest level during the 1997/98

---

[a]The climate sensitivity is defined as the change in global-mean temperature that would ultimately be reached following a doubling of CO_2 concentration in the atmosphere (e.g. from 275 ppm to 550 ppm). The IPCC have previously reported the likely range for this quantity to be between 1.5°C and 4.5°C.

El Niño event, and recent calculations[4] suggest a future rise of between 9 cm and 88 cm by 2100 compared to the average 1990 level. The largest contribution to this sea-level rise comes from the expansion of warmer ocean waters, while melting land glaciers contribute up to 20%.

Mitigating climate change and adapting to its effects

How much of this anticipated climate change can be averted by policy-directed reductions in greenhouse gas emissions? The answer depends both on how carbon and other emissions will evolve in the absence of climate policy and on the extent to which climate policy measures are introduced regionally or world-wide. For example, under the terms of the Kyoto Protocol, signed in 1997 but not yet ratified, greenhouse gas emissions from industrialised countries have to fall by the end of the first commitment period in 2012 to 5.2% below their 1990 levels[6]. This target, if achieved in isolation, would reduce future global warming to 2100 by at most 0.1°C to 0.2°C, depending on how the global economy evolves[7]. Of course, the intention behind the Protocol is for progressively larger reduction targets to be negotiated, ultimately involving a wider set of nations. Such longer-term, planned emissions reductions would achieve greater drawdown in the global warming rate, but most analysts would see such mitigation efforts – even under optimistic assumptions – limiting global warming by 2100 to a minimum of about 1.5°C.

Given this prospect of future climate change it is important that our climate change management strategy includes efforts *both* to slow the pace of change (mitigation by pursuing options for emissions reductions) *and* to anticipate the residual, unmitigated risks (adapting our resource and management systems to cope with changing climate and emerging climate change impacts).

What are climate change scenarios?

The rest of this chapter will translate the above global picture into a set of climate change scenarios for the UK. Climate scenarios present coherent, systematic and internally-consistent descriptions of changing climates. These scenarios are typically used as inputs into climate change vulnerability, impact or adaptation assessments, but are used in many different ways by many different individuals or organisations. Some studies may require only semi-quantitative descriptions of future climates, perhaps as part of a scoping study. Others may need quantification of a range of future climates, perhaps with explicit probabilities attached, as part of a risk assessment exercise. Others still may require information for very specific geographical areas. There is also a range of time horizons that may be considered relevant, depending on the type of decision to be made. Water companies may be concerned with operating conditions over the near-term (10–20 years), while coastal engineers or forestry investment decisions may need to consider longer-term horizons.

Climate change scenarios are most commonly constructed using results from global climate model (GCM) experiments. These model experiments provide fairly detailed descriptions of future climate change that can be used to inform vulnerability and adaptation assessments. GCM-based scenarios, however, are uncertain descriptions of future climate for a number of reasons[8].

One fundamental source of uncertainty in describing future climate originates from the unknown world future. How will global greenhouse gas emissions change in the future? Will we continue to be dominated by a carbon-intensive energy system? What environmental regulation may be introduced to control such emissions? Different answers to these questions can lead to a wide range of possible emissions scenarios[5]. Since any climate change GCM experiment has to choose an emissions scenario, different choices can lead to quite different climate outcomes.

The second main source of uncertainty in climate change prediction stems from different values of the climate sensitivity and from the contrasting behaviour of different climate models in their simulation of regional climate change. These latter differences are largely a function of the different schemes employed to represent important processes in the atmosphere and ocean (known as parameterisations) and the relatively coarse resolutions of the models. In the Hadley Centre GCM, for example, the UK land area is represented by just four gridboxes, making it impossible to differentiate between the climate change predicted for, say, the Lake District and Merseyside or for the Wash and the Thames Estuary.

Given the above difficulties in making firm predictions about future climate, how is it best to proceed? Do we try to make the 'best' judgement or most likely estimate of future greenhouse gas emissions, employ the 'best' model we can find, and then create the 'best' estimate of future climate change? This is the sort of approach that leads to a 'best guess' or 'business-as-usual' climate scenario. Alternatively do we consider a wide range of emissions scenarios and climate modelling uncertainties to try to capture a wide range of possible climate outcomes for a region like the UK? In this case we have to judge where the important extremes in the range of possibilities lie, but still keep the number of resulting climate scenarios to a manageable minimum. A third approach would be to establish probabilities for different levels of climate change within these ranges, rather than regarding each climate scenario as equally likely[9]. This allows uncertainties to be handled using risk management frameworks.

The climate scenarios used in this chapter are based on those published in 1998 for the UK Climate Impacts Programme – the so-called UKCIP98 scenarios[10]. These scenarios adopted the second approach described above, in that four alternative scenarios of climate change for the UK spanning a 'reasonable' range of possible future climates were presented. These scenarios were labelled Low, Medium-low, Medium-high and High, the labels referring to their respective global warming rates. The scenarios rely largely on two sets of GCM experiments completed by the Hadley Centre during 1995 and 1996. These experiments were undertaken using a coupled ocean-atmosphere GCM called HadCM2. This model has been extensively analysed and validated and represents one of the leading global climate models in the world. These UKCIP98 scenarios have been widely used in UK climate impacts assessments over the past four years. New modelling work has now been completed by the Hadley Centre and the next set of national UK scenarios for the UK Climate Impacts Programme will be published in April 2002.

Recent observed trends in UK climate

The UK possesses some of the most extensive instrumental climate time series in the world, the longest being the Central England Temperature series which extends back to 1659. This presents a unique opportunity to examine climate variability in the UK on long time-scales based on observational data. It would be advantageous if we could treat these long time series as describing purely natural climate variability, thus enabling us to better identify what level of human-induced climate change is truly significant. This may not be a correct interpretation, however, since – at least in the most recent century – human forcing of the climate system has been occurring through increased atmospheric concentrations of greenhouse gases. What we are probably observing in these long instrumental data series, therefore, is a mixture of natural climate variability and human-induced climate change, with the contribution of the latter increasing over time. It is nevertheless very instructive, before we progress to examine future climate change scenarios, to look back and appreciate the level of climate variability that the UK has been subject to over recent generations. This involves us in examining year-to-year, decade-to-decade and even century-to-century variations in relevant climate indices. It is within this history of past climate that the British environment, economy and society – including our forest management system – has evolved and to which it has in some measure adapted. Just as future climate change can only be sensibly interpreted against a background of observed climate variability, so too the impacts of future climate change for the UK can only be properly evaluated in the context of environmental and societal adaptation to past climate variability.

Changing temperatures

The annual values of the Central England Temperature (CET) series[11] are plotted in Figure 2.2, together with a version smoothed to emphasise the decadal scale trends. From the CET data three things are evident. First, there has been a warming of UK climate[b] since the 17th century. A linear trend fitted through the time series suggests a warming of about 0.7°C over three hundred years and of about 0.5°C during the twentieth century. Second, this warming has been greater in winter (1.1°C) than in summer (0.2°C). Third, the cluster of warm years at the end of the record means that the 1990s decade – 1990 to 1999 – was the warmest in the entire series, with four of the five warmest years since 1659 occurring in this short period.

The CET series can also be used to examine changes in daily temperature extremes,

Figure 2.2 Central England Temperature annual anomalies (°C) for the period 1659 to 2000 expressed with respect to the 1961–90 mean. The smoothed curve (30-year filter) emphasises decadal scale trends, and the black line is the equivalent global temperature anomaly.

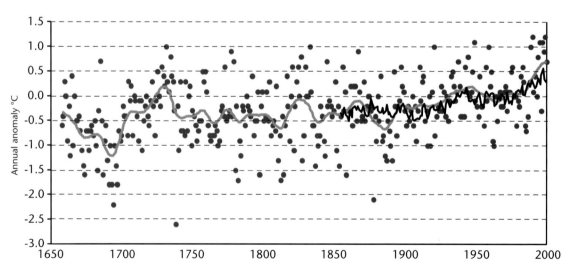

[b]Although the Central England Temperature record is based on measurements in the English Midlands, the year-to-year values are highly correlated with temperature variations over most of the UK.

although in this case only since 1772[11]. Figure 2.3 shows the frequencies of 'hot' and 'cold' days in central England over this period, where hot and cold are defined as days when mean temperature is above 20°C and below 0°C, respectively. There has been a marked reduction in the frequency of cold days since the 18th century particularly during March and November. The annual total has fallen from between 15 and 20 per year prior to the 20th century to around 10 per year over most of the 20th century. There has been a less perceptible rise in the frequency of hot days, although several recent years (1976, 1983, 1995 and 1997) have recorded among the highest annual frequencies of such days. As with annual temperature, the last decade has seen the highest frequency of such days in the entire series averaging about 7.5 hot days per year, nearly twice the long-term average. The warm year of 1995 recorded 26 hot days in central England, the highest total in 225 years of measurements.

Changing precipitation

There are no comparable long-term trends in *annual* precipitation, whether over England and Wales or over Scotland. Variations over thirty-year time-scales have, nevertheless, on occasions exceeded ±10% on an annual basis, or over ±20% on a seasonal basis. These are

Figure 2.3 *Occurrence of 'hot' and 'cold' days derived from daily-mean temperature (T$_{mean}$) in the CET series from 1772–1997. 'Hot' days are with T$_{mean}$ greater than 20°C and 'cold' days are with T$_{mean}$ below 0°C.*

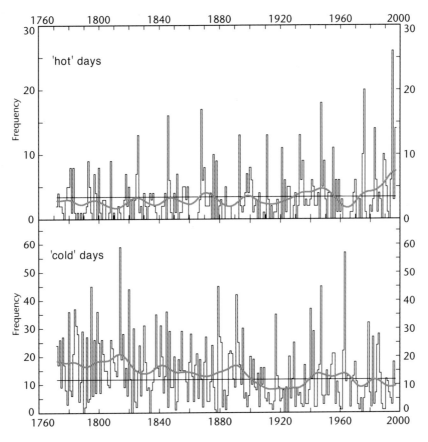

quite large fluctuations in multi-year precipitation and taking such estimates to be the background level of natural precipitation variability on these time-scales has important implications for how water and other moisture sensitive resources are best managed in the UK. There have been systematic changes in the *seasonality* of precipitation, however, with winters becoming wetter and summers becoming drier. This increasing Mediterranean-like precipitation regime has been evident in both Scotland and in England and Wales.

Also noticeable over recent decades has been an increase in the proportion of winter precipitation falling in the heaviest intensity storms, a trend that has been noted across the UK[12]. The shift towards higher intensity precipitation in winter has been mirrored by a shift towards less intense precipitation in summer. There have been no coherent national trends in the precipitation intensity distributions of spring and autumn.

Changing storminess

The available data on gale frequency over the UK only extend back to 1881 and this series shows no long-term trend over the 120-year period. Gale activity is highly variable from year-to-year. For example, a minimum of two 'gales' occurred in 1985 and a maximum of 29 gales occurred in 1887. The 1961–90 average is for just over 12 'severe gales' to occur in the UK per year, mostly in the period November to March. The middle decades of the 20th century were rather less prone to severe gales than the early and later decades and the highest decadal frequency of 'severe gales' (15.4 per year) since the series began in 1881 was recorded during 1988 to 1997.

Changing sea-level

A final indicator of trends in UK climate relates to sea-level, with climate warming anticipated to lead to a rise in global-mean sea-level. Long-term series of tide-gauge data for a number of locations around the UK coastline have been analysed[13]. All of these series indicate a rise in mean sea-level, ranging from 0.7 mm yr^{-1} at Aberdeen to 2.2 mm yr^{-1} at Sheerness. These raw estimates of sea-level change need adjusting, however, to allow for natural rates of coastline emergence and submergence resulting from long-term geological readjustments to the last glaciation. The adjusted net rates of sea-level rise resulting only from changes in ocean volume range from 0.3 mm yr^{-1} at Newlyn to 1.8 mm yr^{-1} at North Shields. These data provide convincing evidence of a rising ocean around the UK coastline.

Future changes in UK climate

This section presents a summary of climate changes for the UK for the four UKCIP98 scenarios[c] referred to earlier[10]. Climate changes are presented for one of three future 30-year periods centred on the 2020s, the 2050s and the 2080s. The climate changes for each of these periods are calculated as the change in thirty-year mean climates with respect to the 1961–90 average. The 2020s are therefore representative of the period 2010–2039, the 2050s of 2040–2069 and the 2080s of 2070–2099. The changes shown here are those anticipated to result from greenhouse gas forcing of the climate system under the assumptions discussed earlier. Natural climate variability (i.e. the noise of the system) will in reality modify these magnitudes and patterns

---

[c] The change patterns for the Low scenario are derived from the HadCM2 GGd experiment and for the High scenario from the HadCM2 GGa experiment. In each of these cases, the GCM patterns are scaled by the respective global warming curves to yield magnitudes of change for the UK consistent with these low (1.1°C warming by the 2080s) and high (3.5°C) rates of global warming. The change patterns for the Medium-low (1.9°C warming by the 2080s) and Medium-high (3.1°C) scenarios are extracted directly from the respective HadCM2 experiments, GGd and GGa.

Figure 2.4 *Change in winter mean temperature (with respect to the 1961–90 mean) for 30-year periods centred on the 2020s, 2050s and 2080s and for the four UKCIP98 scenarios. Top: Low scenario, changes are scaled from the HadCM2 GGd ensemble-mean. Second row: Medium-low scenario, changes are from the HadCM2 GGd ensemble-mean. Third row: Medium-high scenario, changes are from the HadCM2 GGa ensemble-mean. Bottom: High scenario, changes are scaled from the HadCM2 GGa ensemble-mean. Background fields are interpolated from the full HadCM2 grid, while the highlighted numbers show the change for each HadCM2 land gridbox over the UK.*

of change, whether this variability is internally generated or whether it results from external factors such as solar variability or volcanic eruptions.

Changes in temperature

Figure 2.4 shows the changes in winter mean temperature for the four UKCIP98 scenarios. For all scenarios and for all seasons (not shown) there is a northwest to southeast gradient in the magnitude of the climate warming over the UK, the southeast consistently warming by several tenths of a degree Celsius more than the northwest. Warming rates vary from about 0.1°C per decade for the Low scenario to about 0.3°C for the High scenario. Although in general warming is greater in winter than in summer, this is not always the case. In the Medium-low scenario for example, summers over southeast England by the 2080s are 2.4°C warmer than the 1961–90 average, while winters warm by only 2.0°C. The year-to-year variability of seasonal and annual-mean temperature also changes. Winter seasonal-mean temperatures become less variable (because of fewer very cold winters), while summer seasonal-mean temperatures become more variable (because of more frequent very hot summers).

The consequences of rising mean temperature and changing inter-annual temperature variability are changing probabilities of very hot years (and seasons). Table 2.1 shows the changing probabilities that the annual mean temperature anomaly experienced in Central England in 1997 will be exceeded in the future[d]. Under all four scenarios, such an annual anomaly becomes much more frequent, occurring once per decade by the 2020s under the Low scenario

and nearly seven times per decade under the High scenario. By the 2080s, virtually every year is warmer than 1997 in the Medium-high and High scenarios, and between 55 and 90% of years are warmer than 1997 in the Low and Medium-low scenarios.

The distribution of daily temperature extremes also changes in the future. The shapes of the distributions do not change greatly, but they are all displaced by approximately the mean seasonal warming expected by the 2080s. Thus for southeast England in winter, the mildest nights are currently about 12–13°C, but by the 2080s some winter nights reach 15°C. Similarly in summer over Scotland, the hottest days currently reach between 23°C and 24°C, but by the 2080s some daily maxima reach 27°C. Some further specific examples of changing probabilities of model-simulated daily temperature extremes are shown in Table 2.2[e].

Table 2.1 Percentage of years in southern UK exceeding an annual-mean temperature anomaly of 1.06°C above the 1961–90 mean (i.e. the observed 1997 annual anomaly for Central England) under the four UKCIP98 scenarios. The 1961–90 values are based on model simulations and not on observations.

	1961–90	2020s	2050s	2080s
Low	6	13	26	56
Medium-low	6	47	74	88
Medium-high	6	59	85	99
High	6	67	89	100

---

[d]1997 was the third warmest year ever recorded in the UK, nearly 1.1°C warmer than the average 1961–90 temperature.

[e]It should be noted that all these quoted temperatures refer to model-simulations; although the relative changes may be credible, the absolute numbers cited will differ from site observations.

Table 2.2 Probability of daily temperature extremes for Scotland and SE England derived from the HadCM2 model for the UKCIP Medium-high scenario. Note: these probabilities are for climate model gridbox regions (~10 000 km²) and therefore the absolute probabilities will differ from those measured at individual stations.

	Winter nights below freezing		Summer days above 25°C	
	Scotland	SE England	Scotland	SE England
Present (1961–90)	0.28	0.20	0.00	0.06
Future (2080s)	0.11	0.07	0.01	0.18

Changes in precipitation

The patterns of precipitation change are less consistent between seasons and scenarios than the equivalent temperature changes. Annual and winter precipitation increases for all regions, periods and scenarios, although the annual increases by the 2080s for the Low and Medium-low scenarios are very modest at only a few per cent of current precipitation. Winter precipitation increases are largest and reach 20% or more for the 2080s in the High scenario. Increases in winter precipitation of this magnitude are certainly significant. For the summer season, there is a general tendency for drying in the south of the UK and wetting in the north. These summer changes are modest, however, and probably only significant in the southeast of the UK and for the 2080s period in the Medium-high and High scenarios. Autumn displays patterns of change broadly similar to winter, while precipitation changes in spring are generally very small and not significant.

Despite these contrasting changes in mean seasonal precipitation, all seasons experience an increase in the year-to-year relative variability of seasonal precipitation throughout the UK. This means that seasonal precipitation totals will differ from the average level by greater amounts more often in the future than at present. Two examples of what this may mean for future precipitation anomalies are shown in Table 2.3. The probability of summers experiencing rainfall of less than 50% of the long-term average increases very substantially. By the 2080s such dry summers occur once per decade compared to once per century under modelled present-day climate. In contrast, the probability of successive dry *years* – defined as a two-year precipitation deficit of 10% or more compared with the long term average – changes little in the future. By the 2080s, such successive dry years actually become less likely because the increased summer precipitation deficits are more than compensated for by increased precipitation in other seasons. The statistics in Table 2.3 relate to precipitation only and make no allowance for increased moisture deficits induced by higher evaporation losses. The warming UK climate is likely to lead to higher evapo-transpiration rates. For the Medium-high scenario for example, summer potential evapo-transpiration increases by up to 10% or more over southern UK. Summer droughts – when defined in terms of precipitation minus evaporation – are likely to become much more frequent in the future, especially over the southern UK.

Table 2.3 Percentage of years experiencing seasonal precipitation anomalies across southern UK for present climate (1961–90) and for three future 30-year periods for the Medium-high scenario. The 1961–90 values are based on model simulations and not on observations.

Precipitation	1961–90	2020s	2050s	2080s
Summer total below 50% of average	1	7	12	10
2-year total below 90% of average	12	11	14	6

It was noted earlier that the intensity of daily winter precipitation in the UK has been observed to be increasing over recent years. Increases in the intensity of daily precipitation over the UK are also a feature of the UKCIP98 climate scenarios – in both winter and summer seasons. However, the predicted increase in summer precipitation intensities is not consistent with recent observed trends, and indeed, more recent Regional Climate Model simulations from the Hadley Centre show no increase in summer precipitation intensity. The future increase in precipitation intensity in the winter half-year is likely to increase the risk of riverine flooding in various UK catchments. Analysis of the daily precipitation regimes over the UK in the Hadley Centre Regional Climate Model (RCM)[f] confirms these increases in winter precipitation intensity[14], with the most intense daily precipitation events increasing in frequency by up to 75% by the 2080s (Medium-high scenario).

Changes in storminess

Storminess is measured here in terms of gale frequencies derived from large-scale pressure fields. Changes in the frequencies of three different categories of gales are shown in Table 2.4 for the Medium-high scenario. For the winter season, there is a suggestion that overall gale frequencies may decline in the future, although very severe winter gales increase. Note that the sign of the changes in severe gale frequencies varies between the three periods, and this indicates that a clear anthropogenic signal in severe gale frequencies is not easily detectable from the noise of natural climate variability. Summer gales are much less frequent (less than 2 per year) than winter gales and consequently any changes in summer gale frequencies are likely to be small.

Related to this analysis of gale frequencies are changes in airflow characteristics over the UK. Three aspects of airflow can be analysed: flow strength, vorticity (i.e. anticyclonic or cyclonic flow) and flow direction. This analysis suggests a tendency for autumns to experience windier conditions, with a reduction in northerly and easterly flow and an increase in southwesterly and westerly flow. Summers become slightly more anticyclonic in character with more westerly and northwesterly flow, while winter and spring become slightly less anticyclonic. These changes in airflow characteristics may be important for certain

Table 2.4 Changes in seasonal gale frequencies over the British Isles for the 2020s, 2050s and 2080s for the Medium-high scenario shown as per cent changes from the 1961–90 mean. The 1961–90 frequencies are calculated from climate model outputs and not from observations.

	1961–90 Gales per year	2020s % change	2050s % change	2080s % change
Winter gales	10.9	-1	-9	-5
Winter severe gales	8.5	-1	-10	-5
Winter very severe gales	1.4	+8	-10	+11
Summer gales	1.8	+3	0	+14
Summer severe gales	1.1	0	-2	+15
Summer very severe gales	0.1	+25	-16	+9

[f]The RCM operates at a spatial scale of 50 km, compared to the GCM (from which the UKCIP98 scenarios were derived) resolution of about 300 km.

aspects of the UK environment, for example air pollution levels in cities or episodes of acid deposition.

Changes in sea-level

Changes in mean sea-level around the UK coast are likely to be similar to the global average. Results from the HadCM2 simulations indicate that by the 2050s, this rise for the UK region will be within 2–3 cm of the global mean. However, there will be regional differences in the rate of sea-level rise due to regional changes in ocean currents and atmospheric pressure that lead to greater rates of thermal expansion and water accumulation in the northeast Atlantic compared to the global average. What is more important when evaluating these sea-level changes, however, is to consider natural vertical land movements and changing storm-surge regimes.

Vertical land movement (a naturally rising or falling coastline) occurs as a result of isostatic adjustments. The UK is tilting as a result of such adjustment, so that much of southern UK is presently sinking and much of northern UK is rising. Some representative rates for the UK coastline are shown in Table 2.5, alongside the climate-induced changes in sea-level for the 2050s. The two most extreme regions for vertical land movements are East Anglia – sinking by 9 cm by the 2050s – and western Scotland – rising by 11 cm. Under the lower scenarios of climate-induced sea-level rise these natural land movements can be very significant in exacerbating or reducing the estimated climate-induced change in mean sea-level around the UK coast.

A second factor to consider in relation to sea-level rise and coastal flooding risk is the changing nature of storm surges. A rise in mean sea-level will result in a lower surge height being necessary to cause a given flood event, leading to an increase in the frequency of coastal flooding. If surge statistics remain the same in the future this changed flooding risk may be calculated quite simply. However, surge statistics may change for a number of reasons. The tracks and intensity of mid-latitude cyclones may change in the future and the formation and evolution of storm surges may also change, particularly in shallow waters.

Consideration of uncertainties

The future climates of the UK illustrated in this section are scenarios. They are plausible and self-consistent descriptions of future UK climate, but they originate from different assumptions about future emissions of

Table 2.5 Representative changes in sea-level (cm) around the UK coast by the 2050s due to global climate change only ('Climate') and to the combined effect of climate and natural land movements ('Net'). The global-mean climate-induced sea-level changes are used here, but adjusted by 10% to account for slightly higher rates of increase around the UK coastline. Changes are with respect to average 1961–90 levels.

	Low		Medium-low		Medium-high		High	
	Climate	Net	Climate	Net	Climate	Net	Climate	Net
West Scotland	13	2	20	9	28	17	74	63
East Scotland	13	8	20	15	28	23	74	69
Wales	13	18	20	25	28	33	74	79
English Channel	13	19	20	26	28	34	74	80
East Anglia	13	22	20	29	28	37	74	83

greenhouse gases. Furthermore, the transformation of these emissions into future climate change estimates is itself beset with uncertainty due to the role of other climate agents and poorly represented processes in the climate models.

The existence of uncertainties does not imply the absence of knowledge. There are some aspects of future climate change about which there is greater confidence than others. Although formal levels of confidence cannot easily be applied, there is more confidence in predictions of future increases in CO_2 concentrations and in mean sea-level than there is about increases in storminess or more frequent summer droughts.

It is worth briefly rehearsing five of the main sources of uncertainty about future climate prediction since all of these qualify the descriptions of future UK climate summarised here. These five main sources of uncertainty are:

- unknown future greenhouse gas emissions
- natural climate variability
- different responses between different global climate models
- poorly resolved regional and local climate changes
- the possibility of relatively rapid, non-linear changes in the climate system.

Uncertain future greenhouse gas emissions

The UKCIP98 scenarios assume two different future growth rates for greenhouse gas emissions – 1% per annum growth in net atmospheric greenhouse gas concentrations for the High and Medium-high scenarios and 0.5% per annum growth for the Medium-low and Low scenarios. The 1% per annum growth rate approximates to the IS92a emissions scenario which has been widely used as a standard emissions profile, while the 0.5% per annum growth rate approximates to an emissions profile more like IS92d. The 1990s

growth rate in net greenhouse gas concentration was approximately 0.7% per annum. These IS92 emissions scenarios were non-intervention scenarios and were based on different assumptions about future population and economic growth and about different energy futures. It is possible of course that future concentration growth rates may fall outside this range.

The effects of natural climate variability

Other factors that are also not 'predictable' will almost certainly affect climate, in particular cooling due to volcanic dust and both warming and cooling due to the changing energy output of the sun. However, the climate effect of even a major volcanic eruption such as Mount Pinatubo in 1991 disappears after a few years and so, barring an unusual succession of major energetic eruptions, modifications of the climate change scenarios shown here due to volcanoes are likely to be small. Although variations in the direct output of the sun affect climate, this effect has been small over the past 100 years and there are no indications that these quite modest effects will change in the future. There are theories that the sun can affect climate in indirect ways, such as its ability to modify cosmic rays and potentially cloud cover, but they remain speculative.

The natural *internal* variability of the climate system may also modify the climate change scenarios described here. For example, natural internal climate variability may cause the 30-year average climates described here to vary in temperature by up to ±0.6°C in winter and up to about ±0.4°C in summer and in precipitation by up to about ±10% in both summer and winter.

Uncertainties arising from climate modelling

The UKCIP98 climate scenarios are based on results from the HadCM2 climate model experiments – results from other GCM experiments were not used. There are a number of climate laboratories around the world, however, that perform similar climate experiments to the Hadley Centre. Different global climate models yield different regional climate changes, sometimes quite large differences, and it is difficult to know which are inherently more believable. For example, a number of other leading global climate models show more rapid annual warming over the UK compared to the UKCIP98 scenarios, in some cases by almost 1°C. For precipitation, all leading models show an increase in annual and winter precipitation over northern UK, but differ in their response in the south of the country and in summer. Some models show more extreme summer drying than the UKCIP98 scenarios and some models show less drying. Quantifying such differences between models is important if the full range of uncertainty is to be sampled[15].

Obtaining regional scenario information

The climate scenario information for the UK has been depicted at the spatial scale that is resolved by the HadCM2 climate model, namely 2.5° latitude by 3.75° longitude. This model resolves only four discrete regions within the UK – roughly describable as 'Scotland', the 'Scottish/English borders', 'Wales' and 'England'. The coarse resolution of global climate models such as HadCM2 has a number of implications for the climate change scenarios derived from them. First, the coarse GCM-grid greatly simplifies the coastline and topography of a country like the UK. For example, the Shetland Islands do not exist in HadCM2 and the 'Scotland' gridbox has a uniform elevation of 221 metres. These simplifications of geography may alter the larger-scale circulation in the model and make the modelled response to anthropogenic forcing – even at the GCM resolution – different from what it would realistically be.

Second, within each gridbox there is a great deal of heterogeneity in the land cover characteristics that interact with the atmosphere. This heterogeneity cannot be captured by a GCM and, again, means that the large-scale modelled response to external forcing is greatly simplified. Third, and largely because of the first two limitations, within a single GCM gridbox there may in reality be quite different climate responses to anthropogenic forcing. Thus warming over the east of Scotland may be different to warming over the west. The UKCIP98 scenarios cited here cannot discriminate between such local differences, although recent work using higher resolution climate models has explored these questions (e.g. for Scotland[16]).

This coarse spatial resolution of GCM-based scenarios is therefore at first sight a limitation in their application to a wide range of impact assessments. These assessments may either be quite localised, around a single river catchment or urban area, or may operate on a national scale, but with a spatial resolution of kilometres or tens of kilometres rather than hundreds of kilometres – for example a national land use classification assessment. Just how much of a limitation this is requires some consideration of the problem of 'downscaling' climate change information.

Rapid and non-linear climate change

The UKCIP98 climate scenarios have been derived from climate models that include the best possible representation, consistent with current understanding and computing limitations, of processes in the atmosphere, ocean and land that will determine climate change. However, we do not understand the climate system well enough to be able to rule out other outcomes. It has been suggested, for example, that relatively rapid climate change could occur if the climate system shows a non-linear response to increased greenhouse gas concentrations.

One example of this would be a change in the thermohaline circulation (THC) of the world's oceans. The THC consists of strong ocean currents that transport large amounts of heat around the world. It has been suggested for some time that a collapse of the THC in the North Atlantic could cause cooling over northwest Europe. The Hadley Centre model, in common with some others, shows a slow weakening of the THC as greenhouse gas concentrations increase[17]. Recent observational work is also suggesting that we might be detecting the first signs of a weakening in the North Atlantic ocean circulation[18]. It is important to realise, however, that the slow cooling due to this effect will only partially offset the general warming from the increases in greenhouse gases. The North Atlantic will still warm, but parts will warm at a slower rate than if the THC had remained constant. A sudden, more dramatic collapse of the THC has not been seen in any experiment using the most comprehensive climate models. Nevertheless, we must take the possibility seriously because of the potential major impact of such an event. At present, however, we have little way of assigning even a nominal probability to such an event occurring, which makes planning and preparing for this eventuality very difficult.

Another potential non-linearity in the climate system stems from the response of the natural carbon cycle to human-induced climate change; this factor is not included in the UKCIP climate scenarios. The Hadley Centre recently developed a climate model which for the first time included an interactive carbon cycle[19]. This showed that human-induced climate change could result in the dying back of some natural forested areas, with a consequent release of additional CO_2 into the atmosphere. Higher temperatures may also cause soils to give up some of their stored carbon (see Chapter 5). Both these factors lead to a substantially higher model-simulated atmospheric CO_2 concentration in the future,

and hence to a more rapid climate change. This result is preliminary, but at least indicates the potential for amplification of climate change via a positive carbon cycle feedback.

A third area for concern lies in the behaviour of the West Antarctic Ice Sheet (WAIS). It is possible that a much more rapid rise in sea-level than suggested in our scenarios could occur should the WAIS disintegrate. The WAIS is grounded below sea-level and is therefore potentially unstable. If it were to disintegrate completely, global sea-level would rise by about five metres. Predictions about the contribution of the WAIS to sea-level rise are difficult and uncertain for at least two reasons. First, is the complexity of processes determining the stability of the WAIS and, second, is the uncertain relationship between changes in accumulation and discharge of ice due to global warming and the effects of natural millennial-scale trends in climate. One recent assessment[20] suggests that the WAIS contributed relatively little to sea-level rise in the 20th century, but over following centuries higher discharge rates from the ice sheet increase its contribution to sea-level rise to between 50 and 100 cm per century.

Conclusions

This chapter has provided a brief survey of the evidence that global and UK climate is changing and concludes, on the basis of the Third Assessment Report of the IPCC, that it is likely that much of the recent observed warming of climate is due to human activities. This being so, it appears very likely that global and UK climate will continue to warm over the 21st century, the rate of warming depending in large measure on how the global energy economy develops in the future. The chapter draws upon the UKCIP98 climate scenarios to describe some of the possible changes in UK climate over the 21st century; while uncertainties remain, the *least* likely scenario is one in which the weather statistics of the past

100 years provide us with a sound basis for planning and design over the next 100 years. A new set of national UK climate scenarios – UKCIP02 – will be published during the spring of 2002. Although qualitatively similar to the ones summarised here, there will be differences in the numbers and in the level of detail supplied. Users are therefore recommended to work with these new scenarios in undertaking research into climate impacts and adaptation and when conducting strategic planning or design activities.

References

1. FOLLAND, C.K. and KARL, T.R. (2001). Observed climate variability and change. In: *Climate change 2001: the scientific basis,* eds J.T. Houghton, Y. Ding, D.J. Griggs, M. Noguer, P.J. van der Linden and D. Xiaosu. WG1 Report to the IPCC Third Assessment. Cambridge University Press, Cambridge, 91–181.

2. MITCHELL, J.F.B. and KAROLY, D.J. (2001). Detection of climate change and attribution of causes. In: *Climate change 2001: the scientific basis,* eds J.T. Houghton, Y. Ding, D.J. Griggs, M. Noguer, P.J. van der Linden and D. Xiaosu. WG1 Report to the IPCC Third Assessment. Cambridge University Press, Cambridge, 696–738.

3. JONES, P.D., OSBORN, T.J. and BRIFFA, K.R. (2001). The evolution of climate over the last millennium. *Science* **292**, 662–667.

4. IPCC (2001). *Climate change 2001: the scientific basis. Summary for policymakers and technical summary.* Cambridge University Press, Cambridge.

5. NAKICENOVIC, N., ALCAMO, J., DAVIS, G., DE VRIES, B., FENHANN, J., GAFFIN, S., GREGORY, K., GRUBLER, A., JUNG, T.Y., RAM, T.K., LA ROVERE, E.L., MICHAELIS, L., MORI, S., MORITA, T., PEPPER, W., PITCHER, H., PRICE, L., RAIHI, K., ROEHRL, A., ROGNER, H.-H., SANKOVSKI, A., SCHLESINGER, M., SHUKLA, P., SMITH, S., SWART, R., VAN ROOIJEN, S., VICTOR, N. and DADI, Z. (2000). *Emissions scenarios. A special report of Working Group III of the Intergovernmental Panel on Climate Change.* Cambridge University Press, Cambridge.

6. BOLIN, B. (1998). The Kyoto negotiations on climate change: a science perspective. *Science* **279**, 330–331.

7. DESSAI, S. and HULME, M. (2002). Climatic implications of revised IPCC emissions scenarios, the Kyoto Protocol and quantification of uncertainties. *Integrated Assessment* (in press).

8. HULME, M. and CARTER, T.R. (1999). Representing uncertainty in climate change scenarios and impact studies. In: *Representing uncertainty in climate change scenarios and impacts studies,* eds T.R. Carter, M. Hulme and D. Viner. Proceedings of the ECLAT-2 Helsinki Workshop, 14-16 April, 1999. Climatic Research Unit, Norwich, 12–34.

9. SCHNEIDER, S.H. (2001). What is 'dangerous' climate change? *Nature* **411**, 17–19.

10. HULME, M. and JENKINS, G.J. (1998). *Climate change scenarios for the United Kingdom.* UKCIP Technical Report No.1. Climatic Research Unit, University of East Anglia, Norwich.

11. PARKER, D.E., LEGG, T.P. and FOLLAND, C.K. (1992). A new daily Central England Temperature series, 1772-1991. *International Journal of Climatology* **12**, 317–342.

12. OSBORN, T.J., HULME, M., JONES, P.D. and BASNETT, T. (2000). Observed trends in the daily intensity of United Kingdom precipitation. *International Journal of Climatology* **20**, 347–364.

13. WOODWORTH, P.L., TSIMPLIS, M.N., FLATHER, R.A. and SHENNAN, I. (1999). A review of the trends observed in British Isles mean sea-level data measured by tide gauges. *Geophysical Journal International* **136**, 651–670.

14. DURMAN, C.F., GREGORY, J.M., HASSELL, D.C., JONES, R.G. and Murphy, J.M. (2001). A comparison of extreme European daily precipitation simulated by a global and regional

climate model for present and future climates. *Quarterly Journal of the Royal Meteorological Society* **127**, 1005–1015.

15. NEW, M. and HULME, M. (2000). Representing uncertainties in climate change scenarios: a Monte Carlo approach. *Integrated Assessment* **1**, 203–213.

16. HULME, M., CROSSLEY, J. and LU, X. (2001). *An exploration of regional climate change scenarios for Scotland.* Scottish Executive CRU Report, Edinburgh.

17. WOOD, R.A., KEEN, A.B., MITCHELL, J.F.B. and GREGORY, J.M. (1999). Changing spatial structure of the thermohaline circulation in response to atmospheric CO_2 forcing in a climate model. *Nature* **399**, 572–575.

18. HANSEN, B.M, TURRELL, W.R. and OSTERHUIS, S. (2001). Decreasing overflow from the Nordic seas into the Atlantic Ocean through the Faroe Bank channel since 1950. *Nature* **411**, 927–930.

19. COX, P.M., BETTS, R.A., JONES, C.D., SPALL, S.A. and TOTTERDELL, I.J. (2000). Acceleration of global warming due to carbon-cycle feedbacks in a coupled climate model. *Nature* **408**, 184–187.

20. VAUGHAN, D.G. and SPOUGE, J.R. (2001). Risk estimation of collapse of the West Antarctic Ice Sheet. *Climatic Change* **52**, 65–91.

Climate Change Impacts

3. Climate change and damage to trees caused by extremes of temperature   29

4. Climate change impacts: storms   41

5. Implications of climate change: soil and water   53

6. Climate change and the seasonality of woodland flora and fauna   69

7. Effects of climate change on fungal diseases of trees   83

8. Climate change: implications for forest insect pests   99

9. Impacts of increased CO_2 concentrations on tree growth and function   119

10. Impacts of climate change on forest growth   141

CHAPTER THREE   Derek Redfern and Steven Hendry

3

Climate Change and Damage to Trees Caused by Extremes of Temperature

KEY FINDINGS

- The likelihood of injury to trees by winter cold may be slightly lower than at present.
- It is likely that spring flushing will advance as a result of milder winters, but the risk of spring frost injury is unlikely to change; nevertheless, unseasonal frosts will still have the potential to cause damage.
- Autumn frosts may become more damaging in England because of later hardening and predicted increases in diurnal temperature range in the south.
- The widespread planting of southern provenances of species such as Sitka spruce, in anticipation of climate change, should be avoided because of the potential for unseasonal frost damage.
- No prediction is possible for the frequency of the type of winter injury known as 'red belt'.
- 'Top-dying' of Norway spruce is likely to increase in England and eastern Scotland; Norway spruce could cease to be a productive species over much of England.
- Increasing heat and drought in the south and east can be expected to increase losses, particularly among newly established trees and mature trees in hedgerows and urban environments. Defects in coniferous timber due to drought crack are also likely to increase in England.
- An increased incidence of summer drought would make trees more vulnerable to attack by weak pathogens.
- Increased winter rainfall may raise water tables enough to kill roots, thereby reducing effective rooting depth and making trees more vulnerable to summer droughts.
- Higher temperatures in summer may reduce the risk of Brunchorstia damage to Corsican pine, enabling it to be planted more widely in the uplands in the future.

Introduction

The major expansion of forestry in Britain that began in the early part of the 20th century led to the large-scale use of exotic species, principally conifers from western North America, continental Europe and Asia. The British climate is a maritime one; temperatures are generally regarded as equable, particularly in western coastal areas, and this has encouraged use of species and provenances from more southerly latitudes in addition to those that are more closely matched to the present climate. Thus, Corsican pine (*Pinus nigra* var. *maritima*) and southerly provenances (Washington and Oregon) of lodgepole pine (*Pinus contorta*) and Sitka spruce (*Picea sitchensis*) are grown quite widely[1]. Species such as *Pinus radiata, Pinus muricata* and *Nothofagus procera* are also grown but on only a small scale at present, and in the mildest areas. Because of the widespread use of exotic species, forests in Britain are probably more vulnerable to weather-induced injury than those in other countries, where forestry practice generally makes more use of native species and local provenances.

Despite the general mildness of the climate and the proximity of the sea, inland areas experience more continental conditions than the coast, and the risk of damage by unseasonal frost, particularly to Sitka spruce, is readily appreciated by forest managers. Care is generally taken therefore to use planting stock of a more northerly provenance, such as the Queen Charlotte Islands or even Alsaka, in these circumstances. It is, however, less readily appreciated that winter weather may also be damaging. Our climate is characterised by variability and windiness[2]; temperature fluctuations resulting from the interplay of Atlantic and continental weather systems, especially in combination with strong winds, can cause dramatic symptoms, and have the potential to cause significant economic loss. Elsewhere, temperature fluctuations in winter and early spring are thought to have played a part in repeated episodes of large-scale dieback in birch (*Betula pendula*) and other hardwoods in the 20th century in eastern North America[3,4]. Records from the Disease Diagnostic and Advisory Service of Forest Research for the period 1982–1998 provide an analysis for northern Britain of damage attributed to various features of the climate over that period (Table 3.1). Illustrations of the various types of damage can be found in Gregory and Redfern[5].

This chapter firstly describes the effects of temperature extremes on the most important commercial species, considering both direct

Table 3.1 Temperature-related climate injury reported in northern Britain, 1982–1998.

Agent		Number of records	% of climate-induced damage reports	Return period (years)
Unseasonal frost:	Spring	105	19.8	1.3
	Autumn	57	10.8	1.5
Winter cold		22	4.2	8.5
Winter desiccation/exposure		102	19.2	1.2
Top dying of Norway spruce		77	14.5	1.1
Drought		45 (+55*)	18.9	5.7
Heat		0	0	0

* Denotes records in which drought was a contributory factor.

effects and those that develop in conjunction with other abiotic factors such as wind and drought. It then considers how the frequency and severity of various types of damage might change in future using the predictions provided by the UK Climate Impacts Programme[6].

Unseasonal frost damage

Spring

Prompted by the occurrence of late spring frosts in 1927, Day and Peace[7] reviewed the European literature on frost damage and carried out freezing experiments on a wide range of commercially important species. Later they published a detailed description of injury to both broadleaves and conifers by frosts that caused serious damage throughout Britain in 1935, and described the weather conditions and other factors associated[A] with it[8]. A succession of frosts in mid-May, when flushing by most species was well advanced, caused collapse and browning of new foliage. This form of damage is common and occasionally widespread. The most recent example occurred in southern England in 1997. Day and Peace[8] calculated that May frosts severe enough to cause damage would occur in Britain every year and the frequency of damage recorded in Table 3.1 is close to this. Damage can occur even earlier if, as in the south of England in 1995, above-average winter temperatures promote flushing. The immediate effects are often dramatic but species such as oak (*Quercus* spp.) and beech (*Fagus sylvatica*) flush for a second time and crowns are generally fully restored by mid-summer.

Among the conifers, Sitka spruce is most frequently affected by unseasonal frost. Damage has more serious consequences than in broadleaved trees, usually resulting in a loss of height increment for one season. It may also induce stem deformation, the formation of multiple leaders and dieback. Dieback has been recorded to ground level in trees up to 2 m

tall[8]. Trees may also be damaged before flushing, although a lower temperature is probably required. In April 1981, cambium on the main stems of Sitka spruce in north and west Scotland was injured by frost on the night of 22–23 April, when minimum temperatures as low as –10°C were recorded[9]. This followed a 4-week period of generally very warm weather with daily maxima as high as 17–20°C on a number of occasions. Trees up to 5 m tall were affected. At first, affected trees flushed normally, but those that had been girdled by death of the cambium, usually at about the mid-point of the stem, died back during summer (Figure 3.1). Alaskan provenances were less severely injured than those of more southerly origin. Similar damage occurred in late April 1989[10] and in early May 1997. In Denmark, this weather pattern, with similar temperatures, caused the same type of cambium injury to Sitka spruce in 1938 and 1991[11].

Autumn

The earliest autumn frosts can cause dieback of late season (lammas) extension growth, especially in Sitka spruce, but other species, including larches (*Larix* spp.), are affected occasionally. In Sitka spruce, needles remain vulnerable for much longer than shoots and can be damaged even without lammas growth. Symptoms are restricted to current-year needles whereas older needles characteristically escape injury[12]. Damage is often dramatic but generally superficial. Discoloured needles may be shed but buds flush normally in spring, although extension growth and needle length may be greatly reduced. Shoots and buds die only in the most severe cases. This type of injury is most common in forests, on trees up to 5 m tall, but it occasionally occurs in nurseries. Other species are rarely affected. In Sitka spruce, needle damage in autumn occurs most frequently in September, but it has been recorded as late as mid-October. Frost hardiness increases as daily minimum

Figure 3.1 Injury to cambium on the main stem of Sitka spruce caused by frost on 22–23 April 1981. Photograph taken in Fearnoch Forest, Oban, Argyll on 15 June 1981. At this stage only those shoots at the point of injury, in the middle of the main stem and extending a distance of approximately 25 cm, had begun to die. The upper part of the tree died later, while the lower stem survived. The position of the initial cambium injury on the main stem may have been determined by the basipetal development of cell division in the cambium, the temperature gradient above ground level and the protection afforded by the lower branches.

temperatures fall below about 8°C and gradually approach zero, so that in 'normal' years needles can withstand temperatures of −5°C to −10°C without injury by the time the first frosts occur. However, if frosts of this severity are preceded by warm weather, needles will not have become acclimated and may be damaged. The risk increases with the duration of any mild weather since the likelihood of a frost severe enough to cause injury also increases. Damage has been recorded in most years, and almost as frequently as that caused

by spring frost (Table 3.1). Severe and widespread events have been reported on seven occasions in northern Britain during the period 1971–1999 (1971, 1972, 1979, 1986, 1989, 1991 and 1993), but there have been no reports from the south.

The severity of damage varies with provenance. Trees of more southerly origin are more susceptible than those from the Queen Charlotte Islands and Alaska, but individual trees within a provenance vary greatly in resistance[12,13].

Winter injury

Winter cold

In a country like Britain where the comparative infrequency of winter cold provides a temptation to grow less hardy species, damage can be striking[14]. Significant damage has been recorded on two occasions in the last 40 years, in 1962–63 and 1981–82. Lesser events in 1978–79 and 1995–96 affected only the most vulnerable forestry species such as *Cupressus macrocarpa* and species of *Eucalyptus* and *Nothofagus*[15-17]. In January 1982, the lowest temperature ever recorded in Britain (−27.2°C at Braemar) killed a number of species and provenances of southerly origin that had not previously been affected by winter cold[18]. Corsican pine was the principal commercially important species affected but there was minor damage to Douglas fir (*Pseudotsuga menziesii*) and lodgepole pine. Large numbers of long-established Leyland cypress (x *Cupressocyparis leylandii*) were also killed in the south of England. Damage involved death of phloem and cambium girdling the lower stem. Girdled trees died throughout 1982, with some surviving until 1983. Partial damage on surviving trees caused the formation of longitudinal lesions, some of which were sufficiently extensive to reduce growth. Gremmen[19] described similar damage to Corsican pine in Holland in 1956.

Damage in winter associated with temperature fluctuations and wind

Despite the southerly origin of some species grown in Britain, winter cold seems to be less important as a cause of injury than fluctuating temperatures combined with wind. During winter 1978–79, lodgepole pine in north Scotland suffered widespread foliage browning and shoot death. The damage is associated with rapid freeze-thaw cycles, and is known as 'red belt' in Canada and Scandinavia[20–24]. Similar injury was seen on a wider range of conifers in 1984 and 1986. In the first case it occurred on older crops, principally of Sitka spruce, but Scots pine was also affected, at high elevation in northwest England and west Scotland[25]. Damage consisted of foliage browning, defoliation and shoot death, which was concentrated typically in a zone of variable extent below the upper few whorls (Figure 3.2). It was widespread and highly visible but had no long-lasting effects. In 1986 damage

Figure 3.2 Damage to mature Sitka spruce in Glenhurich Forest, Strontian, caused by fluctuating temperatures and wind in winter 1983–84.

again occurred at high elevation, but this time it involved mostly trees less than 10 years old and was particularly serious on trees planted the previous year[26]. A study of weather patterns suggested that on both occasions damage was caused by large and rapid changes in temperature, accompanied by strong winds, but the conditions, or sequence of events, leading to winter injuries are complex and difficult to determine[24]. Some winter injury in Britain may be more closely related to the winter desiccation that occurs elsewhere at natural tree-lines[27].

Top dying of Norway spruce

This is the most serious climatic/physiological disorder of a commercially important conifer in Britain (Figure 3.3). The cause, or causes, of the condition are not fully understood, but several features suggest that it is abiotic in origin. The most convincing hypothesis relates it to excessive moisture loss in winter, although summer drought may be an important factor. Norway spruce (*Picea abies*) occurs naturally in a climate that is more continental than that in Britain. Top-dying therefore differs from frost and winter cold injury to other exotic species in that it is related to the use of a species in a different climatic region, rather than at a more northerly latitude.

In Britain, top-dying of Norway spruce was first described by Murray[28,29], but apart from work by Diamandis[30] it has been little studied. The principal characteristics of the disorder, drawn from this literature and from experience gained through the Pathology Advisory Service, are:

- Basipetal browning of current year needles that usually develops during winter and early spring, but which may begin as early as late summer. Affected crops are generally subject to repeated episodes of browning.
- Needle browning is accompanied by a severe reduction in height increment, but

Figure 3.3 Top-dying of Norway spruce, May 1997, at Northern Research Station, Midlothian.

increment may decline before the onset of obvious browning.

- The condition most commonly affects pole-stage crops.
- It is typically initiated by thinning or by the removal of side shelter.
- It is most severe on crop edges but frequently spreads among susceptible individuals throughout the crop. Small isolated stands and narrow shelterbelts are particularly vulnerable.
- It is associated with mild, windy winters and possibly exacerbated by drought.
- It is most common in the drier, eastern parts of Britain.

After thinning, in vulnerable crops, the onset of foliage browning and subsequent dieback may be sudden and dramatic. Trees can recover from foliage browning but in many cases it recurs so that crowns become thinner and then die back. Thereafter, the disorder tends to be progressive so that affected stands often have a mixture of dead trees, healthy trees and trees in various stages of deterioration. Damage is reported frequently (Table 3.1). There are records for all years since 1982, with peaks in some years, but these do not relate clearly to drought years.

Drought

Drought records are surprisingly numerous, even in northern Britain: in addition to the 45 cases where drought was cited as the primary cause of damage (Table 3.1), a further 55 cases reported drought as an associated factor. Reports of damage are clustered in three periods: 1983–84, 1989–90 and 1995–96. These were also drought years throughout Britain. Outwith the survey period, other notable droughts in the last 50 years were in 1947, 1955, 1959 and 1975–76. The most common symptom is premature defoliation in established broadleaved trees and death of newly planted trees of all species. More serious damage in established trees, leading to dieback and death, affects mainly beech and larch (Figure 3.4). Among plantation-grown conifers, drought crack causes defects in the timber of various species including Sitka and Norway spruce, and most frequently in noble fir (*Abies procera*), grand fir (*Abies grandis*) and western hemlock (*Tsuga heterophylla*). Cracks also

Figure 3.4 A group of beech trees in southern England showing varying degrees of dieback caused by drought in 1976, and photographed in 1977.

provide an entry point for decay, but this may not be as important as the physical degrade[31,32].

The implications of climate change for tree health

Predictions of the future climate have been provided by Hulme and Jenkins[6]. There is expected to be an increase in mean temperature across the UK in all seasons. Other salient features for the purposes of this discussion, based on the Medium-high forecast in that report, are:

Winter
A decrease in the diurnal temperature range correlated with an increase in cloudiness and precipitation. Mean windspeed is expected to decrease slightly in the north and to increase in the south, and there is expected to be a general increase in the frequency of storms.

Spring
A decrease in the diurnal temperature range, again correlated with cloud cover changes.

Summer
Precipitation is expected to increase slightly in the north but in the southeast a marked reduction is anticipated. This is correlated with increased potential evapo-transpiration in the southeast and reduced cloudiness; consequently the diurnal temperature range is also expected to increase slightly.

Autumn
Cloud cover is expected to decrease across the UK, increasing the diurnal temperature range, particularly in the south. At the same time, precipitation is expected to increase.

Apart from anthropogenic causes of injury, the pathology of Sitka spruce in Britain is dominated by the effects of frost. During full winter dormancy, Sitka spruce can withstand temperatures of at least –20°C without injury, but after budburst in spring and before hardening has been completed in autumn, temperatures of –3°C to –5°C can kill tissues[33,34]. Spring and autumn frosts that give rise to temperatures that are lethal to tissues are of fairly frequent occurrence in northern Britain. In spring, the last potentially damaging frosts for Sitka spruce occur several weeks later in Scotland than on the west coast of North America, and in autumn the first frosts occur several weeks earlier[35,36]. Provenance choice is thus a key determinant of the extent of frost damage, particularly since the north–south range of Sitka spruce in North America spans regions that are both warmer and colder than where it is planted in the UK.

Dehardening and flushing in spring are influenced mainly by temperature[34], with the effect of daylength relatively weak[33]. Both processes are therefore likely to be advanced in future. Using a thermal time/chilling model, Cannell and Smith[37] predicted that budburst dates might vary from mid-April to early June, and suggested that any future climate warming could increase the risk of frost damage by advancing the date of budburst. However, further modelling work suggested that there may be little or no increase in the incidence of damage, since budburst would be advanced by only five days and on the date of budburst, temperature would also increase[38]. This conclusion is supported by work showing, first, that the higher the minimum air temperature at the time of budburst the lesser the likelihood of any subsequent damaging frost and, secondly, that elevated carbon dioxide (CO_2) concentrations combined with warming will hasten budburst. However, the advance of budburst by a combination of elevated CO_2 levels and warming is less than that resulting from climatic warming alone[38,39]. It was concluded that warming accompanied by a rise in CO_2 concentrations would reduce the risk of spring frost damage.

Frost damage is most frequently associated with polar airflows and clear night-time skies. The effect of climate change on short-duration weather patterns, and the influence of elevation and topography on flushing date, may therefore complicate predictions based on current models. Nevertheless, for the species and provenances currently grown, risks seem unlikely to increase.

In autumn, hardening is likely to be delayed by higher temperatures, but this may be offset by the effect of daylength, which is more important in autumn than in spring. Hardening may also be advanced by elevated CO_2 concentrations, which tend to advance bud set[12,33,39]. At the present time, the predicted probability of autumn frost damage is lower than that of spring frost damage[40]. However, in contrast to spring, cloud cover is predicted to decrease in autumn, particularly in England. This may increase the risk of frost damage in species that produce lammas shoots, such as Douglas fir, the spruces and also larch. Similarly needle damage to Sitka spruce might also increase.

Photoperiod at the latitude of seed origin has a major effect on growth cessation so that hardening of more southerly provenances is relatively late[33,40,41]. Planting Washington and Oregon provenances of Sitka spruce in more continental climates than those in which they are currently grown, perhaps in anticipation of further climate warming, would therefore be likely to incur increased damage.

In winter, despite the predicted rise in mean temperatures, damaging low temperatures may still be reached, although the frequency should be lower than it is now. On the other hand, this may be counterbalanced to some extent by a decrease in levels of hardiness[42], so that the risk of winter cold injury to species currently in use might only be slightly lower than it is now. Damage of the 'red belt' type, which is caused by temperature fluctuations and wind, is associated more with weather patterns than with temperature extremes. More damage

might be anticipated if there is an increase in the frequency with which continental (blocking) high-pressure systems are displaced quickly by deep low-pressure systems. For Norway spruce, the predicted rise in winter temperature and windiness, combined with reduced summer precipitation, could be expected to increase the incidence of 'top dying', particularly in England.

Higher summer temperatures and reduced rainfall will increase drought damage to established trees of vulnerable species, such as beech, larch, western red cedar (*Thuja plicata*), western hemlock, birch, ash (*Fraxinus excelsior*) and sycamore (*Acer pseudoplatanus*)[43,44]. Trees in hedgerows, on raised banks beside roads and in urban areas are likely to be more vulnerable than most trees grown under forest conditions[45]. The ability of some trees to withstand drought may also be compromised by higher winter rainfall, since this could raise winter water tables sufficiently to kill roots and thereby reduce rooting depth. By contrast, increased summer warmth should reduce the risk of damage to Corsican pine by *Gremmeniella abietina*, so that this tree species could be grown more widely in the uplands in future. The risk of winter cold injury should also be slightly lower. For all species, summer heat and drought can be expected to increase establishment losses.

Table 3.1 illustrates the importance of drought as a contributory factor in damage associated with other agents. Trees stressed by drought are vulnerable to attack by a number of weak pathogens. Outbreaks of sooty bark disease of sycamore caused by *Cryptostroma corticale*, strip cankers in beech caused by *Eutypa spinosa* and dieback of larch caused by *Ips cembrae* and the associated blue stain fungus *Ceratocystis laricicola* are all associated with high summer temperatures and drought. These diseases could all increase in the future[48,49].

Although not directly relevant to the UK, the decline of yellow cedar (*Chamaecyparis nootkatensis*) that has taken place since the

1880s in Alaska has been related to climate warming[46,47], and provides an example of what the future might hold for some species here.

Conclusions

The climate predictions available suggest that for the provenances and species presently grown, the risk of winter cold injury *per se* should be slightly lower in future than it is at present and that the risk of damage by spring frost should be no greater. On the other hand, autumn frosts may be more damaging in England if cloud cover decreases as predicted. The extension of southerly provenances of Sitka spruce into areas that are more continental than those where they are currently grown, in anticipation of climate change, may lead to damage and should be avoided. No prediction can be made about the effect of climate change on the incidence of 'red belt' since this phenomenon depends more on short-term weather patterns than on temperature extremes. However, the broadly similar type of injury known as 'top dying' of Norway spruce can be expected to increase in England and probably in eastern Scotland as well. Norway spruce is unlikely to remain a productive species over much of England.

Increasing heat and drought in the south and east can be expected to kill trees either directly, or indirectly by lowering resistance to weak pathogens. Losses are likely to be greatest among newly planted trees and among mature trees in hedgerows, along roadsides and in urban environments. In the south, defects in coniferous timber caused by drought crack can be expected to increase among all species except the pines.

Acknowledgements

We would like to thank the Finnish Forest Research Institute, Rovaniemi, Finland for permission to reproduce part of the following paper presented at a meeting in Lapland, 3–7 August 1992: Redfern, D.B. (1993). Climatic injury as a problem of introduced species in northern Britain. In: *Forest pathological research in northern forests with a special reference to abiotic stress factors*, eds R. Jalkanen, T. Aalto and M-L. Lahti. *Metsäntutkimuslaitoksen tiedonantoja* **451**, 44–49. We are grateful to Grace MacAskill for collating the data in Table 3.1.

References

1. MACDONALD, J., WOOD, R.F., EDWARDS, M.V. and ALDHOUS, J.R. (1957). *Exotic forest trees in Great Britain*. Forestry Commission Bulletin 30. HMSO, London.
2. MANLEY, G. (1952). *Climate and the British scene*. Collins, London.
3. MILLERS, I., SHRINER, D.S. and RIZZO, D. (1989). *History of hardwood decline in the eastern United States*. General Technical Report NE-126. Northeastern Forest Experiment Station, United States Department of Agriculture.
4. AUCLAIR, A.N.D., WORREST, R.C., LACHANCE, D. and MARTIN, H.C. (1992). Climatic perturbation as a general mechanism of forest decline. In: *Forest decline concepts*, eds P.D. Manion and D. Lachance. American Phytopathological Society, St Paul, Minnesota, USA, 38–58.
5. GREGORY, S.C. and REDFERN, D.B. (1998). *Diseases and disorders of forest trees*. Forestry Commission Field Book 16. The Stationery Office, London.
6. HULME, M. and JENKINS, G.J. (1998). *Climate change scenarios for the United Kingdom*. UKCIP Technical Report No.1. Climatic Research Unit, University of East Anglia, Norwich.
7. DAY, W.R. and PEACE, T.R. (1934). *The experimental production and the diagnosis of frost injury on forest trees*. Oxford Forestry Memoirs No. 16. Clarendon Press, Oxford.
8. DAY, W.R. and PEACE, T.R. (1946). *Spring frosts*. Forestry Commission Bulletin 18. HMSO, London.

9. REDFERN, D.B. (1982). Spring frost damage on Sitka spruce. In: *Report on Forest Research 1982*. HMSO, London, 27.

10. GREGORY, S.C., MACASKILL, G.M., REDFERN, D.B. and PRATT, J.E. (1990). Disease diagnostic and advisory service – Scotland and northern England. In: *Report on Forest Research 1990*. HMSO, London, 47–48.

11. YDE-ANDERSEN, A. and KOCH, J. (1993). Exceptional April frost injury in Sitka spruce plantations. In: *Forest pathological research in northern forests with a special reference to abiotic stress factors*, eds R. Jalkanen, T. Aalto and M-L. Lahti. *Metsäntutkimuslaitoksen tiedonantoja* **451**, 36–43.

12. REDFERN, D.B. and CANNELL, M.G.R. (1982). Needle damage in Sitka spruce caused by early autumn frosts. *Forestry* **55**, 39–45.

13. NICOLL, B.C., REDFERN, D.B. and McKAY, H.M. (1996). Autumn frost damage: clonal variation in Sitka spruce. *Forest Ecology and Management* **80**, 107–112.

14. PEACE, T. R. (1962). *Pathology of trees and shrubs*. Oxford University Press, Oxford.

15. PHILLIPS, D.H. (1965). Effects of winter cold. In: *Report on Forest Research 1964*. HMSO, London, 59–60.

16. TULEY, G. and GORDON, A.G. (1979). *Winter damage on* Nothofagus obliqua *and* N. procera. Research Information Note 45/79/SILS. Forestry Commission, London.

17. STROUTS, R.G. and PATCH, D. (1983). The cold winter of 1981–1982. In: *Report on Forest Research 1983*. HMSO, London, 35–36.

18. REDFERN, D.B. and ROSE, D.R. (1984). Winter cold damage to pines. In: *Report on Forest Research 1984*. HMSO, London, 34.

19. GREMMEN, J. (1961). Vorstschade aan Corsicaanse Dennen. *Nederlands Bosbouw-tijdschrijft* **33**, 328–332.

20. MACHATTIE, L.B. (1963). Winter injury of lodgepole pine foliage. *Weather* **19**, 301–307.

21. ROBINS, J.K. and SUSUT, J.P. (1974). *Red belt in Alberta*. Information Report NOR-X-99. Northern Forest Research Centre, Canadian Forestry Service, Environment Canada, Edmonton, Alberta, Canada.

22. REDFERN, D.B., GREGORY, S.C. and LOW, J.D. (1980). Advisory services – Northern Research Station. In: *Report on Forest Research 1980*. HMSO, London, 34–35.

23. JALKANEN, R. and NÄRHI, P. (1993). Red belt phenomenon on the slopes of the Levi fell in Kittilä, western Lapland. In: *Forest pathological research in northern forests with a special reference to abiotic stress factors*, eds R. Jalkanen, T. Aalto and M-L. Lahti. *Metsäntutkimuslaitoksen tiedonantoja* **451**, 55–60.

24. HAVRANEK, W.M. and TRANQUILLINI, W. (1995). Physiological processes during winter dormancy and their ecological significance. In: *Ecophysiology of coniferous forests*, eds W.K. Smith and T.M. Hinkley. Academic Press, London, 95–124.

25. REDFERN, D.B., GREGORY, S.C., PRATT, J.E. and MACASKILL, G.A. (1987). Foliage browning and shoot death in Sitka spruce and other conifers in northern Britain during winter 1983–84. *European Journal of Forest Pathology* **17**, 166–180.

26. REDFERN, D.B., GREGORY, S.C., MACASKILL, G.A. and PRATT, J.E. (1987). Advisory services – Scotland and northern England. In: *Report on Forest Research 1987*. HMSO, London, 42.

27. TRANQUILLINI, W. (1979). *Physiological ecology of the alpine timberline*. Ecological Studies 31, Springer-Verlag, Berlin.

28. MURRAY, J.S. (1954). Two diseases of spruce under investigation in Great Britain. *Forestry* **27**, 54–62.

29. MURRAY, J.S. (1957). *Top dying of Norway spruce in Great Britain*. Seventh British Commonwealth Forestry Conference, Australia and New Zealand 1957. Forestry Commission, London.

30. DIAMANDIS, S. (1979). 'Top-dying' of Norway spruce, *Picea abies* (L.) Karst., with special reference to *Rhizosphaera kalkhoffii* Bubák. VI. Evidence related to the primary cause of 'top-dying'. *European Journal of Forest Pathology* **9**, 183–191.

31. DAY, W.R. (1954). *Drought crack of conifers.* Forest Record 26. HMSO, London.

32. ALDHOUS, J.R. and LOW, A.J. (1974). *The potential of western hemlock, western red cedar, grand fir and noble fir in Britain.* Forestry Commission Bulletin 49. HMSO, London.

33. CANNELL, M.G.R. and SHEPPARD, L.J. (1982). Seasonal changes in the frost hardiness of provenances of *Picea sitchensis* in Scotland. *Forestry* **55**, 137–153.

34. JALKANEN, R.E., REDFERN, D.B. and SHEPPARD, L.J. (1998). Nutrient deficits increase frost hardiness in Sitka spruce (*Picea sitchensis*) needles. *Forest Ecology and Management* **107**, 191–201.

35. CANNELL, M.G.R. (1984). Spring frost damage on young *Picea sitchensis*. 1. Occurrence of damaging frosts in Scotland compared with western North America. *Forestry* **57**, 159–175.

36. CANNELL, M.G.R. (1985). Autumn frost damage on young *Picea sitchensis*. 1. Occurrence of autumn frosts in Scotland compared with western North America. *Forestry* **58**, 131–143.

37. CANNELL, M.G.R. and SMITH, R.I. (1984). Spring frost damage on young *Picea sitchensis*. 2. Predicted dates of budburst and probability of frost damage. *Forestry* **57**, 177–197.

38. CANNELL, M.G.R. and SMITH, R.I. (1986). Climatic warming, spring budburst and frost damage on trees. *Journal of Applied Ecology* **23**, 177–191.

39. MURRAY, M.B., SMITH, R.I., LEITH, I.D., FOWLER, D., LEE, H.S.J., FRIEND, A.D. and JARVIS, P.G. (1994). Effects of elevated CO_2, nutrition and climatic warming on bud phenology in Sitka spruce (*Picea sitchensis*) and their impact on the risk of frost damage. *Tree Physiology* **14**, 691–706.

40. CANNELL, M.G.R., SHEPPARD, L.J., SMITH, R.I. and MURRAY, M.B. (1985). Autumn frost damage on young *Picea sitchensis*. 2. Shoot frost hardening, and the probability of frost damage in Scotland. *Forestry* **58**, 145–166.

41. PARTANEN, J. and BEUKER, E. (1999). Effects of photoperiod and thermal time on the growth rhythm of *Pinus sylvestris* seedlings. *Scandinavian Journal of Forest Research* **14**, 487–497.

42. LARCHER, W. (1983). *Physiological Plant Ecology.* Springer-Verlag, Berlin.

43. CANNELL, M.G.R. and SPARKS, T.H. (1999). Health of beech trees in Britain. In: *Indicators of climate change in the UK*, eds M.G.R. Cannell, J.P. Palutikof and T.H. Sparks. Centre for Ecology and Hydrology, Natural Environment Research Council, 56–57.

44. STROUTS, R.G. and WINTER, T.G. (2000). *Diagnosis of ill-health in trees.* HMSO, London.

45. REDFERN, D.B., BOSWELL, R.C. and PROUDFOOT, J.C. (1997). *Forest condition in 1996.* Research Information Note 291. Forestry Commission, Edinburgh.

46. HENNON, P.E. and SHAW, C.G. (1994). Did climatic warming trigger the onset and development of yellow-cedar decline in southeast Alaska? *European Journal of Forest Pathology* **24**, 399–418.

47. HENNON, P.E. and SHAW, C.G. (1997). The enigma of yellow-cedar decline. What is killing these long-lived, defensive trees? *Journal of Forestry* **95**, 4–10.

48. REDFERN, D.B., STOAKLEY, J.T. and STEELE, H. (1987). Dieback and death of larch caused by *Ceratocystis laricicola* sp. nov. following attack by *Ips cembrae*. *Plant Pathology* **36**, 467–480.

49. HENDRY, S.J., LONSDALE, D. and BODDY, L. (1998). Strip-cankering of beech (*Fagus sylvatica*): pathology and distribution of symptomatic trees. *New Phytologist* **140**, 549–565.

4 Climate Change Impacts: Storms

KEY FINDINGS

- The UK has a severe wind climate, with the potential for afforestation often limited by wind; current forest management, particularly in the uplands is therefore adapted to extremes of wind climate.
- Since 1945, there has been notable damage to some forests in the UK, on average, every other year.
- Current predictions suggest a modest increase in mean wind speed, while the frequency of gales may increase; the predictions of both are tentative and generally within the magnitude of current inter-annual variability.
- Although the predictions suggest little impact in terms of the wind climate, uncertainty over the frequency of extremes, and the sensitivity of the damage threshold to methods of forest management, indicates no room for complacency.
- Climate change could have indirect consequences for wind risk management, including: changes to the frequency and duration of waterlogging; increased frequency of wet snow leading to more snow damage; larger leaf area resulting in increased wind resistance and thus vulnerability.
- No major adaptation to current management practice is recommended at this stage, but continuation of 'best practice' is appropriate, with review as climate predictions are refined. A number of key points should be considered for site-specific estimates of risk:
  - There are dangers in applying solutions from elsewhere without a careful appraisal of the similarity of the two situations.
  - For stands at high risk the potential options will tend to be limited, while for stands at low risk the options will be wide and goals other than risk-minimising will take precedence; it is those sites at moderate risk where the greatest potential exists to either exacerbate the risk by poor decision-making, or to reduce it through careful management; existing wind-risk models provide guidance.
  - Careful appraisal of future scenarios will be required, to reassess the strategy of continued wind risk-sensitive management and to identify whether more substantial changes in practice are warranted.

Introduction

This chapter reviews the current impact of strong winds on forests, and then considers predicted changes in the incidence of storms. Strong winds cause a variety of effects to trees and forests, including mortality of young plants through desiccation or toppling, restriction of growth, effects upon tree form (through branch and leader loss), and mortality through windthrow and wind snap. The emphasis here is on how climate change may influence the last two of these impacts.

Review of current impacts

The current climatology of strong winds

Across the world, strong winds sufficient to cause damage to trees are delivered by five mechanisms – hurricanes, tornadoes, thunderstorms, local orographic effects and extra-tropical cyclones. Hurricanes, tornadoes and thunderstorms are most prevalent in tropical and sub-tropical regions, and orographic effects are largely associated with major mountain chains such as the European Alps, the Rocky Mountains of North America, and the Southern Alps of New Zealand[1].

Extra-tropical cyclones are most significant in temperate regions of the world. These low pressure systems (depressions) form on the polar front, the junction between warm tropical air and cold polar air, and develop and intensify as they track in an easterly direction, before filling and declining. Britain's maritime location, on the edge of the European land mass, puts it close to the track of approximately 160 depressions each year, many of which are still vigorous when they reach its coastline. As a consequence, Britain has one of the most severe wind climates of the temperate regions, with equivalent areas being southeast Alaska, southern Chile, and other maritime fringes of Europe. Air masses rotate anti-clockwise in the northern hemisphere, and as a consequence of

their characteristic track and behaviour, the strongest winds are from the southwest, and the prevailing wind over Britain is between westerly and southwesterly.

Depressions frequently occur in families of events, due to the pattern of the wide-scale pressure fields, and such families may have an important fatiguing effect on trees. The track of individual storms can mean that the affected area may vary markedly from the pattern produced by the majority of the systems. However, in general there is a strong gradient in windiness and the frequency of strong winds, increasing from central Europe to Britain, and within Britain, from southeast to northwest. Winds are also stronger at high elevation than at low elevation, and in areas of high topographic exposure rather than in areas of high topographic shelter. The effect of strong winds on trees may be enhanced by snow or ice-loading, and damage to foliage can also occur when winds are salt-laden.

Effects on forests

There is a long recorded history of damage and disturbance to forests due to wind. There are documented accounts from the 13th century, and palaeo-ecological evidence (in peat bogs and in submerged forests exposed on foreshores) from even earlier. In the 20th century there were several major storms that caused substantial damage within individual regions, and on exposed sites, chronic (endemic) damage was common. The review of documented cases of damage between 1945 and 2000 shown in Table 4.1 indicates that some notable damage to forests occurred in Britain on average every other year.

Forest management in a windy climate

Forest management in Britain, particularly in upland Britain, has been developed to reduce the impacts of strong winds. A number of techniques are now used to prevent or

Table 4.1 *Storm catalogue from 1945–2000 only for events known to have damaged forests or trees*[2–4]. *Date gives first day if multiple day storms.*

Date	Main area affected	Notes
26.12.1998	Central and W Scotland	Damage to many old trees; forests in Kintyre – 850 000 m³
24.12.1997	Ireland, Wales, NW England	Clocaenog, Wales; Eire – 360 000 m³
06.11.1996	Central and W Scotland	
08.12.1993	SW England, Midlands	
17.01.1993	S Scotland, N England	Kelso area
26.02.1990	England, Wales and S Scotland	
03.02.1990	England	
25.01.1990	S and W Britain	'Burn's Day' storm – 1 260 000 m³ (1–3% growing stock)
16.01.1990	N Scotland	
16.12.1989	SW England	
13.02.1989	NE Scotland	Black Isle (Record low-level gust of 123 knots at Fraserburgh)
14.01.1989	N Scotland	
21.12.1988	N Scotland	
03.03.1988	NE Britain	
09.02.1988	SW England, Wales, SW Scotland	
16.10.1987	SE England	3 910 000 m³ (13–24% of growing stock)
25.08.1986	Ireland	Hurricane Charley, flooding and tree damage – especially old deciduous
13.01.1984	SW Scotland	
02.03.1982	Central Scotland	
02.01.1976	Midlands, mid Wales, E England	960 000 m³ (<5% growing stock)
12.01.1974	S Scotland	
02.04.1973	E England	
12.11.1972	Midlands and E England	
14.01.1968	Central Scotland	1 320 000 m³ (15–30% of growing stock)
21.07.1965	S England	Tornado RHS garden at Wisley – 179 trees uprooted
16.02.1962	NE England	'Sheffield' storm
16.09.1961	N Ireland	Hurricane Debbie
04.02.1957	Scotland	220 000 m³
01.03.1956	NE England	Pennine foothills Barnsley/Barnard Castle 28 000 m³
31.01.1953	NE Scotland	1 800 000 m³ (10–25% of growing stock)
30.12.1951	N/NW Scotland	FC – Borgie, Culloden, Alltcailleach – 8500 m³; private estates – Alvie, Fyvie, Kiethhall, Dunkeld, Doune – 113 000 m³
18.12.1949	Argyll	

minimise damage, including choice of site preparation, thinning regime and rotation length[5]. In addition, research has provided predictive tools to help managers select the appropriate techniques to match the appropriate level of risk. However, these techniques are inevitably, costly.

Sensitivities in threshold for damage

The winds recorded at conventional Meteorological Office sites during catastrophic storms in the 20th century have been reviewed[6]. In broad terms these indicate that gusts of 35 m s[-1] (hourly mean wind speeds of 22 m s[-1]) experienced at low-lying sites are associated with low percentages of damage (i.e. less than 5% of vulnerable growing stock), and that gusts of more than 40 m s[-1] (hourly mean wind speeds of 25 m s[-1]) result in widespread damage (10–30%). Damage is rarely noted when gusts less than 30 m s[-1] (hourly mean wind speeds of 19 m s[-1]) are recorded, and only a fraction of the current storm systems contain winds sufficient to cause damage (Figure 4.1).

The level of damage is thus very sensitive to the wind speed experienced, and substantial changes in strength and frequency of strong winds could have important effects on severity of windthrow.

Evidence for climate change

Instruments capable of measuring wind speed, or as pressure measurements, deriving wind speed, have only been available for approximately 120 years. Measurements at individual sites show substantial variability between years and between decades (see Figure 4.2), and regional differences in the year of highest wind speed. As a consequence of this variability, it is not as yet possible to observe any signal of climate change in wind speed records. In addition there have been substantial changes in the extent and character of forests in Britain. For example, during the 20th century, there was an increase in forest area from 5% to 12%, with much of this expansion on exposed sites in the north and west of the country which had not held forest for hundreds of years. The lack of a static population means that changing trends in damage are also impossible to observe.

Figure 4.1 An example of a typical frequency distribution of wind speed for a hilltop site in northern Britain (Strathlachlan), indicating the small fraction >19 m s[-1] which represents possible damaging events. Bars represent recorded data, and the line represents the fitted Weibull probability function.

Figure 4.2 Time-series indicating the high between year and between decade variability that makes detection of any climate change signal almost impossible. [Source: Hulme and Jenkins[7]].

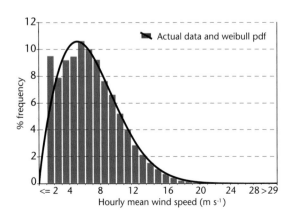

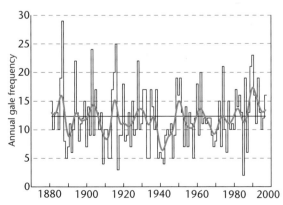

Potential impacts of climate change

The potential for enhanced storminess

Global warming will introduce more energy into the atmosphere, leading to accentuated pressure differences and increased windiness. However, which regions of the world will experience this enhanced windiness are difficult to predict.

Changes that would have a significant impact on forestry in Britain include those to the delivery mechanism (e.g. increased thunderstorm activity), the frequency, timing or magnitude of storms, the direction of the strongest winds, or the coincidence with other significant events (e.g. periods of heavy rain or wet snow).

What are the predictions?

There are acknowledged difficulties in predicting the magnitude and location of any change in windiness. However, the current predictions to 2080[7] propose modest changes in wind speed and seasonality, and modest differences between regions within Britain.

Mean wind speed

The scenarios suggest a 1–5% increase in wind speed, with, for example, those for the Medium-high scenario (see Chapter 2) suggesting a 1–2% increase by 2080 (Figure 4.3).

Seasonality

The scenarios suggest a shift in the seasonal pattern of windiness, with an increase in autumnal windiness, and a decline in summer windiness. For example, those for the Medium-high scenario indicate an increase of 2–7% in autumn wind speeds, an increase of 2–3% in spring windiness, a reduction of 1 to 2% for summer wind speeds, and little change (–1 to +1%) for winter wind speeds by 2080. The increase in autumn windiness is most pronounced in northern Britain (Figure 4.3).

Intense storms

An analysis of the probabilities of occurrence of daily wind speed (Figure 4.4) show more frequent high summer wind speed days in northern Britain, but little change in winter extremes; for southern Britain there is little consistent change in the extreme daily wind regime for summer or winter.

A further analysis of the scenario data yields a table of gale frequencies[7]. There is a suggestion of a decline in overall gale frequencies, but a possible increase in very severe winter gales. The authors note that '*the changing sign of the changes in severe gale frequencies between the three periods indicates that a clear anthropogenic signal in severe gale frequencies is not easily detectable from the noise of natural climate variability*'. A modest increase in summer gales is also forecast, although the frequency of these is very small (Table 4.2).

Figure 4.3 Annual and autumn predictions for changes (%) to mean wind speed relative to the 1961–1990 baseline for the Medium-high scenario (2080s) of UKCIP98. [Source: Hulme and Jenkins[7]].

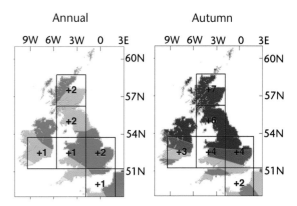

Figure 4.4 Occurrence of daily extremes – climate change predictions for extreme winds; black = 1961–90, green = 2080s. [Source: amended figure from Hulme and Jenkins[7] courtesy of Hadley Centre for Climate Prediction and Research].

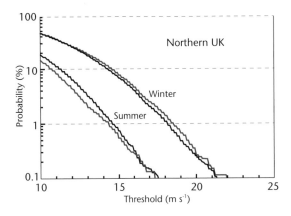

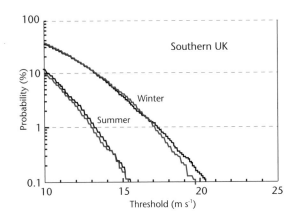

Table 4.2 Frequency of very severe gales per year. [Source: adapted from Hulme and Jenkins[7]].

	1961–90	2020s	2050s	2080s
Winter storms	1.4	1.5	1.3	1.6
Summer storms	0.10	0.12	0.08	0.11

What would be the potential impact of these changes?

The magnitude of predicted changes is less than the variability from one year to another experienced in the recent past. This implies that the predicted changes are likely to have little observable impact. A change of mean wind speed of 1–2% is likely to be invisible, but if it were to have an impact, this would most likely be to reduce growth rates in general, or possibly to alter the location of upper tree-lines. However, the effects of the increasing wind speed may be masked by those caused by increasing temperatures.

The effect of the predicted seasonal shift in windiness is also unlikely to be great. An increase in summer winds may have a subtle effect on the form of trees, through increased damage to branches and leaders before hardening is complete. It is arguable that an increase in windiness in autumn would be less damaging to trees than an equivalent increase in winter. Trees are probably better anchored in autumn than after repetitive stormy periods and subsequent fatiguing of the soil/root strength during the winter.

Any increase in intense storms is likely to be significant, but the predictions are so tentative, and the magnitude of the predicted effects so small, as to imply little change – particularly when wind damage is already a subject of management and mitigation measures. However, there are two aspects of the interaction between strong winds and storms that should be emphasised to caution against complacency. These are the sensitive nature of the link between mean and extreme wind climate (apparently small increases in mean wind speed can have a substantial effect on the probability of extreme wind speeds), and the powerful influence that forest management can exert on the wind speed that causes damage.

Uncertainties with prediction of strong winds

The strongest winds in Britain come from a small fraction of the large population of extra-tropical cyclones. As a result, there are reasonable statistical relationships between the mean windiness and the extreme windiness. This enables the likelihood of strong winds to be calculated from estimates of the mean windiness. However, the method is very sensitive to assumptions about the shape of the distribution. One of the parameters reflects the magnitude of the windiness (cf. intensity of storms), but the other reflects the relative frequency. The present climate change predictions provide indications of the magnitude but are not sufficiently informative regarding the frequency. This is illustrated in Figure 4.5 which shows the effect of an increase in mean wind speed of 10%, coupled with varying assumptions about the shape of the distribution. If the increase involved a change in spread of the distribution (light green), the impact could be more significant than the current predictions imply; this is shown by the black dashed line in Figure 4.6.

Use of the ForestGALES model to illustrate sensitivities to climate change

ForestGALES is a deterministic/probabilistic risk assessment model for managing wind risk to British forestry[8,9]. The model is stand-based (i.e. it works at the standard forest management unit) and is designed to assist tactical/strategic management decisions. The first part of the model involves entering the characteristics of the site and stand. The strength and the overturning resistance of the mean tree, and the wind loading on the tree are then calculated. The critical wind speeds required to overturn and break the tree are found by an iterative solution and are then converted into an annual probability of damage. This represents the probability that damaging winds will occur at the site occupied by the stand within any one year.

The ForestGALES model can be run for a specific stand at a point in time for which the necessary input data are known. Alternatively the model can calculate the change in damage probability over the life span of the stand from knowledge of the stand Yield Class and by

Figure 4.5 Uncertainties due to extreme parameters. Hourly mean wind speed for Strathlachlan (solid black line) together with simulations of the effect of a 10% increase assuming the same (dotted line), and two different distribution shapes.

Figure 4.6 Sensitivity to parameter assumptions. Return period for extreme wind speeds at Strathlachlan (solid grey line) together with three simulations assuming a 10% increase and different distribution shapes given in Figure 4.5.

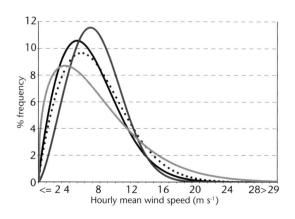

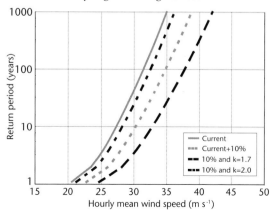

accessing mensurational data from yield tables stored as computer files. This allows differences in thinning patterns and initial planting spacing to be compared.

To demonstrate the sensitivity of damage to windiness and management choices, two scenarios have been selected for calculation by the ForestGALES model. In both, species and growth rate are held constant, assuming Sitka spruce (*Picea sitchensis*) of moderate growth rate (Yield Class 14, i.e. maximum mean annual increment of 14 m^3 ha^{-1} yr^{-1} with a top height of 19 m at age 50 years).

Windiness comparisons

The effect of subjecting the example stand to different wind climates is modelled by varying the DAMS scores[10]: values of 5, 10, 15 and 20 units (arbitrary DAMS windiness scores) equate to a range of wind climate from sheltered continental to exposed maritime. A DAMS score of 10 is equivalent to an annual mean wind speed of approx 2.5 m s^{-1} and a one-in-fifty year extreme hourly mean wind speed of 21 m s^{-1}; a DAMS score of 20 would equate to an annual mean wind speed of approx 7 m s^{-1} and a one-in-fifty extreme hourly mean wind speed of 35 m s^{-1}. Current predictions suggest a change in DAMS score of no more than 1–2 units at any one location. To illustrate the effects of soil type the calculations were performed using resistive turning moments representing brown earth and gley soils. On freely-draining brown earth soils, rooting depth of Sitka spruce is effectively unrestricted and may achieve depths well in excess of 1 m; on wet gley soils the rooting depth is restricted by winter water table and may be limited to 30 cm or less. A major change in site wetness may produce a change of soil type over centuries, but short-term saturation of soils will also weaken soil strength (see Chapter 5). At present the precise effect of this is difficult to quantify, but these results provide an illustration of the importance of soil type.

Silvicultural comparisons

Two options for initial site preparation are demonstrated: turf planting which permits good radial root development and little restriction of lateral root spread, and deep spaced-furrow ploughing which, although very successful as an aid to plant establishment, gives rise to very asymmetrical root systems.

A range of initial spacings were chosen to include narrow (1.4 m), standard (1.7 m) and wide (2.6 m) inter-tree distances. When subsequently managed to a 'no thin' regime, these spacings result in height:diameter ratios ranging from 81.5 to 114 at age 50. The 'no thin' regime has no artificial manipulation of spacing after planting and changes in stocking result only from competition-induced mortality. In addition, comparisons were made between the 'no thin' regime and a selective thinning regime in which space is manipulated to favour dominant stems.

Results of model runs

For ease of comparison in this review the annual figures calculated for the age of 50 (approximate economic rotation in British conditions) are used both for threshold wind speed of overturning (cf. hazard function) and for the probability of damage. Table 4.3 presents the results for a comparison of windiness and site type, for the standard spacing model (1.7 m) under a selective thinning regime. Threshold wind speed does not vary between wind climates but does vary between site types. However, the variation in wind speed alone is difficult to interpret. Once the wind speed is converted into the probability of damage, the significance of wind climate is apparent, and the difference between site types becomes more meaningful. In low wind speed climates the choice of management strategy may be unimportant, but choice will be crucial in high wind speed climates. For example, compare the differences in

Table 4.3 Results from ForestGALES illustrating the influence of windiness and soil type. Sitka spruce, 1.7 m initial spacing, selective thinning regime, shallow spaced furrow ploughing.

DAMS score (windiness)	Threshold wind speed for overturning at age 50 (m s^{-1})		Annual probability of exceedance of threshold wind speed at age 50	
	Brown earth	Gley	Brown earth	Gley
DAMS 5	27.4	23.8	0.0	0.0
DAMS 10	27.4	23.8	0.0	0.0
DAMS 15	27.4	23.8	0.005	0.059
DAMS 20	27.4	23.8	0.290	0.779

probability of damage between the two soil types in Table 4.3 for high and low DAMS scores. This emphasises the need for estimates of risk if we are to make sensible (context-specific) decisions. Note that it is not possible to generalise over strategy, as it is situation-dependent. Consequently, a strategy that provides discrimination in one location or climate (high DAMS score) may not in another location or climate (low DAMS score). In the same way it would not be appropriate to transfer a strategy from one climate regime, for example, maritime to continental or vice versa, or from past to the future *if* major changes were involved. At present, such changes are not forecast.

Table 4.4 presents the effects of silvicultural choice on threshold wind speed and annual probability of damage assuming a gley soil and a DAMS score of 15. Threshold wind speed again provides relativities between treatments and would permit the selection of the most stable on the basis of ranking. However, the importance of the choices is only apparent when the wind speeds are transformed into probabilities. The 'no thin' regime results in substantially lower probabilities than the other thinning regimes and, in comparison, the effect of initial spacing is relatively trivial. Selection of the most stable regime (i.e. turf plant and 'no thin') rather than the least stable (plough, wide space and thin) results in an almost 100-fold difference in probability – for the same site type and location. This graphically illustrates the potential for management to influence risk, and reinforces the need for objective tools to support decision-making. Surprisingly little is known about the sensitivity of decision making

Table 4.4 Results from ForestGALES illustrating the influence of spacing, thinning and site preparation choices. Sitka spruce, gley soil and a DAMS score of 15.

Spacing and thinning choice	Threshold wind speed for overturning at age 50 (m s^{-1})		Annual probability of exceedance of threshold wind speed at age 50	
	Turf	Plough	Turf	Plough
1.7 m No thin	29.8	25.9	0.001	0.015
1.7 m Selective thin	23.8	18.8	0.059	0.685
1.4 m Selective thin	24.5	19.4	0.038	0.567
2.6 m Selective thin	24.7	17.6	0.034	0.876

to levels of probability (annual or cumulative) and so it is not possible to set thresholds. These may also be situation-specific and also dependent upon economic and organisational factors.

Conclusions

Britain has a severe wind climate, and a long history of forest damage and disturbance. As a consequence, the forest management that has evolved, particularly in the uplands, is already well-adapted to this form of climatic extreme. Current predictions indicate modest changes to wind speed and frequency of intense wind storms. The magnitude of these changes is generally less than the inter-annual variability, and the predictions for the extremes are particularly tentative, so that the potential impact of climate change does not seem great. However, the uncertainty over the frequency of extremes, and the sensitivity of the damage threshold to methods of forest management, indicates no room for complacency. We propose that no major new adaptation of wind risk management is warranted in response to the climate change scenarios, but that continuation of 'best practice' is appropriate, with review as climate predictions are refined.

Recommendations for managers

Managers must make site-specific estimates of risk, and then develop site-specific management strategies; there are dangers in applying solutions from elsewhere without a careful appraisal of the similarity of the two situations. For stands at high risk the potential options will tend to be limited, while for stands at low risk the options will be wide and goals other than risk-minimising will take precedence. It is those sites at moderate risk where the greatest potential exists to either massively exacerbate the risk or to reduce the risk through careful management. For example, planting trees at wider spacing produces higher taper which

may reduce the risk of stem breakage due to the wind; at the same time it may increase the risk of crown damage from snow because of the production of a larger more exposed crown. Careful appraisal of future scenarios will be required, to reassess the strategy of continued wind risk-sensitive management and to identify whether more substantial changes in practice are warranted.

References

1. QUINE, C.P., HUMPHREY, J.W. and FERRIS, R. (1999). Should the wind disturbance patterns observed in natural forests be mimicked in planted forests in the British uplands? *Forestry* 72, 337–358.

2. ANDERSEN, K.F. (1954). Gales and gale damage to forests, with special reference to the effects of the storm of 31st January 1953, in the north east of Scotland. *Forestry* 27, 97–121.

3. ANDERSON, M.L. (1967). *A history of Scottish Forestry*, vols 1 and 2. Nelson, London.

4. LAMB, H.H. (1991). *Historic storms of the North Sea, British Isles and Northwest Europe*. Cambridge University Press, Cambridge.

5. QUINE, C.P., COUTTS, M.P., GARDINER, B.A. and PYATT, D.G. (1995). *Forests and wind: management to minimise damage*. Forestry Commission Bulletin 114. HMSO, London.

6. QUINE, C.P. (1991). Recent storm damage to trees and woodlands in southern Britain. In: *Research for practical arboriculture*, ed. S.J. Hodge. Forestry Commission Bulletin 93. HMSO, London, 83–94.

7. HULME, M. and JENKINS, G.J. (1998). *Climate change scenarios for the United Kingdom*. UKCIP Technical Report No. 1. Climatic Research Unit, University of East Anglia, Norwich.

8. DUNHAM, R., GARDINER, B., QUINE, C. and SUAREZ, J. (2000). *ForestGALES: a PC-based wind risk model for British forests - User's guide*. Version 1.3. Forestry Commission, Edinburgh.

9. GARDINER, B.A. and QUINE, C.P. (2000).

Management of forests to reduce the risk of abiotic damage – a review with particular reference to the effects of strong winds. *Forest Ecology and Management* **135**, 261–277.

10. QUINE, C.P. and WHITE, I.M.S. (1993). *Revised windiness scores for the windthrow hazard classification: the revised scoring method*. Research Information Note 230. Forestry Commission, Edinburgh.

Implications of Climate Change: Soil and Water

KEY FINDINGS

- Climate change can be expected to have a fundamental effect on soil properties and processes, and a direct impact on water resources.
- There is concern that global warming could result in a long-term loss of soil carbon stocks; however, the general view for temperate forests is that productivity currently exceeds soil organic matter decomposition, and global warming plus rising CO_2 concentrations are likely to enhance carbon storage for at least the next 50–100 years.
- Good forest management can help to promote soil carbon retention by selecting species best suited to the changed climate and by adopting practices that increase forest productivity and reduce carbon losses.
- Soil wetness, waterlogging and flooding are predicted to increase in winter throughout the UK; wetter soils will reduce trafficability and increase the risk of soil damage and erosion; an increased incidence of waterlogging will also reduce root survival and tree stability.
- Opportunities for the restoration of floodplain woodland are likely to increase, with possible attendant benefits of flood control.
- An increased frequency and severity of summer droughts is thought likely, and would threaten tree health and survival.
- An increased risk of water shortages in the south will require greater consideration to be given to the water use of trees and the need for better catchment management planning.
- The mobility, retention, dilution and in-stream processing of pollutants may be affected by climate change; enhanced acidification, eutrophication and the discoloration of water supplies will continue to be important issues.
- Freshwater biota could be threatened by higher water temperatures and altered river flows.
- Soil and water changes normally associated with afforestation and forest management practices can exceed those expected from climate change; judicious forest management and the development of best practice offer much scope for ameliorating the effects of climate change.

Introduction

The UK Climate Impacts Programme's (UKCIP) most probable climate change scenario[1] suggests a gradual warming across the whole of the UK, with mean summer and winter temperatures rising by some 2–3°C by the end of this century. Winters are predicted to be around 20% wetter, while summers could be 20% drier in the south and 5% wetter in the north (Chapter 2). Furthermore, recent Regional Climate Model (RCM) simulations (see Chapter 2) suggest that in Scotland there will also be a difference between the east and west, with a much larger increase in both the intensity and total volume of precipitation in the west[2]. Logic tells us that such changes are likely to have a fundamental effect on soil properties and processes, and a direct impact on water resources. Chief among soil concerns is the impact on soil organic matter turnover and thus carbon storage, a key element of the global warming debate. However, the concomitant effects on nutrient availability and soil erodibility are also very important, with significant implications for sustainable forest management. Changes to rainfall and evaporation will have more obvious effects, including the potential for more frequent winter flooding and summer water shortages, especially in the south. Wetter soils would reduce trafficability and increase the risk of soil damage and erosion, while an increased incidence of waterlogging would have a direct and potentially serious impact on root mortality and distribution. This chapter summarises current knowledge on these and other effects of climate change for UK forest soils and water resources, and considers the likely interactions with forest management.

Implications for soil

The soil is the basic living resource that underpins the whole forest ecosystem (Figure 5.1). It is a dynamic layer supported by many

Figure 5.1 A typical forest soil showing the accumulation of organic matter in the upper profile.

complex chemical, physical and biological activities. The majority of these are strongly regulated by climatic factors, the most important of which are temperature and moisture. Key soil properties and processes that will be affected by climate change include soil organic matter, soil water balance and soil erodibility.

Soil organic matter

Organic matter is a vital soil component affecting soil structure, water holding capacity, fertility, pollutant retention and biodiversity. It is also a critical pool in the carbon cycle and thus has a major role to play in greenhouse gas balance. The core issue is the stability of the organic matter store and whether climate change, combined with forest mangement, will lead to long-term loss or gain (Figure 5.2). In general terms, forest soils have a higher carbon content than soils associated with most other land uses[3] (Table 5.1), and it is this potential to sequester or emit large quantities of carbon, relative to the living biomass that they sustain,

Table 5.1 *Average soil carbon density (tC ha⁻¹) for different land covers in the UK. [Source: Milne, 2001[3]].*

Land cover	Region			
	England	**Scotland**	**Wales**	**Northern Ireland**
Natural	487	1048	305	551
Woodland	217	580	228	563
Arable	153	156	93	151
Pasture	170	192	200	178
Other	33	141	43	102

that is a key element over the discussion of soils and climate change.

On the input side of the equation is the question of the balance between the primary productivity of the forest, i.e. the production of organic matter by photosynthesis and the amount of energy used by the tree in respiration. Both are predicted to increase with temperature but the fraction of photosynthate consumed by respiration is expected to remain roughly the same, in the range 40–75%[4]. The general view for temperate forests, therefore, is

that the combined effects of a rise in temperature, a lengthened growing season, increased soil moisture and raised carbon dioxide levels ($[CO_2]$), is likely to result in an overall increase in tree growth and organic matter inputs to the soil[5].

There are, however, some concerns about whether increases in net primary productivity can be sustained in the long-term. A number of complicated negative feedbacks are possible, the most important of which is likely to be the effect on the soil nutrient supply, particularly in

Figure 5.2 *A summary of the processes and factors regulating net ecosystem productivity.*

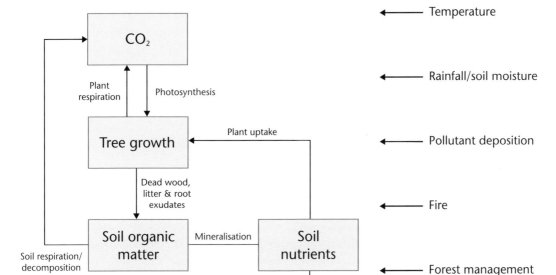

terms of nitrogen availability. Increased forest growth under elevated $[CO_2]$ has been shown to produce plant litter with a higher C:N ratio[6], at least in part a result of N limitation. Unless climate change speeds up soil nitrogen mineralisation and release (which is thought likely), this litter with a high C:N ratio may accumulate and induce nitrogen deficiency, limiting growth. Future changes to nitrogen deposition will also have a role to play, since it is widely believed that such inputs have been responsible for enhancing tree growth rates across much of northern Europe in recent decades[7]. EU nitrogen emissions are expected to decline significantly in the future as emission control policies increasingly take effect, although uncertainties remain over future trends in ammonia concentrations and hence deposition.

On the debit side of the carbon balance equation is the effect of climate change on the processes regulating soil carbon losses, principally the decomposition of soil organic matter. This is driven by soil microbial respiration, which in common with many biological and chemical processes, increases exponentially with temperature. As a rule of thumb, soil respiration rates approximately double for a 10°C rise in temperature, although the actual factor, termed Q_{10}, has been shown to vary widely between different soils. The central question is how the relative temperature sensitivities of organic matter decomposition and net primary productivity compare; if the former exceeds the latter then this could lead to a long-term decline in carbon storage. This issue remains the subject of considerable debate among the research community. A brief discussion of the implications of rising $[CO_2]$ on soil respiration is given in Chapter 9, together with a summary of initial findings relating to soil carbon balance from a Free Air Carbon Enrichment experiment (FACE).

The northern peatlands, which represent a major global carbon store, are thought to be most at risk of changing from a net sink to a net source of carbon. This is based on laboratory incubation studies that show the temperature sensitivity to be greatest at the lower end of the temperature spectrum, with Q_{10} values of 4–8 at temperatures of less than 5°C[8]. This contrasts with Q_{10} values of around 2 for net primary productivity. However, more recent field-based work in Scandinavia has found little evidence of any significant change in organic matter decomposition with soil warming, suggesting that peatland respiration is less sensitive to temperature than previously thought[9]. Possible reasons include the effect of the quality of the organic matter, with recalcitrant material of a high C:N ratio being more resistant to microbial decomposition[10]. Another important factor controlling soil respiration is water availability, rates being limited by waterlogging, which can be expected to increase with higher rainfall.

Forest management has an important role to play in the overall carbon balance. Clearly, factors such as forest age distribution, stand structure, species choice, harvesting regime, cultivation, drainage and fertiliser operations can all have an effect on forest net primary productivity and soil organic matter decomposition. While most practices that are designed to improve productivity will increase the value of the forest as a carbon sink, this is not always the case. Important exceptions include the burning of lop and top, and forest fires in general, both of which can cause large losses of soil and plant carbon and nitrogen to the atmosphere (Figure 5.3). The drainage of peatlands is another example, with the resulting improved soil aeration enhancing the decomposition of soil organic matter. Research in the UK has shown that in the long-term, this carbon loss will exceed the gain due to reduced soil methane and nitrous oxide production with soil drying, which are important greenhouse gases, and the increased net primary productivity with improved forest growth on the better drained soils[11].

Figure 5.3 Forest fires can have a major effect on net ecosystem productivity by reducing soil carbon and nitrogen pools, and altering the age distribution of forests.

In conclusion, most models suggest that the net primary productivity of temperate forests currently exceeds organic matter decomposition. They also predict that climate change combined with rising $[CO_2]$ is likely to enhance the forest carbon sink for at least the next 50–100 years. However, there remains much uncertainty, and time will tell whether this positive scenario is the correct one. Good forest management can help to promote carbon retention by selecting species and provenances best suited to the changed climate and by adopting practices that increase forest productivity or reduce carbon losses.

Soil water balance

Changes to rainfall and evaporation will have a direct effect on soil water balance. Concern naturally focuses on the two extremes of soil waterlogging and drought, with their attendant implications for tree stability and survival, as well as runoff generation and groundwater recharge. A clear distinction can be drawn between the likely effects of climate change in the north and the south. The increased winter and summer rainfall that is predicted for the north is likely to exceed the seasonal rise in evaporation, resulting in an all-year-round increase in soil wetness and waterlogging. This may necessitate a revision and extension of forest drainage and cultivation practices, with implications for organic matter decomposition, carbon storage and soil erosion. Winter waterlogging would present the added problem of restricting rooting depth, rendering trees more liable to summer drought stress.

The situation, however, is more complicated in the south, where there could be the dual disadvantage of greater soil wetness in the winter and increased drying in the summer. An increased frequency and severity of summer droughts could threaten tree health and survival. Previous events such as the 'long, hot summer' of 1995 have caused widespread problems for sensitive species such as beech, birch, ash and sycamore[12,13] (Figure 5.4). However, there is considerable uncertainty about the future susceptibility of trees to drought. Studies suggest that the rise in atmospheric $[CO_2]$ could increase the water use efficiency of trees by reducing stomatal opening, through which water is lost by transpiration[14]. Others argue that this could be offset by an increase in leaf area associated with the predicted rise in productivity due to climate change[15]. Another complicating factor is that greater winter rainfall is less likely to lead to the carry-over of a soil moisture deficit from one year to the next. This aspect has

Figure 5.4 Birch was one of the species to be severely affected by the 1995 drought, as shown by widespread leaf yellowing, browning and defoliation.

played a major part in the severity of past droughts, such as in 1976, when one dry year followed on from another. A fully re-wetted soil will mean more available water for tree growth during a subsequent summer drought, although this will be partly countered by any increase in tree water use.

Soil erodibility

An increase in both the quantity and intensity of rainfall can be expected to increase the risk of erosion in forest soils. This will have implications for the planning and management of forest operations in erosion-prone areas, especially within sensitive water catchments (Figure 5.5). Additional protective measures in terms of the timing and scale of operations, machine choice and sediment control are likely to be required to tackle the greater threat of soil damage from site trafficking and the resultant loss of sediment to streams, especially in connection with harvesting work[16].

Culvert design is another example of where change is likely to be required. Increased winter rainfall may exceed the design criteria for existing culverts in many areas, leading to more frequent failures and damage to the freshwater environment from downstream siltation (Figure 5.6).

Figure 5.6 Culvert failure may become a more regular occurrence with wetter winters.

Greater soil drying in the south of Britain will pose a different set of problems. Exposed soils may become more susceptible to wind erosion, particularly if warming and thus increased decomposition rates lead to a reduction in soil organic matter. This is more likely to arise with arable soils and could generate a need for more woodland planting in the form of shelterbelts or riparian buffers. The effect on clay soils could also be troublesome, with increased drying promoting shrinkage and swelling (Figure 5.7). The resulting soil cracking and ground subsidence could reduce tree survival on recently planted sites, and accentuate damage to buildings.

Figure 5.5 Frequent heavy rainfall and wet soils can cause particular problems for the harvesting of forest crops on erodible sites.

Figure 5.7 Soil drying and cracking can result in large plant losses on sensitive sites.

Implications for waters

It is readily apparent that a change to the rainfall climate is likely to affect both the timing and volume of river flows and the extent of groundwater recharge. Less clear, however, are the knock-on effects for water quality and freshwater biology. All of these aspects are considered below.

Water yield

It is helpful to separate the north and south of Britain when considering the effects of climate change on water yield, although the recent regional climate model (RCM) simulations also indicate an east-west split in Scotland[2] (see Chapter 2). The predicted increase in winter and summer rainfall in northern Britain can be expected to result in higher run-off and catchment water yields. Since only a small fraction of the water resource in these parts is currently utilised, this increase is unlikely to have any implications for water supplies. The main exception is for catchments that are used for the generation of hydroelectricity, where the additional yield could benefit production.

Of greater concern is likely to be the impact on flood risk. Recent wet winters have caused a number of serious flooding incidents and highlighted the threat to both rural and urban communities. Such events are expected to become more frequent in the future, requiring greater attention to be given to the issue of flood protection and control.

Forestry is viewed by many as having an important role to play in reducing flood risk. This is mainly due to the greater water use of conifer forest, which results from the higher interception loss from forest canopies compared with other vegetation types. For every 10% of a catchment covered by a mature conifer crop, there may be some 2% reduction in water yield[17]. A completely forested catchment may therefore have the effect of increasing evaporation by an amount that is equivalent to the predicted increase in annual rainfall under climate change. However, it does not follow that a higher forest water use will equally affect all flows. Interception by conifers varies during the year and tends to decline in proportion with the size and intensity of a given rainstorm. This is because the evaporation process effectively becomes 'saturated' during large events. Consequently, the scope for forests to reduce the severity of major floods that are derived from an extended period of very heavy rainfall or an intense storm is rather limited. The main exception could be for floods generated by snow melt, although climatic warming is likely to reduce the importance of such events; evaporation is greater from snow-covered forests and the rate of melting is slower for snow on the forest floor, both of which could help to reduce flood flows.

Cultivation and drainage practices can exert a strong effect on the timing of run-off from forest catchments. Deep ploughing and intensive drainage have the greatest impact since they increase the density of water channels by 60 times or more. This can increase flood flows by up to 20–30% and decrease the time to peak by about one-third for completely drained catchments[18]. The effect is long lasting, although it declines through time with soil subsidence and the infilling of drains. Badly designed drainage systems and the diversion of run-off from one catchment to another can also cause local flooding problems.

One location where forestry could make a net positive contribution to flood control is in the actual floodplain itself[19]. The removal of river embankments in less sensitive locations would allow floodwaters to spread out and thus help to reduce downstream flood peaks at high risk sites. Woodland would be a natural alternative on the farmland released in this way and could provide wider benefits for both flood retention and the freshwater environment in general. The greater 'hydraulic roughness' of woodland in terms of the physical presence of the trees and woody material on the ground surface, which can create 'debris dams', can be expected to delay and thus reduce flood flows (Figure 5.8). Floodplain woodland expansion is not without risks, however, and consideration needs to be given to sites that could be threatened by the backing-up of floodwaters, problems of restricted access to rivers, and the impact of a higher water use on water supplies during periods of summer drought.

The effects of climate change on the opposite flow extreme, namely low river flows, is another issue. Low flows are mainly controlled by the frequency of summer rainfall and the nature and extent of groundwater stores within a catchment. The predominantly hard geology underlying most of northern Britain means that groundwater storage is relatively small and many areas suffer from a low flow problem during summer months. This has led to concerns about the effects of new forest planting in some locations, although recent research suggests that forestry will generally have little impact on the generation of low flows[20]. Since summer rainfall is predicted to increase and evaporation to decrease slightly in northern Scotland by the end of this century, such problems may be eased in the future.

Figure 5.8 Trees, fallen branches and leaf litter can create a dynamic network of multiple channels and dams which can help to slow down flood flows.

Turning to the south of Britain, the predicted increase in winter rainfall may pose a similar threat of flooding, but it is the effect of the decrease in summer rainfall and increased evaporation that is likely to present an even greater cause for concern. Water demand already exceeds supply during dry summers in the south and is predicted to rise by 15–27% between 1990 and 2021 due to population growth and warmer temperatures[21]. A scenario of increasing water shortages is likely to focus efforts on protecting existing supplies and developing new sources.

Areas with more impermeable geology such as southwestern England and upland Wales will be most at risk. These will suffer from the dual problem of much of the increased winter rainfall directly running off into rivers, contributing to an increased flood risk, as well as reduced flows in summer. This could require the construction of more storage reservoirs to aid flood control and water supply during summer droughts.

The impact of a greater summer drying on water supplies, however, remains unclear. Much will depend on the nature of the underlying geology in terms of its ability to store and release higher winter rainfall. Porous rocks such as chalk and sandstone underlie much of southern England and represent major groundwater aquifers. These supply up to 75% of water needs in some regions and sustain summer flows in many major river systems, such as the River Thames. Recharge normally takes place between mid-winter and early spring once the summer soil moisture deficit has been met. Provided that the increased winter rainfall is sufficient to exceed any enhanced deficit, then the effect on groundwater supplies is likely to be positive. There are reasons to expect that this could well be the case since plant physiological controls will limit how far the soil moisture deficit can extend. The browning-off of shorter vegetation such as grass and the ability of trees to limit transpiration rates when atmospheric demand is high by closing leaf stomata, means that the increase in actual evaporation is likely to be much less than that of potential evaporation.

It has already been noted that conifer forests generally use more water than shorter vegetation and while this is thought to have little effect on the generation of flood flows, the impact on water supplies in the south is a different matter. Research has shown that mature conifer crops can cause a disproportionately large reduction in groundwater recharge in drier regions due to the smaller quantity of rainfall and thus effective drainage. Reductions of 80% or more are possible, making any significant expansion of conifer woodland a cause for concern in drought prone areas[22].

Broadleaved woodland has a much lower water use compared to conifers and thus poses less of a threat to water resources. In fact, studies on chalk actually show greater recharge under beech woodland compared to managed grassland and therefore new planting could help to enhance water supplies in some locations[23]. However, woodland on drier soils overlying sandstone may have the opposite effect; this remains the subject of ongoing research[24] (Figure 5.9). Other situations where broadleaved woodland is likely to diminish water yields include the large-scale planting of short rotation coppice crops of poplar and willow. These species have been shown to have a fairly luxuriant use of water where water is not limiting, with the potential to reduce water yields by 50% or more compared to grass[22]. It is important to note though that the relative balance of water use between different species and vegetation types could alter in the future, depending on changes to the length of the growing season and in water use efficiency with climate warming and increased [CO_2].

The wide ranging nature of the possible effects of forestry on water yield is likely to make land use a more important consideration in future water resource planning. Forest and woodland design has a key role to play in this

Figure 5.9 Soil moisture probes are being employed in Clipstone Forest in Nottinghamshire, along with other techniques, to compare the water use by oak, Corsican pine, heath and grass.

process, since the scale, species mix and age distribution of the forest cover, as well as the nature of forestry practices, will all affect the amount of water evaporated. For example, it is more than likely that the effect of a well-managed, mixed-age and mixed-species forest will be much smaller than that comprising a uniform mature crop (Figure 5.10). Judicious forest design and management could therefore play a role in helping to offset some of the effects of climate change on future water supplies within existing forested catchments.

Water quality

Increased rainfall and temperature can be expected to affect the deposition, mobility, retention, dilution and in-stream processing of pollutants, with consequent effects on water

Figure 5.10 *Forest design planning is leading to the creation of a more open and diverse forest structure in Britain, which will help to protect water supplies.*

quality. One important issue is the effect on surface water acidification, which remains a serious problem in some parts of the UK (Figure 5.11). While emission control is succeeding in reducing acid deposition and aiding chemical recovery, this could be partly offset by climate change.

Firstly, higher annual rainfall could increase the loading of acid deposition and the leaching of soil base cations. This would be made worse if, as some predictions suggest, there were more frequent storms leading to more frequent and possibly accentuated acid events, driven by both sea-salts and acid deposition. Such events will probably become more common during summer months in the north as a result of higher rainfall and the effects of intervening, warmer dry periods. The latter will increase the mineralisation of soil organic matter, resulting in the greater release and consequent flushing of stored sulphur and nitrogen compounds, contributing to acidification. Freshwater life is particularly vulnerable to acid spates at this time of the year.

Secondly, forests are known to contribute to the problem of surface water acidification as a result of the increased capture of acid deposition by their aerodynamically rougher canopies[25]. This scavenging effect is largest when the forest is covered by cloud, which is

Figure 5.11 *Monitoring is under way in a number of acid sensitive areas, such as in the River Halladale catchment in north Scotland, to assess the longer-term effects of forestry, emission control and climate change on water quality.*

greatest at higher altitudes, particularly above 300 m elevation (Figure 5.12). Wetter winters could be expected to increase the extent and duration of cloud cover and thus the magnitude of pollutant scavenging.

On the positive side, higher soil temperature and moisture may increase soil mineral weathering rates, helping to neutralise acidity. Increases in forest productivity will also enhance nitrate uptake and so reduce nitrate leaching, providing uptake exceeds any enhancement in soil nitrification. This could help to counter the emerging problem of nitrogen saturation in some forest soils, which threatens to increase nitrate release and thus acidification[26]. An increase in soil wetness and waterlogging would also assist by promoting denitrification.

Eutrophication is another issue likely to be affected by climate change. Phosphate is the principal nutrient limiting algal growth in freshwaters and an increase in temperature could stimulate its release from soils and sediments. Warmer conditions would also promote algal growth and winter survival, although this would be offset by the increased dilution and flushing due to higher rainfall. An increase in the growth of terrestrial plants could help to lock up some of the released nutrients, but an enhanced productivity of

aquatic plants would mean greater weed problems. In terms of forestry, there would be raised concern about the leaching of phosphate following fertiliser applications, and to a lesser extent harvesting operations, in sensitive water catchments (Figure 5.13). Wetter conditions would increase the risk of fertiliser run-off from forests, although the need for applications could reduce if soil nutrients became more available.

Finally, climatic warming has already been linked with an observed rise in dissolved organic carbon (DOC) concentrations in stream waters, thought to result from the increased mineralisation of soil organic matter. Long-term monitoring studies reveal that concentrations have increased by some 10% over the last ten years[27]. Aside from representing a loss of carbon from the terrestrial ecosystem, DOC is directly associated with water colour and thus could lead to increased discoloration of water supplies. High water colour is a serious problem in a number of parts of upland Britain, causing the formation of toxic trihalomethane chemicals when waters are chlorinated for public supply[28]. Both forest drainage and soil drying due to the higher water use of forest crops have been implicated in this issue[29] (Figure 5.14).

Figure 5.12 '*Cloud collectors' are used to quantify the additional capture of acid deposition by forest canopies, which could be greater under a wetter climate.*

Figure 5.13 *There is already a debate in some areas about the relative contributions of forestry and fish farms to phosphate levels in sensitive waters.*

Figure 5.14 Site cultivation will promote soil drying and the mineralisation of soil organic matter, which could contribute to the increased discoloration of some water supplies.

Water biology

The freshwater biota may be threatened by raised water temperatures and altered river flows. Fish, and salmonids in particular, are very sensitive to changing temperature, with potential effects on the timing of spawning, fish growth rates and even survival. Salmonid fish, which predominate in upland waters, require temperatures of between 5 and 15°C for normal growth[30]. While upward shifts into or within this range would benefit growth rates, rises to 21°C and above would have the opposite effect, and could be lethal. Higher water temperatures could also be expected to lead to more disease outbreaks and fungal infections, particularly within fish farms.

The situation with cyprinid fish in lowland waters is more positive, with most species likely to benefit from increased water temperatures. The main caveat concerns those waters that are subject to organic pollution from sewage works and farmland. Since a rise in water temperature decreases the amount of oxygen that water can hold and will increase the microbial oxygen demand, warming is likely to increase the risk of oxygen starvation and fish death.

The wider freshwater biota in forests is also sensitive to temperature change, with increases possibly affecting the composition of invertebrate and aquatic plant communities, and the distribution of individual species. Precise impacts are difficult to predict due to the complex interactions between species tolerances and optima, food availability, competition, predation and susceptibility to disease.

Higher winter and lower summer river flows could affect habitat quality and accessibility. More frequent high flow events would increase the erosion of river gravels and thus the washout of fish eggs. There could also be a rise in siltation resulting from greater soil erosion and bank collapse. Both factors would have a detrimental effect on fisheries and on the wider freshwater environment. Reduced summer flows would restrict habitat availability and fish movements while, in contrast, a greater frequency and extent of winter flooding would have wide benefits for wildlife.

Forestry could help to moderate the predicted rise in water temperature through the management of shade[31]. Heavy shade has generally been found to reduce stream productivity, although benefits can result where high stream temperatures exceed tolerance limits[32]. Current clearance and redesign of the riparian zone within upland forests in Britain is aimed at maintaining about half the length of a watercourse open to sunlight, with the remainder being under dappled shade from mainly broadleaved species. Judicious management of riparian woodland offers a means of achieving a sensible balance between light and shade and thus the most favourable water temperature (Figure 5.15). An expansion of woodland planting along lowland rivers would be particularly helpful in this respect, by providing much needed shade and shelter from high summer temperatures. There would also be many other environmental benefits, including the retention of diffuse pollutants draining adjacent agricultural ground[19]. However, such advantages must be carefully balanced against the increased threat to water flows and supplies by the greater water use of woodland vegetation, particularly involving species with a high water demand, such as willow and poplar.

Figure 5.15 Riparian woodland has an important role to play in protecting the freshwater environment from the wider effects of climate change.

Conclusions

Climate change could have wide ranging impacts on forest soils and the quality and quantity of drainage waters. Among the most important soil effects predicted are an increase in soil organic matter and thus carbon storage, increased soil wetness and waterlogging in winter, increased soil drying in the summer, particularly in the south, and an increased risk of soil damage and erosion. Probable key water impacts include higher river flows in winter leading to an increased flood risk, reduced or enhanced groundwater recharge and summer low flows in the south, an increased risk of surface water acidification in acid sensitive areas, an increased risk of eutrophication and discoloration of water supplies, and changes to the diversity and abundance of aquatic flora and fauna.

Forest management could help to enhance the beneficial effects of climate change and moderate the threats. Attention to species choice and good silvicultural practice will improve net primary productivity and carbon storage, as well as helping to tackle the adverse effects of increased summer drought, both for tree health and the impacts of woodland on water supplies. Some restrictions on the type and scale of future planting on sandstone may be required to protect water resources, while an expansion of broadleaved woodland on chalk could actually enhance groundwater supplies. The application and development of good practice offers much scope for reducing the threats to soil and water quality. Upland forestry probably has a minor role to play in controlling future flood risk but the restoration of floodplain woodland could make a significant contribution to flood defence. Woodland planting and management in the riparian zone presents an effective way of moderating water temperature changes through achieving a sensible balance between light and shade, with wider benefits for the freshwater environment. In the light of the complexity of the issues outlined in this chapter, and also the lack of definitive answers to guide forest management, it is clear that the continuation of monitoring and research will be very important.

References

1. HULME, M. and JENKINS, G. (1998). *Climate change scenarios for the United Kingdom*. UKCIP Technical Report No. 1. Climatic Research Unit, University of East Anglia, Norwich.

2. HULME, M., CROSSLEY, J. and LU, X. (2001). *An exploration of regional climate change scenarios for Scotland*. Scottish Executive Central Research Unit, Edinburgh.

3. MILNE, R. (2001). Land use change and forestry: The 1999 greenhouse gas inventory for England, Scotland, Wales and Northern Ireland. In: *Greenhouse gas inventories for England, Scotland, Wales and Northern Ireland: 1990, 1995, 1998 and 1999*, eds A.G. Salway *et al.* National Environmental Technology Centre, AEA Technology, Harwell.

4. SAXE, H., CANNELL, M.G.R., JOHNSEN, Ø., RYAN, M.G. and VOURLITIS, G. (2001). Tree and forest functioning in response to global warming. Tansley Review No. 123. *New Phytologist* **149**, 369–400.

5. BROADMEADOW, M.S.J. (2000). *Climate change – implications for forestry in Britain*. Forestry Commission Information Note 31. Forestry Commission, Edinburgh.

6. HU, S., CHAPIN III, F.S., FIRESTONE, M.K., FIELD, C.B. and CHIARIELLO, N.R. (2001). Nitrogen limitation of microbial decomposition in a grassland under elevated CO_2. *Nature* **409**,188–191.

7. CANNELL, M.G.R., THORNLEY, D.C., MOBBS, D.C. and FRIEND, A.D. (1998). UK conifer forests may be growing faster in response to increased N deposition, atmospheric CO_2 and temperature. *Forestry* **71**, 277–295.

8. KIRSCHBAUM, M.U.F. (1995). The temperature dependence of soil organic matter decomposition, and the effect of global warming on soil organic

C storage. *Soil Biology and Biochemistry* **27**, 753–760.

9. JARVIS, P.G. and LINDER, S. (2000). Constraints to growth of boreal forests. *Nature* **405**, 904–905.

10. GIARDINA, C.P. and RYAN, M.G. (2000). Evidence that decomposition rates of organic mineral soil do not vary with temperature. *Nature* **404**, 858–861.

11. CANNELL, M.G.R., DEWAR, R.C. and PYATT, D.G. (1993). Conifer plantations on drained peatlands in Britain: a net gain or loss of carbon? *Forestry* **66**, 353–360.

12. REDFERN, D., BOSWELL, R. and PROUDFOOT, J. (1996). *Forest condition 1995*. Research Information Note 282. Forestry Commission, Edinburgh.

13. CANNELL, M.G.R. and McNALLY, S. (1997). Forestry. In: *Economic impacts of the hot summer and unusually warm year of 1995*, eds J.P. Palutikof, S. Subak and M.D. Agnew. Department of the Environment and University of East Anglia, Norwich, 33–44.

14. MEDLYN, B.E., BARTON, C.V.M., BROADMEADOW, M.S.J., CEULEMANS, R., DE ANGELIS, P., FORSTREUTER, M., FREEMAN, M., JACKSON, S.B., KELLOMAKI, S., LAITAT, E., REY, A., ROBERNTZ, P., SIGURDSSON, B.D., STRASSEMEYER, J., WANG, K., CURTIS, P.S. and JARVIS, P.G. (2001). Stomatal conductance of forest species after long-term exposure to elevated CO_2 concentration: a synthesis. *New Phytologist* **149**, 247–264.

15. BROADMEADOW, M.S.J. and JACKSON, S.B. (2000). Growth response of *Quercus petraea*, *Fraxinus excelsior* and *Pinus sylvestris* to elevated carbon dioxide, ozone and water supply. *New Phytologist* **146**, 437–451.

16. NISBET, T.R. (2001). The role of forest management in controlling diffuse pollution from UK forestry. *Forest Ecology and Management* **143**, 215–226.

17. FORESTRY COMMISSION (1993). *Forests and water guidelines*. Forestry Commission, Edinburgh.

18. ROBINSON, M., MOORE, R.E., NISBET, T.R. and BLACKIE, J.R. (1998). *From moorland to forest: the Coalburn catchment experiment.* Institute of Hydrology Report 133. Institute of Hydrology, Wallingford.

19. KERR, G. and NISBET, T.R. (1996). The restoration of floodplain woodlands in lowland Britain: A scoping study and recommendations for further research. Environment Agency Report W15. Foundation for Water Research, Marlow, Bucks.

20. NISBET, T.R. and STONARD, J.S. (1995). The impact of forestry on low flow regime – an analysis of long-term streamflow records from upland catchments. In: *Proceedings of the British Hydrological Society's 5th National Hydrology Symposium*, eds A.R. Black and R.C. Johnson. Institute of Hydrology, Wallingford, 7.25-7.30.

21. NATIONAL RIVERS AUTHORITY (1994). *Water: Nature's precious resource.* National Rivers Authority, Bristol.

22. HALL, R.L., ALLEN, S.J., ROSIER, P.T.W., SMITH, D.M., HODNETT, M.G., ROBERTS, J.M., HOPKINS, R., DAVIES, H.N., KINNIBURGH, D.G. and GOODY, D.C. (1996). *Hydrological effects of short rotation coppice.* Final Report (B/W5/00275/REP) to ETSU (July 1996). Institute of Hydrology, Wallingford.

23. HARDING, R.J., HALL, R.L., NEAL, C., ROBERTS, J.M., ROSIER, P.T.W. and KINNIBURGH, D.G. (1992). *Hydrological impacts of broadleaf woodlands: implications for water use and water quality.* Project Report 115/03/ST. National Rivers Authority, Bristol.

24. CALDER, I.R., REID, I., NISBET, T.R., BRAINARD, J., GREEN, J. and WALKER, D. (2000). Impact of lowland community forests on groundwater resources. In: *Proceedings of the British Hydrological Society's 7th National Hydrology Symposium.* Newcastle University, Newcastle, 2.83-2.88.

25. FOWLER, D., CAPE, J.N. and UNSWORTH, M.H. (1989). Deposition of atmospheric pollutants on forests. *Philosophical Transactions of the Royal Society, London,* **B324**, 247–265.

26. EMMETT, B.A. and REYNOLDS, B. (1996). Nitrogen critical loads for spruce plantations in Wales: is there too much nitrogen? *Forestry* **69**, 205–214.

27. MONTEITH, D.T. and EVANS, C.D. (2000). *UK acid waters monitoring network: 10 year report.* ENSIS Publishing, London.

28. MILOT, J., RODRIGUEZ, M.J. and SERODES, J.B. (2000). Modelling the susceptibility of drinking water utilities to form high concentrations of trihalomethanes. *Journal of Environmental Management* **60**, 155–171.

29. REYNOLDS, S.E., KNEALE, P.E. and MCDONALD, A.T. (1996). Quantifying the store of water soluble colour in upland peaty soils: the effect of forestry. *Scottish Forestry* **50**, 22–30.

30. ARNELL, N.W., JENKINS, A. and GEORGE, D.G. (1993). *The implications of climate change for the National Rivers Authority.* National Rivers Authority R&D Report 12. National Rivers Authority, Bristol.

31. NAKAMURA, F. and DOKAI, T. (1989). Estimation of the effect of riparian forest on stream temperature based on heat budget. *Journal of the Japanese Forestry Society* **71**, 387–394.

32. BESCHTA, R.L., BILBY, R.E., BROWN, G.W., HOLTBY, L.B. and HOFSTRA, T.D. (1987). Stream temperature and aquatic habitat: fisheries and forestry interactions. In: *Streamside management: forestry and fisheries interactions*, eds E.O. Salo and T.W. Cundy. Institute of Forest Resources, University of Washington, Washington, USA, 191–232.

6

Climate Change and the Seasonality of Woodland Flora and Fauna

KEY FINDINGS

- Phenology is a significant resource allowing us to examine how species have responded to natural temperature variation in the past, and also to ongoing anthropogenically-driven climate change.
- The temperature response of spring activity has been examined for a wide range of native flora and fauna.
- Documented changes in timing in recent decades have been very marked with spring activity of several species advancing by up to a month.
- Changes appear to be more marked in the UK than elsewhere in Europe and are stronger for plants and invertebrates than for vertebrates.
- Differences in species response to temperature may result in an altered competitive advantage and thus to a changed community composition in the future.
- The consequences of a changed phenology must not be considered in isolation from other direct climate-change-related problems such as changed frequency of extreme events (drought, flood, storms) or through indirect effects such as land use change or habitat fragmentation.
- Populations of deer and squirrels are adversely affected by cool, wet weather, through reducing food availability and increasing mortality. Predicted climate change is therefore likely to result in increased population densities and ranges if appropriate control measures are not put in place.
- A phenology network has been established to provide monitoring information and to raise awareness of climate change issues.

Introduction

The seasonality or timing of natural events in woodland ecosystems is a key factor determining their composition, character and survival. In many cases, woodland fauna are dependent on the flushing of trees or the regrowth of herbaceous species in spring for food. Furthermore, the growth of trees is itself a function of the length of the growing season, with, as a rule of thumb, an extension in growing season of one week equating to an increase in growth potential of 10%. Changes to the timing of budburst are likely to have larger impacts on productivity than a delay in the onset of autumn senescence since energy input from the sun is much larger in spring (April–May) than autumn (October). This chapter therefore concentrates on the timing of spring events, and discusses them in terms of climate change and natural climate variability.

The study of the timing of naturally recurring events, phenology, has a long history in the UK, and has now evolved from being a pastime for nature lovers to being recognised as a valuable tool in monitoring the impacts of climate change. The reason for this rise in importance is that the wealth of long-term phenological data-sets that are available represents a resource that is present in few other fields of research. While the observations summarised in this chapter may not have been recorded exclusively in woodland, an attempt has been made to restrict the examples given to species that occur in woodland. Phenology, typically but not always, involves simple observations of first events, such as first leafing. As such, it goes against the grain of recent scientific studies of climate change impacts on British wildlife that are using increasingly sophisticated and expensive equipment and approaches, such as the modelling of climate response surfaces[1], or the examples given in Chapters 11 and 12. In contrast, phenology can be carried out by a competent naturalist with only a pencil and notebook. This chapter details some of the temperature-related changes in UK phenology that have been reported by a variety of sources, and in some cases, over periods exceeding two hundred years. These examples refer only to past events and are not used here in a predictive manner, but they demonstrate how British wildlife has responded to natural climate variability. In addition, the more complex interactions between climate, the phenology of forage and activity are discussed for squirrels and deer, both important inhabitants of British forests.

Sources of data

Phenological observations in Britain date back to 1736. Until the latter half of the 19th century records largely exist from the diary entries of dedicated naturalists acting independently. Undoubtedly, many of these will have now been lost forever, although old records continue to be unearthed as phenology receives greater attention. From the 1870s, phenology became co-ordinated under the auspices of the Royal Meteorological Society, but in the post-war period, with the exception of the British Naturalists' Association, phenology again became largely an unco-ordinated activity. Despite these organisational changes, a wealth of data for the last fifty years is available, and it represents the period when the majority of migrant bird information was collected both by county bird recorders and at coastal bird observatories. It was also the period in which some institutional monitoring schemes, such as the Butterfly Monitoring Scheme became established. In the recent past, monitoring networks such as the Environmental Change Network[2] (ECN) and the UK Phenology Network[3] have also been established, and continue to provide valuable data.

The Marsham record

Robert Marsham FRS (1708–1798) is considered to be the father of British phenology. Marsham inherited an estate a few miles north of Norwich and displayed an intense interest in trees and established a series of replicated experiments with the aim of increasing their productivity. In 1736 he commenced recording 27 'Indications of Spring'. These included first leafing dates of 13 tree species, first flowering of snowdrop, hawthorn and two other species, arrival dates of some migrant birds, the nesting activities of rooks and the first croaking of amphibians. These records were continued by successive generations of the Marsham family up to 1958, and one member of the family continues to contribute to the current UK phenology network, although not from the original location. As with most data-sets, the Marsham record has gaps in it, but there are between 160 and 200 years of data for the tree species and these give us a unique opportunity to examine how trees have responded to natural variability in climate.

The relationship between flushing date of mountain ash (*Sorbus aucuparia*) and mean temperature in the period 1 February to 30 April is shown in Figure 6.1. As is the case throughout this chapter (unless specifically mentioned), the temperatures quoted are the Central England Temperature (CET) record[4]. The response of flushing in mountain ash is of the order of an advance of six days for every degree Celsius rise in temperature. Sparks and Carey provide a comprehensive analysis of the data from 1736 to 1947[5].

Although most species seem to fit this general relationship, there is sufficient variation in the response of individual species, for example between ash (*Fraxinus excelsior*) and oak (*Quercus robur*), to suggest that climate warming could result in perceptibly different impacts on the flushing of individual species (Table 6.1). In turn, competition between species could be affected by a differential response of flushing date, potentially resulting in altered woodland composition at the community level. Such a threat is of considerable interest in mainland Europe[6], particularly for commercial forestry.

Figure 6.1 The relationship between first leafing date of mountain ash and mean February–April temperature (°C). A strong negative relationship is apparent, suggesting earlier leafing in warmer years.

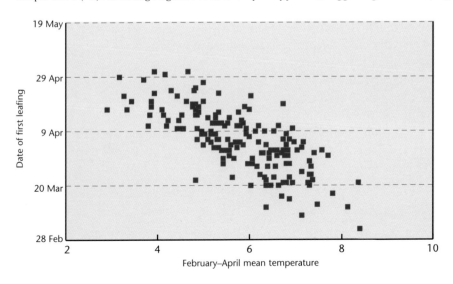

Table 6.1 *Estimated response to a 1°C increase in temperature in the first quarter of the year for 13 woody species. Data taken from the Marsham record.*

English name	Scientific name	Estimated response*
Hawthorn	*Crataegus monogyna*	9.9
Sycamore	*Acer pseudoplatanus*	6.7
Birch	*Betula pendula*	5.2
Elm	*Ulmus procera*	5.7
Mountain ash	*Sorbus aucuparia*	5.6
Oak	*Quercus robur*	5.6
Beech	*Fagus sylvatica*	3.0
Horse chestnut	*Aesculus hippocastanum*	4.8
Sweet chestnut	*Castanea sativa*	5.5
Hornbeam	*Carpinus betulus*	6.1
Ash	*Fraxinus excelsior*	3.5
Lime	*Tilia* spp.	5.2
Field maple	*Acer campestre*	4.4

*Advance of flushing in days per 1°C increase in January–March temperatures.

In the UK, one of the key areas of interest is whether the current character of our ancient woodland can be conserved if these impacts of climate change are realised. It should, however, be borne in mind that some of the more direct impacts of climate change on the performance or survival of individual species are likely to have at least as large an effect on woodland character and composition as the indirect effects acting through competition outlined above.

Royal Meteorological Society

From 1875 until 1947, the Royal Meteorological Society co-ordinated a phenological network for the British Isles. The aim was to investigate the link between climate and the periodicity of natural life. The scheme involved phenological records of flowering events from hazel (*Corylus avellana*) at the beginning of the season to ivy (*Hedera helix*) at the end. The scheme consistently recorded the appearance dates of three butterfly species and the return dates of four migrant bird species. At various times in its 73-year history, the phenology of additional species was recorded. Results were reported annually in the *Quarterly Journal of the Royal Meteorological Society*. This significant data-set is now available as a database.

Recently, a 58-year portion of the data-set has been analysed[7]. All of the 24 species examined showed a strong relationship to temperature with earlier flowering in warmer years. Figure 6.2, for example, shows how wood anemone (*Anemone nemorosa*) flowering dates averaged over the British Isles responded to temperatures in the January–March period. A stronger relationship was apparent for the flowering date of horse chestnut (*Aesculus hippocastanum*) relative to mean March–May temperatures (Figure 6.3). An analysis of the complete data-set suggests that for the 24 species included, flowering events advanced by 2–10 days for every degree Celsius warming[7].

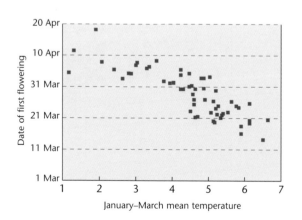

Figure 6.2 *Mean British Isles first flowering dates for wood anemone for the period 1891–1948 in relation to mean January–March temperature (°C).*

Figure 6.3 *Mean British Isles first flowering dates of horse chestnut for the period 1891–1948 in relation to mean March–May temperature (°C).*

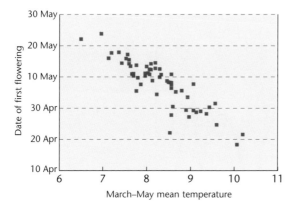

One important observation derived from this data-set is that the same temperature response is evident for both the first appearance of the orange tip butterfly (*Anthocharis cardamines*) and the flowering of garlic mustard (*Alliaria petiolata*)[8]. Garlic mustard is one of the foodplants of the larvae of the orange tip, which lays its eggs into the seed heads. This relationship indicates that over the range of observed temperatures, synchrony between the two species has been maintained. A similar synchrony was reported between oak (*Quercus robur*) and winter moth (*Operophtera brumata*)[9]. These limited results hint that synchrony could be maintained in a warmer environment, perhaps because the species have co-evolved and respond to similar environmental drivers. Species which did not

co-evolve may not be so fortunate. Further discussion of synchrony between species is given in Chapter 8, relating to climate impacts on host–insect pest relationships.

Combes record

Jean Combes' records of the budburst of oak, ash, horse chestnut and lime (*Tilia x vulgaris*)[10] date from 1947, and are summarised in Table 6.2. These represent an example of how the data from a single recorder have influenced a range of different studies. Not only has oak budburst been adopted as a UK government indicator of climate change[11], largely on the basis of this data-set, but it has also been used to validate a model of budburst with encouraging results (see Figure 6.4) and to investigate recent tree ring studies.

The Combes record shows a remarkable change in budburst dates in the post-war period (Table 6.2), and the advance in oak budburst of several weeks in only fifty years (Figure 6.4) gives an indication of the likely rate and magnitude of change that we might anticipate in this century. The largest rate of change appears to have been between the 1980s and the 1990s which saw the mean date of budburst advance by 6–12 days (Table 6.2), coinciding with a rise in temperature during the first three months of the year of 1.3°C. The large variation in the response of different species that was evident in the Marsham record is again apparent in the Combes data-set, although the reasons behind these differences

Table 6.2 *Mean budburst dates in Surrey in the last five decades of the 20th century.*

	1950s	1960s	1970s	1980s	1990s
Oak	April 30	April 26	April 24	April 20	April 10
Ash	May 6	May 7	May 7	April 30	April 24
Horse chestnut	March 25	March 27	March 31	March 27	March 15
Lime	April 7	April 9	April 12	April 14	April 3

Figure 6.4 Budburst date of oak in Surrey 1959–1999 (green). The black line represents the modelled date of budburst, based upon the synthesis model of Hänninen[12] using meteorological data for Wisley (courtesy of British Atmospheric Data Centre). [Source: after ECOCRAFT[13]].

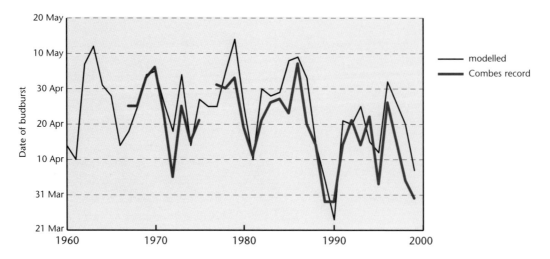

are uncertain, and remain an area for future research. It is, however, likely that a number of different factors, including temperature, chilling requirement and day length control the timing of budburst, and that it is the balance between these factors that determines the response of an individual species.

A further comparison to make from these data is the excellent agreement between the temperature response of oak from the Combes record with the long-term data-set from the Marsham record (Figure 6.5). This gives us confidence that the relationship between flushing of oak and temperature has been the same over the last 50 years as it was during the preceding two centuries, i.e. it has not changed over time, and gives even greater value to the database of historical events.

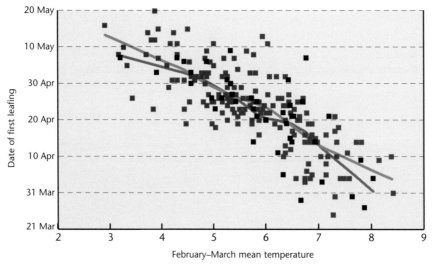

Figure 6.5 Relationship between date of first leafing and temperature (°C) for oak in Surrey (black) compared to that from the historical Marsham record (green). Smoothed lines (locally weighted sum of squares: LOWESS) have been superimposed to identify the underlying trends.

Manning record

Mary Manning's records on flowering of garden species only date from 1965[14], but they are valuable in representing a number of woodland ground vegetation species for which, otherwise, records might be absent. Figure 6.6 shows the change in the timing of winter aconite (*Eranthis hyemalis*) flowering, which is now advanced by about a month compared with the 1960s, while Figure 6.7 details the relationship

Figure 6.6 Winter aconite first flowering dates in Norwich 1965–2000. A smoothed line (LOWESS) has been superimposed to identify the underlying trend.

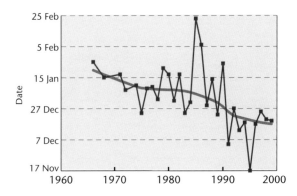

Figure 6.7 The relationship between daffodil first flowering dates in Norwich 1965–2000 and mean January–February temperature (°C).

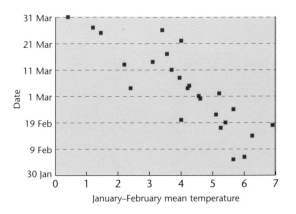

between the flowering date of daffodil (*Narcissus pseudonarcissus*) and temperature.

The magnitude of the response observed in the Manning record may not be due solely to climatic warming. Urban areas are generally one to two degrees warmer than the surrounding countryside (the heat island effect), and Norwich has expanded during the period in question. However, the contribution from urban growth to the heat island effect cannot account for all of the observed response. As with the Combes record, these data have been influential in demonstrating the magnitude of recent changes in the phenology of British wildlife.

Other sources of data

Butterfly Monitoring Scheme

The Butterfly Monitoring Scheme consists of fixed route recording of the presence of butterflies throughout the period from April to September. The scheme started in 1976 and now extends to some 120 sites nationally. The primary aim of the scheme is to monitor butterfly abundance, but details on phenology can be derived from the weekly recordings. As with the other taxa described previously, there have been rapid changes to species phenology, with the first appearance of most butterfly species advancing in recent decades[15]. One good example is the orange tip butterfly which has also been adopted as a UK government indicator of climate change[11]. This shows an advance in both first appearance and peak flight date over the monitoring period (Figure 6.8). Other woodland species, such as the ringlet (*Aphantopus hyperantus*) and brimstone (*Gonepteryx rhamni*), have shown similar responses.

The activity of other insects, such as aphids and moths, is also displaying a relationship with temperature[11]. This may manifest itself in earlier phenology, increased abundance, increased generations, enhanced migration and

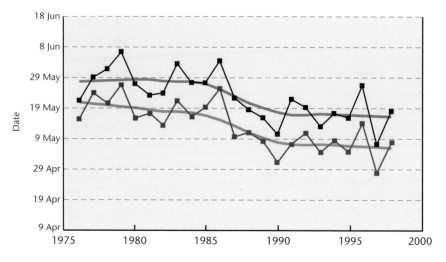

Figure 6.8 First appearance (green) and peak flight date (black) of the orange tip butterfly. Smoothed lines (LOWESS) have been superimposed to identify the underlying trends.

range expansion. Since these are not independent measures, it is difficult to identify exactly how climate warming is affecting the ecology of these species. However, as outlined in Chapter 8 (Table 8.1), it is likely that impacts on a combination of life stages and other factors are involved.

Ornithological records

The co-ordinated recording of migrant bird arrival times at the county level dates back, for some localities, to the end of the 19th century. The earliest coastal bird observatories were established in the 1920s. For both sources of information, there has been a marked increase in record keeping in the post-war period. Unfortunately the recording of migrant bird arrivals remains an unco-ordinated activity with little exchange of information between either counties or observatories. Figure 6.9 shows first arrival dates of blackcap (*Sylvia atricapilla*) and chiffchaff (*Phylloscopus collybita*) averaged over four coastal bird observatories. A trend towards earlier arrival is apparent. The picture for chiffchaff is also repeated in Figure 6.10 using a longer series from the Hertfordshire Natural History

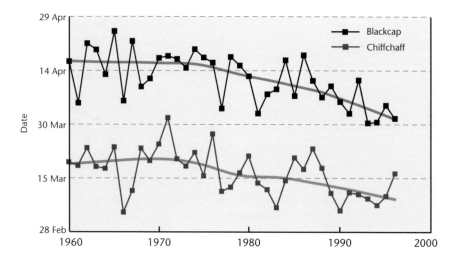

Figure 6.9 The mean first appearance dates of blackcap (black) and chiffchaff (green) taken from four coastal bird observatories. Smoothed lines (LOWESS) have been superimposed to identify the underlying trends.

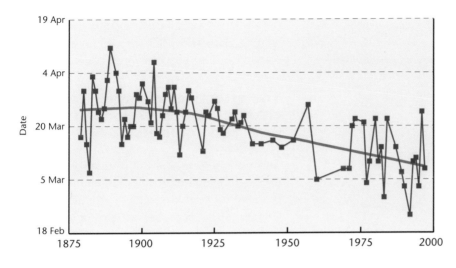

Figure 6.10
Chiffchaff arrival dates reported from the Hertfordshire Natural History Society 1879–1998. A smoothed line (LOWESS) has been superimposed to identify the underlying trend.

Society for which records began in 1879. Both species are becoming more common as winter residents in this country, to the extent that some county reports have stopped reporting arrival dates as they are resident throughout the year. The body of data is increasing and international collaboration is showing trends towards the earlier arrival of migrating species in many European countries.

In addition to records on the arrival of migrant birds, a large volume of data on the nesting and productivity of resident species is available through the British Trust for Ornithology's Nest Record Scheme. This information has shown clear trends towards earlier nesting by many different types of bird over recent years, influenced by warmer temperatures. Figure 6.11 shows how the median nest date of chaffinch (*Fringilla coelebs*) correlates with early spring temperatures.

International Phenology Garden Project

A Europe-wide network of phenological gardens was established in the 1960s to record phenological events of a number of clonal tree species. Unfortunately there are no extant sites in the UK, although data from one (Farnham) were used to calibrate the oak budburst model shown in Figure 6.4. Two of the co-ordinators of the scheme have recently reported changes in leafing and leaf fall across Europe[16]. They report a greater response in the 'British Isles/Channel Coast' region than elsewhere in Europe with spring (defined as the mean date of flushing of three tree and one shrub species) some 18 days earlier over the last 30 years. The onset of autumn (defined as leaf fall of the same four woody species used to define spring) also appears to have been delayed by some 6 days over the same period. The net result is an indicative extension of the growing season by 24 days in three decades, although the magnitude of this extension will vary greatly between species.

Frog spawning

There is also evidence that amphibian activity is related to temperature. As an example, the relationship between the first spawn date of frogs (*Rana temporaria*) at a site in Grange-over-Sands, Cumbria and temperature over the last 14 years is shown in Figure 6.12.

The list of species whose phenology is seemingly affected by temperature continues to grow as more data are accrued; for example, a recently acquired historic data-set on honey bees demonstrates clear patterns in activity and

Figure 6.11 The relationship between median laying date of the chaffinch and mean March–April temperature (°C). Data courtesy of Humphrey Crick, BTO.

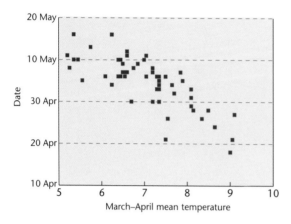

Figure 6.12 The relationship between first spawn date of common frog and January–March mean temperature (°C). Data courtesy of David Benham.

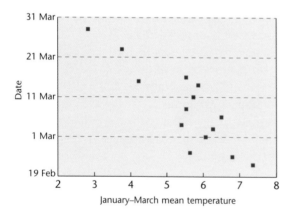

honey yields related to climate. As our knowledge grows researchers will become better placed to identify the effects of climate on the ecology of species and thus more competent to predict what the consequences of a warming climate in the current century will be to our native flora and fauna. Steps are being taken towards using data-sets similar to those described in this chapter for predicting

the impacts of climate change on British wildlife, through work such as that of Roy and co-workers[17] on butterfly abundance.

The effects of climate change on populations of deer and squirrels

The timing, availability and quality of plant forage play important roles in determining the population size of some mammal species. Climate also affects the activity of mammals directly. Complex interactions between climate, forest management and the physiology of the mammals exist and, therefore, data-sets demonstrating clear patterns of climate related impacts alone are rare and difficult to interpret. This section explores how changing climate is thought likely to affect both the seasonality and activity of squirrels and deer, both of which are relevant to forestry in the UK.

Climate patterns are increasingly being recognised as a major influence on animal populations. Broadly speaking, weather can affect mammals in two main ways: either *directly*, by affecting energy balance or movement, or *indirectly*, by altering plant growth and habitat conditions or susceptibility to disease. In most mammals, activities such as growth, mating, reproduction and dispersal are strongly seasonal and, as a result, the influence of unusual or extreme weather will depend largely on the time of year in which it occurs.

In Britain, the most pronounced *direct* effects occur during winter. Wind and rain increase the rate of heat loss, and snow can hamper mobility and increase the effort required for foraging[18]. Following severe winters, deer are more likely to be found with reduced body weights, delayed antler growth or depleted kidney or marrow fat[19–21] – changes in condition that are often associated with increased mortality. As a rule, however, mortality *en masse* is usually evident only after a severe winter when other conditions are also unfavourable, for example when population density is high, causing chronic food shortage[22-24]. A reduction in the frequency or severity of cold winters would therefore have the effect of maintaining higher over-wintering populations, with a sustained impact on vegetation.

In deer, reproduction is timed to coincide with the period of greatest vegetation productivity. Gestation and lactation create increased nutritional demands on females with the result that changes in winter and spring weather, which can affect the timing of vegetation growth, can have a marked effect on reproductive performance[25]. The temperature in April and May, for example, has been found to affect the weight at birth of red deer calves[26]. Birth weight is an important determinant of performance: both the chance of subsequent survival as well as reproductive performance in adult females increases with increasing birth weight[27]. Thus warm springs tend to produce not only more calves that survive to adulthood but also females with greater reproductive output.

An additional factor affecting deer populations would be changes in habitat caused by storms. By creating openings in the canopy, the productivity of ground vegetation increases providing more food for deer in the years following storm damage[28]. These areas are actively selected by deer and if extensive, the additional browse available will result in increased recruitment rates. The influence on deer populations will of course depend on the number and size of openings. In one case where approximately two-thirds of the woodland was felled, the density of deer was two to three times greater 13 years after the clearing was created[29]. Density subsequently declined as the growth of young trees eventually shaded out the understorey.

Tree seeds form an important food source for many mammals, including squirrels, mice, voles and deer. Seed production in many species varies substantially both from year to year and from site to site. Populations of squirrels and wood mice reach peak densities during or shortly after a particularly good seed year. In oak woodlands, acorn production can vary from zero to more than one tonne per hectare in a year, and as much as 80–90% is likely to be consumed by animals[30]. Although the mechanisms affecting seed production are still not fully understood, it is clear that climatic conditions can have varied effects on different tree species. In oak, for example, warm weather stimulates acorn development directly. In beech and ash on the other hand, temperature and leaf flushing date, respectively, have been found to affect flower development, often resulting in increased seed production the following year[31]. Weather patterns may also affect squirrels and other small mammals directly. During a long-term study of squirrel populations in mature oak-dominated woodland in Surrey, the lowest density of grey squirrels was only 2 per hectare following a cold winter and a failure of the acorn crop the previous autumn. In contrast, the density was 16 per hectare in 1977, one year after a good mast year[32].

In summary, populations of both deer and squirrels are adversely affected by cool weather which can act to reduce food availability or increase mortality at various times of year. As a result, the projected warming trend in the climate strongly suggests that populations will increase in range or density unless appropriate control measures can be implemented. However, responses to climate change are unlikely to be confined to a simple increase or decrease in relation to average temperatures. By affecting food supplies, the balance of competition between species may be altered, with the result that changes in abundance of some species may be disproportionately large or small, depending on the influence on their competitors[33]. At lower latitudes, deer populations are known to be affected more by summer conditions than winter[34], with the result that in the future, summer conditions may become more significant than winter or spring weather patterns. Models linking population performance to climate variables are likely to provide a useful means of predicting future trends in wildlife populations.

Conclusions

The phenological data-sets described here have allowed us to examine how species have responded to natural temperature variation in the past, and also to ongoing climate change. Documented changes in the timing of spring activity of a wide range of species, including examples of plants, birds and insects indicate that there has been a marked advance in recent decades – for some species, of up to one month. Reports in the literature suggest that changes in phenology appear to be more marked in the UK than elsewhere in Europe and are stronger for plants and invertebrates than for vertebrates. Differences in the relationships between temperature and spring activity of individual species may result in an altered competitive advantage and thus to a changed community composition in the future. The consequences of a changed phenology must not be considered in isolation from other direct climate-change related problems such as changed frequency of extreme events (drought, flood, storms) or through indirect effects such as land use change or habitat fragmentation.

An analysis of the impact of a wide range of issues, including both climate and land use change is particularly important for some vertebrates as a result of the complex interactions that are involved in the relationship between climate and population performance. For example, populations of deer and squirrels are adversely affected by cool, wet weather, through reducing food availability and increasing mortality. As a consequence, predicted climate change is likely to result in increased population densities and ranges, and appropriate control measures may therefore be required to limit their damage to forests.

Phenology is likely to become an increasingly important area for defining the progress of climate change. To this end, a series of recent initiatives, including the UK Phenology Network (www.phenology.org.uk) and the Environmental Change Network (www.ecn.ac.uk) have been established to provide relevant data-sets, and also to raise awareness of issues associated with climate change.

Acknowledgements

A chapter of this nature relies heavily on all those dedicated individuals who have diligently recorded observations, and to all of them we are grateful.

References

1. HUNTLEY, B., BERRY, P.M., CRAMER, W. and MCDONALD, A.P. (1995). Modelling present and potential future ranges of some European higher plants using climate response surfaces. *Journal of Biogeography* **22**, 967–1001.

2. SYKES, J.M. and LANE, A.M.J. (1996). *The United Kingdom Environmental Change Network: Protocols for standard measurements at terrestrial sites*. The Stationery Office, London.

3. SPARKS, T.H., CRICK, H.Q.P., BELLAMY, D. and MASON, C.F. (1998). Spring 1998. A summary of the first pilot year of a revived UK phenological network. *British Wildlife* **10**, 77–81.

4. PARKER, D.E., LEGG, T.P. and FOLLAND, C.K. (1992). A new daily central England temperature series, 1772–1991. *International Journal of Climatology* **12**, 317–342.

5. SPARKS, T.H. and CAREY, P.D. (1995). The responses of species to climate over two centuries: an analysis of the Marsham phenological record, 1736–1947. *Journal of Ecology* **83**, 321–329.

6. KRAMER, K. (1995). Phenotypic plasticity of the phenology of seven European tree species, in relation to climatic warming. *Plant, Cell and Environment* **18**, 93–104.

7. SPARKS, T.H., JEFFREE, E.P. and JEFFREE, C.E. (2000). An examination of the relationship between flowering times and temperature at the national scale using long-term phenological records from the UK. *International Journal of Biometeorology* **44**, 82–87.

8. HARRINGTON, R., WOIWOD, I.P. and SPARKS, T.H. (1999). Climate change and trophic interactions. *Trends in Ecology and Evolution* **14**, 146–150.

9. BUSE, A. and GOOD, J.E.G. (1996). The synchronisation of larval emergence in winter moth (*Operophtera brumata* L.) and budburst in pedunculate oak (*Quercus robur* L.) under simulated climate change. *Ecological Entomology* **21**, 335–343.

10. SPARKS, T.H., CAREY, P.D. and COMBES, J. (1997). First leafing dates of trees in Surrey between 1947 and 1996. *The London Naturalist* **76**, 15–20.

11. CANNELL, M.G.R., PALUTIKOF, J.P. and SPARKS, T.H., eds (1999). *Indicators of Climate Change in the UK*. Department of the Environment, Transport and the Regions, London.

12. HÄNNINEN, H. (1990). Modelling bud dormancy release in trees from cool and temperate regions. *Acta Forestalia Fennica* **213**, 1–47.

13. ECOCRAFT (1999) *Predicted impacts of rising carbon dioxide and temperature on forests in Europe at stand scale.* Final project report (ENV4-CT95-0077). IERM, University of Edinburgh, Edinburgh.

14. SPARKS, T. and MANNING, M. (2000). Recent phenological changes in Norfolk. *Transactions of the Norfolk and Norwich Naturalists' Society* **33**, 105–110.

15. ROY, D.B. and SPARKS, T.H. (2000). Phenology of British butterflies and climate change. *Global Change Biology* **6**, 407–416.

16. ROETZER, T. and CHMIELEWSKI, F-M. (2000). Trends growing season in Europe. *Arboreta Phaenologica* **43**, 3–13.

17. ROY, D.B., ROTHERY, P., MOSS, D., POLLARD, E. and THOMAS J.A. (2001). Butterfly numbers and weather: predicting historical trends in abundance and the future effects of climate change. *Journal of Animal Ecology* **70**, 201–217.

18. HART, J.S., HEROUX, O., COTTLE, W.H. and MILLS, C.A. (1961). The influence of climate on metabolic and thermal responses of infant caribou. *Canadian Journal of Zoology* **39**, 845–856.

19. WATSON, A. (1971). Climate and the antler-shedding and performance of red deer in north-east Scotland. *Journal of Applied Ecology* **8**, 53–67.

20. RUNGE, W. and WOBESER, G. (1975). *A survey of deer winter mortality in Saskatchewan.* Wildlife Report No. 4. Saskatchewan Department of Tourism and Renewable Resources, Regina.

21. CLUTTON-BROCK, T. H. and ALBON, S. D. (1984). Climatic variation and body weight of red deer. *Journal of Wildlife Management* **48**, 1197–1201.

22. KLEIN, D. R. (1968). The introduction, increase and crash of reindeer on St. Matthew Island. *Journal of Wildlife Management* **32**, 350–367.

23. MITCHELL, B. (1984). Effects of the severe winter of 1962–63 on red deer (hinds and calves) in north-east Scotland. *Deer* **6**, 81–84.

24. TAKATSUKI, S., SUZUKI, K. and SUZUKI, I. (1994). A mass-mortality of Sika deer on Kinkazan Island, Northern Japan. *Ecological Research* **9**, 215–223.

25. LANGVATN, R., ALBON, S.D., BURKEY, T. and CLUTTON-BROCK, T.H. (1996). Climate, plant phenology and variation in age of first reproduction in a temperate herbivore. *Journal of Animal Ecology* **65**, 653–670.

26. ALBON, S. D., GUINNESS, F. E. and CLUTTON-BROCK, T.H. (1983). The influence of climatic variation on the birth weights of red deer (*Cervus elaphus*). *Journal of Zoology* **200**, 295–298.

27. ALBON, S. D., CLUTTON-BROCK, T. H. and GUINNESS, F.E. (1987). Early development and population dynamics in red deer II. Density-independent effects and chart variation. *Journal of Animal Ecology* **56**, 69–82.

28. HALLS, L.K. and ALCANIZ, R. (1968). Browse plants yield best in forest openings. *Journal of Wildlife Management* **32**, 185–186.

29. GILL, R.M.A., JOHNSON, A. L., FRANCIS, A., HISCOCKS, K. and PEACE, A. J. (1996). Changes in roe deer (*Capreolus capreolus* L) population density in response to forest habitat succession. *Forest Ecology and Management* **88**, 31–41.

30. WORRELL, R. and NIXON, C.J. (1991). *Factors affecting the natural regeneration of oak in upland Britain – a literature review.* Occasional Paper 31. Forestry Commission, Edinburgh.

31. HARMER, R. (1994). Natural regeneration of broadleaves in Britain II. Seed production and predation. *Forestry* **67**, 275–286.

32. GURNELL, J. (1987). *The natural history of squirrels.* Christopher Helm, Bromley, Kent.

33. DAVIS, A.J., LAWTON, J.H., SHORROCKS, B. and JENKINSON, L. S. (1998). Individualistic species responses invalidate simple physiological models of community dynamics under global environmental change. *Journal of Animal Ecology* **67**, 600–612.

34. GAILLARD, J.M., DELORME, D., BOUTIN, J.M., VANLAERE, G. and BOISAUBERT, B. (1996). Body mass of roe deer fawns during winter in two contrasting populations. *Journal of Wildlife Management* **60**, 29–36.

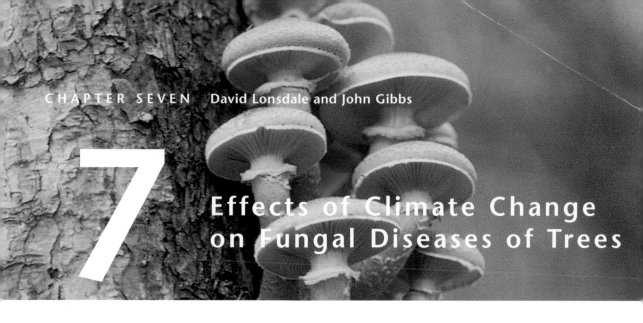

CHAPTER SEVEN

David Lonsdale and John Gibbs

7 Effects of Climate Change on Fungal Diseases of Trees

KEY FINDINGS

- The effects of predicted climate change on fungal diseases of trees can, to some extent, be judged by analysing the existing roles of climate and of fluctuations in weather; it is, however, more difficult to predict the effects of climate change on host–pathogen relationships than on the individual organisms.

- The impact on those pathogens whose reproduction or dispersal is clearly affected by temperature is relatively predictable.

- Warmer summers may in particular favour certain thermophilic rust fungi on poplar, which are currently rare or non-native in Britain; this has important implications for poplar breeding programmes.

- Insect vectors of pathogens such as the fungi causing Dutch elm disease are likely to respond to warmer summers by extending their geographic ranges and hence the ranges of disease incidence.

- The likely effects of higher year-round temperatures have been modelled in the case of *Phytophthora cinnamomi*, a very widespread fungus which causes root and stem-base diseases of a wide range of broadleaved and coniferous species. The models show a probable significant increase in the activity of this fungus across the UK and Europe in general.

- Warmer winters may increase the activity of some weak pathogens, such as *Phacidium coniferarum*, which are active only when the host is dormant.

- An increased incidence of summer drought would probably favour diseases caused by fungi whose activity is dependent on host stress, particularly root pathogens and latent colonisers of sapwood.

- A reduction in the number of summer rain-days may reduce the incidence of various foliar diseases such as *Marssonina* leaf spot of poplar. Generally, however, it is difficult to predict the impact of climate change on pathogens whose reproduction or dispersal is strongly affected by rainfall or humidity.

- The protective effects of mycorrhizas against various root diseases may be altered by changes in the relative fitness of different mycorrhizal fungi under conditions of altered soil temperature or moisture regime.

Introduction

Climate has been of great importance in the development of associations between trees and fungal pathogens[1]. In particular, the geographic range of each species of tree or pathogen is delimited by factors such as temperature, moisture, light intensity and snowfall which affect growth, reproduction and dispersal. Such factors affect the incidence of diseases by determining the distribution of a particular pathogen in relation to the geographic range of a potential host. Also, within a region where both host and pathogen are present, the severity of disease can vary with climate. Such variations can result from the direct effects of climatic factors on the pathogen, or from their effects on aspects of host physiology which determine resistance to attack. Other effects may involve other organisms with which either the host or pathogen interact.

In natural ecosystems, associations between particular tree and pathogen species are often of great antiquity and have evolved in ways which tend to avoid mutual destruction. Environmental stability may have been a prerequisite for the development of many of these host–pathogen associations and, if that is the case, it follows that they will be perturbed by major climate change. Less stable relationships tend to occur in the simpler ecosystems that initially exist in man-made plantations, often involving new combinations of host and pathogen species that have been artificially transported beyond their natural geographic ranges. In such cases, it can be envisaged that climate change could encourage major changes in disease incidence and severity.

In an attempt to evaluate the effects of climate change in these diverse situations, the scope of this chapter has been narrowed to consider only some of the most widely predicted changes – namely that temperatures in temperate regions of the world can be expected to be a few degrees higher than at present and that there will be greater climate instability with an increased frequency of drought (see Chapters 2 and 5). Also, the whole topic of saprotrophic survival has been excluded from consideration, as this would demand a chapter in its own right.

Direct effects on the pathogens

Effects on the geographic range of pathogens

The geographic ranges of tree pathogens are, to some extent, determined by the temperature ranges over which they can grow, although many species are prevalent only in regions where temperature and other climatic factors are sufficiently close to optimal values to allow rapid growth and reproduction during part of the year. A very wide range of pathogens could be expected to show alteration of their geographic ranges in response to climate change. This potential is best illustrated by examples of pathogens that respond to the year-to-year fluctuations that already occur.

Leaf rust of poplars (*Populus* spp.), caused by *Melampsora allii-populina*, is an example of a disease which, near the edge of its present climatic range in the UK, appears only sporadically due to temperature fluctuation. It is a topical example, since poplar growing is now being encouraged in many European countries as an alternative to producing agricultural surpluses. Many of the new fast-growing varieties that are favoured for this purpose were bred in Belgium, where they were screened for field resistance to rust in the 1970s[2]. It appears that *M. allii-populina* was virtually absent from the trial grounds in central Belgium at this time. Thus, the varieties were in effect screened only against another rust species, *M. larici-populina*, which, unlike *M. allii-populina*, is well established through-out Belgium and in much of northern Europe. In 1985, some of the varieties were quite heavily infected by rust in Belgium, and the fungus was found to be *M. allii-populina* which, as shown in Figure 7.1, occurs regularly only in regions further south[3]. There have been similar outbreaks in southern England following the importation of these varieties for commercial use.

As shown by Somda and Pinon[3], *M. allii-populina* is more thermophilic than *M. larici-populina* at some stages of its life cycle – especially urediniospore germination – and, as a wind-dispersed foliar pathogen, it can become prevalent north of its usual range during years with warmer than average temperatures. Other poplar rusts are also quite temperature-sensitive, including one, *M. medusae*, which has been accidentally imported into southwest France and which has shown no sign of spreading from this region into other climate zones[4]. However, the possibility of future climate warming has important implications for poplar breeding programmes, as well as for plant quarantine controls.

The example of *M. medusae* raises a further issue in relation to some pathogens which are climatically confined to certain regions but which could find suitable conditions elsewhere, if they were able to bypass natural geographical barriers such as mountain ranges. Such barriers are, of course, often circumvented by human interference, as has been the case with the introduction of *M. medusae* into Europe and with the relatively recent appearance of *M. larici-populina* in North America[5]. However, under conditions of climate amelioration, some barriers might become less of an obstacle, allowing 'natural' spread to extensive areas formerly outside the geographic ranges of the fungi concerned.

The accidental transfer of plant pathogens to new regions of the world is always of concern but could become more significant in the face of climate change. A good example is that of *Phytophthora cinnamomi*, an oomycete that appears to have originated in the Pacific Celibes region, but which now also occurs over wide areas of Australasia, North America and Europe[6,7]. This fungus has an extremely wide host range, causing root and stem-base diseases

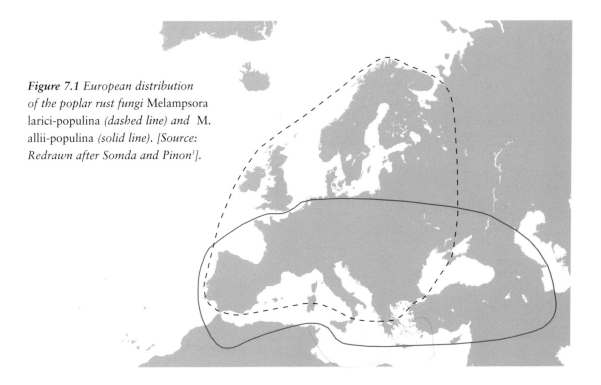

Figure 7.1 European distribution of the poplar rust fungi Melampsora larici-populina *(dashed line) and* M. allii-populina *(solid line). [Source: Redrawn after Somda and Pinon[3]].*

of broadleaved and coniferous trees. It has caused severe damage to some Australian eucalypt and floristically rich heathland systems and, in Europe is also associated with a major dieback problem in Iberian oak forests[8]. Although the fungus can grow at 5°C, and now occurs in areas representing a wide climatic range, its pathogenic activity is greatest at 25–30°C, making it particularly destructive in sub-tropical and Mediterranean climates. In cool-temperate maritime areas, such as Britain, it causes occasional disease outbreaks but might be expected to become more prevalent with global warming, as suggested by the output of a model developed by Brasier and Scott[6].

The development of a model to predict the effects of climate warming on the activity of *P. cinnamomi*[6] was made possible because there were high quality data on the existing pathogenic activity and geographic distribution of this fungus (Figure 7.2). The data were examined in relation to a range of different global warming regimes projected in the CLIMEX climate matching programme developed by CSIRO in Australia[9]. Also, the

model was adjusted for the known temperature preferences and tolerances of the pathogen and for projected changes in soil moisture content. In particular, host susceptibility under an increased frequency of drought was taken into account.

As a test of the model, there was a good fit between the known distribution of the pathogen in Europe and its geographically modelled patterns of activity, based on current climate regimes (Figure 7.2a). The effects of global warming on the activity of the fungus could therefore be predicted with reasonable confidence. The example in Figure 7.2b, which shows the situation predicted for an average warming of 3°C, suggests a considerable northward extension of the range where the fungus would be active, especially in maritime areas such as the UK. Brasier and Scott[6] stress, however, that the activity of the pathogen would also be influenced by the availability of susceptible host species and by the activity of its natural enemies.

The same model has been used by Brasier[7] to predict the activity of *P. cinnamomi* worldwide. As in the case of Europe, a good fit

Figure 7.2 (a) Current activity of Phytophthora cinnamomi *in Europe, modelled using the CLIMEX programme on the basis of present-day climate; (b) activity of the fungus predicted after a warming of 3°C. Dot size signifies relative suitability of climate for survival and growth of the fungus, and thus its relative activity. Maps pre-date recent national boundary changes. [Source: After Brasier and Scott[6]].*

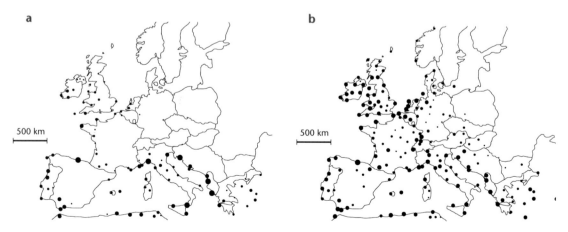

was found between the known distribution of the pathogen and the modelled map of its activity, based on current climate regimes (Figure 7.3a). With an average 3°C warming, the model showed a widespread increase in activity towards the poles and some loss of activity in the equatorial zone (Figure 7.3b). This change is highlighted in Figure 7.3c, which identifies the regions that would show either increased or decreased activity. It is interesting to note the similarity between the zones of increased activity of *P. cinnamomi* and the asynchronous dormancy zone illustrated in Figure 7.7.

Effects on the reproduction and dispersal of pathogens

A wide range of pathogens, especially those that infect leaves or green shoots, show large annual fluctuations in their incidence and severity of attack, and these events can often be attributed to weather conditions. Many fungi are favoured by moist conditions during the growing season, due to an enhancement of spore production and, in many cases, dispersal by rain-splash. Others, such as some of the powdery mildews, are favoured by low humidity. Winter conditions are also important in determining the success of the saprotrophic survival of many leaf-infecting fungi.

In view of the effects of existing weather fluctuations on the severity of various foliar diseases, climate change could be expected to affect their relative prevalence in the long term. A reduction in the number of rain-days in the summer might, for example, decrease the dispersal of many leaf-spot fungi such as *Marssonina* species on poplars[10] and *Cristulariella pyramidalis* on black walnut (*Juglans nigra*)[11]. By contrast, wetter weather in the spring would be expected to encourage infection early in the growing season.

In the UK, one of the most striking pathological phenomena of recent years has been the prevalence and severity of scab on

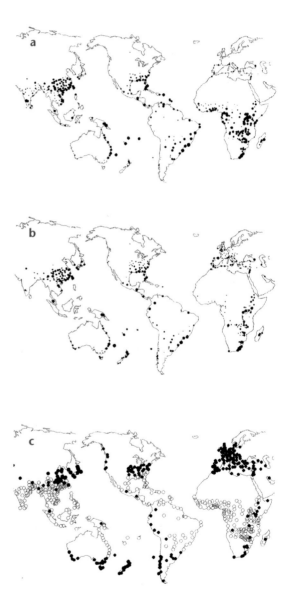

Figure 7.3 World-wide activity of P. cinnamomi *under (a) current climates, (b) assuming a 3°C increase in mean annual temperatures, and (c), the contrast between (a) and (b). In (a) and (b), dot size represents the climatic suitability for the growth and activity of the fungus, and in (c), open and filled circles represent decreased or increased predicted activity, respectively. [Source: After Brasier[7]].*

Figure 7.4 Venturia salicopia *infection of crack willow.*

willow (*Salix* spp.) caused by *Venturia* (Figure 7.4). Many trees of susceptible species such as crack willow (*S. fragilis*) have died as a result of the destruction of the foliage and young shoots year after year. This disease would seem to be a good candidate for detailed epidemiological studies to determine if some shift in climate is involved, although it would also be necessary to investigate the possibility that a new form of the pathogen has either evolved or arrived. The research would have to be undertaken on a broad front, however, as the effects of climate on cycles of disease are complex. The research would need to address the effects of climate change not only on hosts and pathogens, but also on the microbial interactions which influence the survival of pathogens during dormancy or saprotrophic development.

Effects on the activity of pathogens in winter

In the dormant season, the host's physiological responses to temperature and day-length may to some extent inactivate its defensive reactions, but the temperature can be high enough to allow the pathogen to remain active.

Thus, there are many diseases caused by weak parasites which develop mainly at this time of year.

Although many diseases are known to develop mainly in the dormant season, there are few quantitative data which demonstrate the onset or cessation of pathogenesis. One example comes from the work of van Vloten[12] on the bark-killing pathogen *Phacidium coniferarum* (syn. *Phomopsis pseudotsugae*). In Japanese larch, *Larix kaempferi*, this fungus invades wounds made during the winter months, such as can be created by pruning operations, and develops until it is checked by the onset of renewed cambial activity in spring (Figure 7.5).

Working in a stand of 13-year-old Japanese larch, van Vloten[12] made wound inoculations with *P. coniferarum* at monthly intervals and measured the size of the resulting lesions. As the results in Figure 7.6 show, the size of the lesions following dormant-season inoculation was proportional to the length of time available to the fungus for host invasion before the onset of the growing season. This work was conducted in the relatively maritime climate of Wageningen in the Netherlands during the mild winters of 1949–50 and 1950–51. The results might have been rather

Figure 7.5 Canker of Japanese larch caused by Phacidium coniferarum, *a dormant season pathogen.* '*A*' *denotes living tissue, and* '*B*', *cankered areas.*

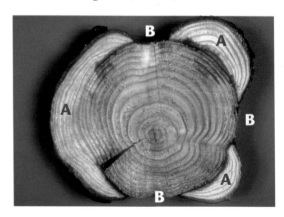

Figure 7.6 *Stem lesions induced by the dormant-season pathogen* Phacidium coniferarum *on Japanese larch inoculated in different seasons: bars represent an index of canker incidence and length.* [*Source: After van Vloten[12]*].

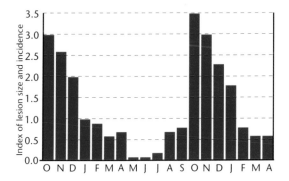

different during colder winters when the limiting effects of low temperature on the fungus would have been important.

For pathogens like *P. coniferarum* that have little ability to overcome host resistance during the growing season, winter temperature is likely to be critically important. In climates where temperatures are too low during most of the dormant season to allow such micro-organisms to grow within host tissue, there is little opportunity for them to cause disease. However, there are geographic zones, mainly in temperate latitudes, in which winter dormancy of woody plants coincides with periods when temperatures are high enough for microbial activity. Thus, in these zones of 'asynchronous dormancy', disease can be caused by fungi which would otherwise be largely non-pathogenic.

The poleward boundaries of the 'asynchronous dormancy zone' (ADZ) will obviously differ for varying host-pathogen combinations. However, the 2°C isotherm for January in the Northern Hemisphere, and for July in the Southern Hemisphere (adjusted to sea-level) provide a possible demarcation for most diseases, although a more realistic parameter would need to be based on a detailed analysis of temperature records throughout the winter. Also, there are many cold upland regions within the zone which should be excluded from it. A suggested global 'asynchronous dormancy zone' based on the 2°C isotherm is shown in Figure 7.7. Towards the equator, this zone is shown as including all regions with a distinct winter, that is, with the coolest monthly mean below 18°C. However, it could in reality be much narrower since, as shown here, it includes the subtropical zones where there are many evergreen tree species, including some which should perhaps not be regarded as showing winter dormancy. This uncertainty applies particularly in much of the Southern Hemisphere, where genera such as *Eucalyptus* and *Nothofagus* are often dominant.

According to some computer-generated models[13], global warming would cause the ADZ in each hemisphere to migrate slightly and irregularly polewards (Figure 7.7). In Europe, it would also expand somewhat eastwards. These projected shifts in the zone (based on climate predictions for the period 2058–2067) are superimposed on the existing situation depicted in Figure 7.7. The changes appear to be fairly small, compared with other effects such as the increased incidence of summer drought that could occur in many mid-latitude regions. However, the range of fungi which could respond to a 'window of opportunity' in mild winters is considerable, since it would include many of the most common causes of stem cankers and shoot diebacks.

Even in regions of the world where winters are colder than in the zone demarcated in Figure 7.7, certain fungi have evolved the ability to invade host tissues in the winter. Temperatures rarely fall far below freezing under snow cover, and certain low-temperature pathogens termed 'snow-moulds' have exploited this phenomenon. An example of such a fungus is *Phacidium infestans*, which attacks the needles and shoots of various

pathogenic growth within the sapwood and into the overlying bark. Their activity is often revealed by the production of extensive stromatic fruiting structures on the surfaces of the branches or stems that these fungi have helped to kill. An important example is that of *Biscogniauxia mediterranea*, which has caused serious damage to oak species such as *Quercus cerris* and *Q. suber* following droughts in southern Europe[24,25]. In Britain, similar strip cankers on beech (*Fagus sylvatica*) are caused by *B. nummularia* and *Eutypa spinosa*[23,26], and these were particularly prevalent in southern Britain after the 'double' drought years of 1975–76, 1983–84 and 1989–90.

Climate change could affect the European distributions of *B. mediterranea* and *B. nummularia*. The former causes strip-cankers only in relatively warm climates, such as occur in the Mediterranean countries. The latter is common as far north as southern Britain but becomes rare in the cooler and damper north and west of Britain, and has its northernmost outposts in southern Scandinavia, where its host is *Prunus* rather than *Fagus*[27]. Interestingly, *B. mediterranea* has also been found in southern Britain, although not as the cause of a strip-canker[28]. Increased summer temperatures and droughtiness could be expected to help shift the distributions of these fungi northwards within the range of potential hosts, or at least to increase the geographic range over which they behave as pathogens.

Another stress-related disease akin to the strip cankers is sooty bark disease of sycamore, *Acer pseudoplatanus*, caused by *Cryptostroma corticale* (Figure 7.8). Here again, the fungus is latent or endophytic within the tissues of the healthy tree[29,30]. In hot dry summers, it can rapidly develop within the xylem and subsequently within the bark[31,32]. Curiously, we are only aware of this disease in southeast England and northern France, even though sycamore occurs as a native species over a much wider area of Europe, including the mountains of the south.

In forests where a more frequent incidence of summer drought exacerbates stress-related diseases, increased tree mortality can open the canopy structure. This, in turn, enhances transpiration stress in the remaining trees, due to their increased exposure to insolation and wind.

An apparent exception to the above examples of drought-induced disease susceptibility seems at first sight to be provided by Dutch elm disease (DED). Drought conditions have been reported to suppress the typical wilting symptom of DED in both the English elm, *Ulmus minor* and the American elm, *Ulmus americana*[33,34]. However, when such cases have been investigated by examination of the xylem, the presence of extensive vascular streaking has indicated that fungal invasion has not been prevented. The suppression of wilting in such cases has not been investigated in detail, but may be due to stomatal closure during periods of water stress.

Although foliar symptoms of DED may indeed be suppressed by drought stress, there is

Figure 7.8 Sooty bark disease of sycamore caused by Cryptostroma corticale, *a pathogen dependent on host stress.*

evidence that they may also be affected by concomitant factors such as temperature and sunshine. By analysing data from the experimental inoculation of *Ulmus procera* with *Ophiostoma novo-ulmi*, Sutherland and co-workers[35] found that the most severe foliar symptoms of DED occurred when the mean air temperature exceeded 17°C and the duration of sunshine was moderate (5 to 7 h day[-1]). The least severe symptoms occurred under two sets of conditions; either in sunny weather (> 7.5 h day[-1]) irrespective of temperature, or in cool, dull weather with mean air temperature less than 15.5°C and sunshine less than 4.5 h day[-1].

The example of DED illustrates that a situation such as a drought involves a number of different environmental factors, all or any of which may affect disease development and symptom expression in their own right. As these factors are usually interrelated, as in the example of sunshine and summer temperature, a careful analysis of their effects is desirable, although not always feasible. It is also important to bear in mind that they may influence host-pathogen interactions, as well as having direct effects on the susceptibility of the host and the activity of the pathogen.

Effects of altered winter temperatures on the host

During winter dormancy, direct effects of climate on the host are generally less important than those involving the pathogen. The only well-reported effect on the host is that of frost damage, which can encourage the development of certain fungal cankers. Examples for which this has been demonstrated include Botryosphaeria canker of rowan, *Sorbus aucuparia*, caused by *Botryosphaeria dothidea*[36] and canker of *Pinus resinosa* caused by *Diplodia pinea*[37]. In areas such as Britain, where climate-change modelling predicts a decrease in the incidence of frost[13], diseases of this type could become less prevalent.

Effects involving interactions between trees or pathogens and other organisms

Interactions with vector organisms

The spread of certain fungal pathogens depends on insect or other vectors which, like the host and pathogen, are influenced by climate. Their involvement therefore complicates predictions about the effects of climate change on the geographic range of disease incidence. Dutch elm disease provides an interesting example, since *Scolytus scolytus* and *Scolytus multistriatus*, the most important of the beetle vectors in western Europe, do not readily fly at a temperature below about 22°C[38]. Thus, cool conditions do not favour the spread of the fungus[39,40] and may have been responsible for evident delays in the northward advance of the epidemic within some regions where elms occur. Outbreaks of the disease have, however, eventually occurred further north, perhaps aided by the sporadic occurrence of warm summers and by the abundant provision of beetle breeding habitat following the killing of entire trees by the aggressive form of the pathogen, *Ophiostoma novo-ulmi*.

In regions where a pathogen already occurs, weather conditions may favour outbreaks of its vectors only in certain years, suggesting that climate change could influence the long-term prevalence of the disease. One such case is that of the fungus *Ceratocystis laricicola*[41], which was described less than fifteen years ago. It infects the bark, cambium and sapwood of larch trees, causing death and dieback, and is probably transferred between trees by an insect vector, the bark beetle *Ips cembrae*. Redfern and co-workers[41] found that this disease occurred mainly in areas affected by drought, which favours bark beetle attacks by inducing host stress and therefore reducing resistance.

For many fungal diseases involving vectors, the effects of climate and weather on the development of outbreaks and epidemics have not been studied in detail. However, the importance of such effects is to some extent self-evident, since the geographic ranges of insect vectors are determined largely by climate, while their activity and abundance are influenced by the vagaries of weather. Climate change, involving an increase in temperature or in the incidence of drought, could extend the range of any such diseases into areas where the host and fungus can already both exist but in which vectors are not yet operative.

Effects on mycorrhizas

There is evidence that ectomycorrhizas can protect trees against various root pathogens and that they can in some cases mitigate the effect of stress in exacerbating disease susceptibility[42,43]. There is also evidence that not all ectomycorrhizal fungi are equally protective. For example, it has been reported that mycorrhizal roots of *Pinus* and *Castanea* were protected against *Phytophthora* spp.[44,45], but Malajczuk[46] found that some ectomycorrhizal fungi were much more effective than others in protecting *Eucalyptus* roots against *P. cinnamomi*. Differences in protectiveness were similarly found in mycorrhizal *Picea* roots challenged by *Cylindrocladium floridanum*[47].

If soil temperature and moisture affect the fitness of ectomycorrhizal fungi associated with a particular tree species, a change in climate is likely to alter the range of species and thus to affect disease incidence indirectly. Although an indirect effect of this type has not been documented, there is evidence of population shifts in ectomycorrhizal fungi exposed to altered temperature or moisture. For example, an increase in temperature suppressed species of the putative *Rhizopogon* group, while favouring *Cenococcum* spp.[48]. Similarly, *Boletus edulis* was favoured by dry conditions but declined under irrigation in favour of *Cortinarius*, *Lactarius* and *Russula* species[49].

The effects of drought on mycorrhizas involve not only the fitness of different fungal species under moderate moisture stress, but also their ability to colonise new roots formed when rainfall follows a period of drought sufficient to have caused extensive death of fine roots. Transplantation into dry soil may similarly provide competitive pressure, as in a case involving seedlings of *Pinus caribaea*, which were planted in the dry zone of Sri Lanka. Their mycorrhizal symbiont, a *Boletus* species, was totally replaced by a drought-tolerant *Cenococcum* species[50].

Summary and conclusions

The effects of possible climate change on fungal diseases of trees can to some extent be judged by analysing the existing roles of climate and of fluctuations in weather. For pathogens whose geographic ranges or pathogenic activity are clearly affected by temperature, either positively or negatively, the effects of climate warming are probably predictable. Such pathogens include those that become either less or more active at relatively high summer temperatures. Warming in winter is likely to favour pathogens that require mild temperatures in the dormant season, because it is only then that they can attack the host. If these roles are well understood, predictive modelling may be an informative approach, at least for certain categories of pathogen.

The impact of any increase in the frequency of summer droughts is also reasonably predictable, since the role of host stress in allowing attack by many pathogens, especially root pathogens, is well known. In particular, it can be predicted that such a climate change would alter the stability of associations between tree species and various members of their endophytic mycofloras, some of which would more frequently be triggered into curtailing such associations through killing their hosts.

Prediction is more difficult in the case of pathogens whose reproduction and dispersal is strongly affected by rainfall and atmospheric humidity. This is also true of pathogens that are strongly affected by interactions with other organisms, such as insect vectors or protective mycorrhizal fungi. Furthermore, even in the relatively simple cases described in this chapter, the effects of climate on the interactions between a host and its pathogens are more difficult to predict than the direct effects on each of these organisms.

Acknowledgements

We are grateful to C.M. Brasier for providing information on *Phytophthora cinnamomi* and to him, D.B. Redfern and D. Donnelly (University of Wales, Cardiff), for other contributions and useful comments on the text. We also thank the following individuals and organisations for permission to reproduce data: R.F. Patton (University of Wisconsin-Madison, USA); J. Pinon (INRA, Nancy, France); C.M. Brasier (Forest Research, UK); The European Plant Protection Organisation; The American Phytopathological Society; Blackwell Scientific Publications; The Royal Scottish Forestry Society. This chapter is an adaptation of a paper produced for a British Mycological Society Symposium[1].

References

1. LONSDALE, D. and GIBBS, J.N. (1996). Effects of climate change on fungal diseases of trees. In: *Fungi and environmental change*, eds J.C. Frankland, N. Magan and G.M. Gadd. Cambridge University Press, Cambridge, 1–19.

2. PINON, J., VAN DAM, B.C., GENETET, J. and DE KAM, M. (1987). Two pathogenic races of *Melampsora larici-populina* in north-western Europe. *European Journal of Forest Pathology* **17**, 47–53.

3. SOMDA, B. and PINON, J. (1981). Ecophysiologie du stade urédien de *Melampsora larici-populina* Kleb. et de *M. allii-populina* Kleb. *European Journal of Forest Pathology* **11**, 243–254.

4. PINON, J. (1973). Les rouilles du peuplier en France; systematique et repartition du stade uredien. *European Journal of Forest Pathology* **3**, 221–228.

5. NEWCOMBE, G. and CHASTAGNER, G.A. (1993). First report of the Eurasian poplar leaf rust fungus, *Melampsora larici-populina*, in North America. *Plant Disease* **77**, 532–535.

6. BRASIER, C.M. and SCOTT, J.K. (1994). European oak declines and global warming: a theoretical assessment with special reference to the activity of *Phytophthora cinnamomi*. *OEPP/EPPO Bulletin* **24**, 221–232.

7. BRASIER, C.M. (2000). The role of Phytophthora pathogens in forests and semi-natural communities in Europe and Africa. In: *Phytophthora diseases of forest trees*, eds E.M. Hansen and W. Sutton. IUFRO Working Party 7.02.09. Proceedings from the First International Meeting on *Phytophthora* in Forest and Wildland Systems, Grants Pass, Oregon, USA, 30 August to 3 September 1999. Oregon State University Press, Corvalis, USA, 6–13.

8. BRASIER, C.M (1992). Oak tree mortality in Iberia. *Nature* **360**, 539.

9. SUTHERST, R.W., MAYWALD, G.F and BOTTOMLEY, W. (1991). From CLIMEX to PESKY, a generic expert system for pest risk assessment. *OEPP/EPPO Bulletin* **21**, 595–608.

10. CELLERINO, G.P. (1979). Le Marssoninae dei pioppi. *Cellulosa e Carta* **30**, 3–23.

11. NEELY, D., PHARES, R. and WEBER, B. (1976). *Cristulariella* leaf spot associated with defoliation of black walnut plantations in Illinois. *Plant Disease Reporter* **60**, 587–590.

12. VAN VLOTEN, H. (1952). Evidence of host-parasite relations by experiments with *Phomopsis pseudotsugae* Wilson. *Scottish Forester* **6**, 38–46.

13. ANON. (1992). *The Hadley Centre transient climate change experiment*. Hadley Centre, Meteorological Office, Bracknell.

8

Climate Change:
Implications for Insect Pests

KEY FINDINGS

- Climate change is likely to alter the balance between insect pests, their natural enemies and their hosts; predictions of the impact of climate change on insect damage to UK forests are therefore difficult to make.

- One of the most important effects of climate change will be to alter the synchrony between host and insect pest development, particularly in spring, but also in autumn; the predicted rise in temperature will also generally favour insect development and winter survival, although there will be some exceptions.

- The green spruce aphid is one example of an insect that is likely to benefit from the increase in winter survival, leading to more intense and frequent tree defoliation. A decline in the productivity of Sitka spruce might therefore be expected.

- Modelling work suggests that under a warmer climate, exotic pests such as the southern pine beetle could establish populations in Europe, and that climatic warming could make UK forests susceptible to damage; other bark beetles such as *Ips typographus*, which is present in some parts of Europe, but not the UK, could become a serious problem.

- Rising atmospheric CO_2 concentrations may lead to a decline in food quality for plant-feeding insects, as a result of reduced foliar nitrogen levels.

- The planting of exotic tree species may exacerbate the beneficial effects of climate change on insect pests, as the natural predatory fauna may not be present to limit population growth.

- Changes have already been observed in the distribution of native European butterfly populations, with northern ranges extended and southern ranges reduced. The same is likely to be the case for forest insect pests.

- The combined effects of increased global trafficking of timber and wood products and climate change are likely to result in exotic pests such as Asian longhorn beetle becoming more prevalent; it is therefore essential that we remain vigilant in reporting new pests and altered patterns of damage.

Introduction

Over evolutionary time, insects have shown that they can adapt to a very wide range of habitats by exploiting available resources as well as demonstrating the ability to tolerate and exploit wide climatic variability. Many insect species show this plasticity by having extensive distributional ranges, covering a wide spectrum of climates, with responses to average climate varying across that range – for example southern pine beetle (*Dendroctonus frontalis*) in the USA[1]. Although the performances of individual populations of a given species of insect will be responsive to climatic variability, the number of species will also vary with climate, usually reflected in latitudinal range. For example, Virtanen and Neuvonen[2] analysed species richness of Lepidoptera on a latitudinal gradient in Finland and showed that a mean summer temperature increase of 1°C gave an increase of around 93 species. Against this background of adaptability, it is not surprising that changes in insect diversity and abundance can be expected as a result of climate change in the future. This will be reflected both in direct effects on the insects themselves and also on the host plants and other habitat variables that affect resource utilisation, and the ability to withstand natural mortality factors.

Responses of insect herbivores to climate change

In recognition of the principal subject matter of this Bulletin, namely climate change and UK forests, this chapter deals primarily with insect herbivores and their interactions both with the host tree and with associated factors such as natural enemies. However, although examples of insects in the UK forest ecosystem will be included, other examples from world literature will be used to illustrate some of the key points that are likely to determine responses to climate change. It is also important to distinguish situations where forest insects have co-evolved with their hosts, where both would be expected to be well adapted to local climatic conditions, and situations where either, or both, insect and host is an exotic species and potentially at a climatic extreme. In these situations, the effects of climate change will depend considerably on how close to the edge of climatic suitability the insect–host interaction is likely to be. Western spruce budworm (*Choristoneura occidentalis*) and gypsy moth (*Lymantria dispar*) are sensitive to a combination of regional host tree availability and to parameters linked to climate. Projections of various climate change scenarios have produced a range of results, depending on the average predicted temperatures and precipitation values entered into phenological models[3]. In general, increases in temperatures and declines in precipitation resulted in predicted decreases in defoliation and range, whereas there was a sharp rise in defoliated area if both temperature and precipitation rose. Results were also sensitive to use of general circulation models rather than regional projections of temperature and rainfall shifts. More recent projections for the eastern spruce budworm (*C. fumiferana*)–spruce/fir system suggest that increases in temperature will result in northward shifts in both the optimal tree mix and in the distribution of the moth[4]. Such studies show that effects of climate change will be felt through both direct changes in insect performance and in the ways in which both tree availability and suitability vary over time and space.

Biological factors determining insect population responses

The wide variety of insect species present in forest ecosystems reflects the complexity of those ecosystems, especially in relation to the interactions of herbivores with their host plants. There have been many studies of insects on trees in Britain, where there is a long tradition of both professional and amateur insect collecting, thus allowing qualitative and sometimes quantitative assessment of interactions with host plants and the environment. Seminal studies by Southwood[5] and Kennedy and Southwood[6] have provided detailed analyses of datasets and much debate about the main factors that determine species diversity and abundance of insects on British trees. Factors such as time that a tree has been present, area occupied by the tree, taxonomic relatedness, tree size, and leaf size explained most of the variance in insect diversity noted on British trees. The data strongly supported the concept of the species–area relationship (larger geographic areas support a larger number of species[7]) and also brought in the hypothesis that Britain, as an island that had been glaciated, had for some tree species, a relatively short period of colonisation. Furthermore, the widespread planting of exotic tree species during the 20th century has added to the number of species present without their native insect fauna. It might also be expected that some of these exotic tree species are close to their northern geographical limits and are more likely to be adversely affected by some of the climate change scenarios. For example, Redfern and Hendry (Chapter 3) note that the widespread use of exotic tree species in Britain makes them vulnerable to climatic injury arising from the extremes of winter cold, drought and other factors.

Insect life cycles: effects on different growth stages

Studies of whole faunas can provide overviews of how species diversity can change over time, but the use of historical faunal lists does not provide a biological explanation for the observed trends and, particularly, does not provide biological links with climate change. In this respect, it is worth noting that because insects exhibit wide biological variability, it is not possible to be definite concerning the ways in which they might respond to climate change.

However, some generalisations can be made in order to illustrate how direct and indirect climate effects can influence performance of many insect species. Thus, Table 8.1 provides a simplified framework for the assessment of how seasonal shifts in temperature and precipitation patterns might affect insects having different life stages present at different times of the year. The framework fits coleopteran (beetle) and lepidopteran (butterfly and moth) life cycles directly and could be adapted easily for other insect orders, e.g. Homoptera (aphids) where the larval and pupal stages would be combined. Climate effects would be manifested through temperature, precipitation, exposure to increased carbon dioxide and ultraviolet light and changes in wind speeds (see Chapter 2).

Synchrony: a key factor in determining insect population performance

Taking winter moth (*Operophtera brumata*) as an example, Table 8.1 can be used to assess how climate change parameters affect each stage of the life cycle and, therefore, how population performance as a whole would alter. Analysis starts in the fourth row of the table, reflecting the fact that winter moth overwinters in the adult stage. Following a period of dormancy, the adult is actually active during the early winter period and so is already well adapted to tolerate winter frosts or early spring frosts. Eggs are also laid during the early winter period and so might be subject to potential frost damage. However, eggs are known to be capable of withstanding low temperatures, especially in the early spring when they are close to hatching[8]. Climate change predictions of decreased winter frosts would, therefore, have little effect on overwinter survival.

The early larval stages can be regarded as critical in determining population survival because they must feed on newly expanding leaves of their principal deciduous hosts,

Table 8.1 Relationship between the overwintering developmental stage of insect herbivores and the potential for climate change impacts as a function of season. For each overwintering strategy, those developmental stages represented in each season are given, together with the ways in which climate may affect them.

Overwintering developmental stage	Winter (dormancy)	Transition →	Spring (early activity)	Summer (peak activity)	Transition →	Autumn (reduced activity, early dormancy)
	Key factors controlling population development					
	Likelihood of surviving winter cold	Synchrony of dormancy with host tree	Temperature dependency of development and number of generations		Synchrony with host tree development	Choice of dormancy site. Risks from early frosts
Egg	**Egg** Frost tolerance, survival.	*Timing of budburst determines suitability of oviposition and feeding sites. Strong link to nutritional and defensive status of foliage. Likelihood of mortality from late frosts.*	**Egg** Hatch date; early survival.	**Larva** Peak growth rate. Duration of stage. **Pupa** Timing of pupation and duration of stage. **Adult** Timing of emergence, duration and rate of oviposition. Effects on realised fecundity.	*Leaf fall or dormancy. Links to declining nutritional suitability, loss of foliage (deciduous) and likelihood of early frosts.*	**Adult** End of stage and of oviposition. **Egg** Hardiness (chorion, possible protective mechanisms).
Larva	**Larva** Frost tolerance, survival.		**Larva** Commencement of feeding activity. Rate of development/ duration of stage.	**Pupa** Timing of pupation and duration of stage. **Adult** Timing of emergence, duration and rate of oviposition. Effects on realised fecundity. **Egg** Duration. Hatch rate.		**Larva** Hardiness. Selection of overwintering sites.
Pupa	**Pupa** Frost tolerance, survival.		**Pupa** Completion of development. **Adult** Timing of emergence, duration and rate of oviposition. Effects on realised fecundity. **Egg** Duration. Hatch rate.	**Larva** Peak growth rate. Duration of stage.		**Pupa** Hardiness. Probability of frost tolerance depending on pupation site.
Adult	**Adult** Frost tolerance, survival.		**Adult** Emergence and commencement of oviposition. Effects on realised fecundity. **Egg** Duration. Hatch rate.	**Larva** Peak growth rate. Duration of stage. **Pupa** Timing of pupation and duration of stage.		**Adult** Selection of overwintering site. Probability of frost tolerance.

particularly oak (*Quercus* spp.)[9]. Any delay in commencing feeding is compromised by rapid increases in secondary metabolites, such as phenolics, in the leaves, leading to poor larval uptake of nutrients and increased mortality[10]. Synchrony between egg hatch and bud burst is, therefore, critical for winter moth survival on oak and, to a lesser extent, on Sitka spruce (*Picea sitchensis*) which has been colonised by this moth in Britain[11]. Climate change scenarios and existing evidence indicate that oak budburst has already advanced by up to 20 days during the late 20th century (see Table 6.2), although there is still considerable variation between years. The key question is, therefore, whether winter moth populations are also responding to these changes in climate and are maintaining synchrony with bud burst. Studies by Hunter[12] indicated that populations of winter moth appear to thrive on trees having the earliest budburst within an oak forest, correlating particularly with the taller trees present. Similarly, Buse and co-workers[13,14] produced results in controlled environment laboratory studies that suggest that warmer temperatures advance budburst and egg hatch by a similar amount and synchrony is maintained in warmer springs, even though leaf and larval development periods are shortened. These data and field observations indicate that development of eggs must also accelerate and so maintain the co-evolved relationship between the moth and its principal host. By contrast, studies of winter moth on an exotic host, Sitka spruce, indicated that, although egg hatch was occurring earlier under higher average accumulated temperatures in late winter and early spring, budburst was not advanced, thus leading to asynchrony[15]. This suggests that larval survival and development are likely to be detrimentally affected by climate change[11]. However, this effect may be diluted by the ability of larvae of winter moth to feed inside the buds of Sitka spruce prior to budburst, at least in young trees[15].

Development of the larval stages of winter moth are governed both by late spring and early summer temperatures and by the requirement for larvae to complete their early feeding on young leaves. The moth is univoltine (one generation per year), and therefore pupation and development to the adult stage occurs during the summer, and also into winter, when adult moths emerge to re-commence the cycle. Temperature effects on larval survival are likely to be small, provided that early feeding commences at the time of budburst. The direct and indirect effects of elevated carbon dioxide concentration ($[CO_2]$) on winter moth have also been measured[14,16–18]. There were no direct effects on larval performance but some changes in nutritional quality, manifested in reduced nitrogen availability, and in leaf defensive properties, indicated by increased concentrations of phenolics, respectively. The indirect effect on the host tree illustrates how climate change effects will be complex but will tend to be driven by subtle changes of timing of nutritional quality during particularly vulnerable stages, such as early feeding phases.

Climate change and insect overwintering strategy

Using Table 8.1 as a template, the question of whether any particular life cycle strategy, particularly for the overwintering stages, is likely to benefit from climate change can be posed. The analysis of macrolepidoptera in Finland by Virtanen and Neuvonen[2] suggests that insect species overwintering in the egg or adult stage will benefit from current climate change predictions compared with those that overwinter as larvae or pupae. On trees in particular, the authors showed that overwinter diapause in the egg and pupal stages is more prevalent than on perennial or annual plants. However, overwintering in the egg stage is less common in moths typically found in the more northern parts of Finland. The European pine sawfly (*Neodiprion sertifer*) provides an example of a species that overwinters as an egg and which is likely to benefit from higher average winter temperatures, especially lower frequencies of severe frosts[19]. Although local site factors, especially infertile soils prone to drought, were implicated in the frequency of sawfly outbreaks, the most critical factor was the likelihood of winter temperatures below −36°C. These low temperatures led to significant egg mortality, even though the eggs are relatively protected within pine needles. The authors predicted that milder winters would lead to increased frequency of N. sertifer outbreaks arising from improved egg survival.

Adaptation to climate/tree host combinations may also shift if average temperatures and associated factors, such as precipitation, change. This can be illustrated by reference to larch budmoth (Zeiraphera diniana) which has been well studied in its native range in Europe and has also colonised other countries. Z. diniana has two forms adapted to different climatic zones with particular linkage to overwinter temperatures. The overwintering egg requires a set period of low temperatures to break diapause and if this is not achieved there may be asynchrony between egg hatch and budburst of the host. Thus Baltensweiler[20] recognised a larch race of the moth that is adapted to higher alpine conditions with egg diapause termination dependent on low winter temperatures. He contrasted this with a pine race found outside the alpine zone and linked more to milder climates where diapause termination is not so dependent on low winter temperatures. Outbreaks of the larch race at high altitudes in the Alps (between 1400 and 2000 m) have been features of the landscape, particularly in the Engadine region of Switzerland, and severe defoliation occurs regularly. A milder winter than normal in 1990 was cited as the main factor in breaking the regular outbreak pattern of the larch race of Z. diniana for the first time since 1850[21]. If milder alpine winters increase as a result of climate change then there may be

a reduction in damage from the larch race of the moth but an increase in damage from the pine race. The ability of the pine race to damage Pinus, Picea and Larix species is apparent in most of the range of the moth in Europe, including Scotland where the moth caused considerable damage to young lodgepole pine (Pinus contorta) stands[22].

Effects on natural enemies

In addition to the direct effects of higher temperatures, greater $[CO_2]$ and other aspects of climate change on herbivorous insects, and indirect effects mediated through host plants, climate change will also affect populations of parasites, predators and pathogens. However, too little is known about the vast majority of natural enemy species to even attempt to predict how they might modify or override the response of pest species to changing conditions. This is the largest unknown factor when assessing the likely consequences of climate change for forest insects. With this uncertainty, it is perhaps more profitable to look at current abundance and distribution of species in relation to current climate, which is the summation of all the factors influencing the population, and attempt to predict how abundance and distribution will shift under different climate change scenarios.

Rates of development, in particular, will tend to be linked to spring and summer temperatures and will also require synchrony with the target herbivore prey. Thus, increased rates of prey development might lead to accelerated numerical responses by natural enemies, potentially linked to density-dependent reductions in prey densities.

The concept of buffering against the impacts of climate has been investigated in a model system involving predator–prey interactions of protists (Protozoa) compounded by variable climate[23]. Despite increases in intrinsic growth rates of over 200% when temperatures were elevated, it was shown that interspecific competition, specifically from predatory protists, prevented the prey populations from exploiting the higher growth rates. Although the study by Fox and Morin[23] involved an 'artificial' microcosm, it did indicate that studies involving multiple trophic interactions will be necessary in order to understand the full effects of climate change.

Indirect effects on insect performance

A considerable rise in atmospheric $[CO_2]$ is predicted to occur during this century. A large number of experiments have explored the consequences of this rise for trees and the insects that feed on them. It is now generally accepted that an increase in atmospheric $[CO_2]$ will cause a decline in food quality for chewing insects: leaf nitrogen concentrations decrease and the concentration of secondary plant compounds may increase. Consequently, the growth and survival of leaf-chewing insects tends to be poorer under elevated $[CO_2]$, the magnitude of the impact on insect performance being closely related to the impact on plant nitrogen[18]. The impact of atmospheric $[CO_2]$ on phloem-feeding insects is less clear and most of the studies showing positive impacts of atmospheric $[CO_2]$ have been on aphids[24]. However, studies on tree-dwelling aphids suggest that they will not be beneficially affected by elevated $[CO_2]$[25].

The major indirect effect through the host tree on forest pests is likely to be through the relative effect of temperature on insect and tree phenology, particularly larval emergence in spring-feeding Lepidoptera and budburst. If, as discussed above in relation to the winter moth, climate warming results in asynchrony, then some forest pests may be predicted to become less significant. However, research on host-specific races of spring-feeding Lepidoptera[26] suggests that they will become quickly adapted to changes in the timing of budburst of their host plants.

A further possible indirect effect on forest pests through the host tree is the increase in the frequency of drought stress-induced outbreaks. Although the theory that pest outbreaks are induced by drought does not apply to all types of pest[27,28], some, such as bark beetles, may be expected to become more serious as the incidence of drought increases. Even where the incidence of outbreaks is unlikely to be affected by drought, such as with Lepidoptera and sawflies, the ability of trees to withstand outbreaks is likely to be negatively affected if climate change results in an increase in the frequency of drought.

Case studies to illustrate insect responses to climate change

Green spruce aphid *Elatobium abietinum*

Many insect species that currently occur over much of the UK are likely to show an increase, or decrease, in population size in response to climate change, or a shift in the area where they are most abundant. One species that is particularly likely to show changes in abundance in relation to a rise in mean temperatures is the green spruce aphid (*Elatobium abietinum*) (Figure 8.1). This aphid is the most important defoliator of Sitka spruce, and to a lesser extent Norway spruce, in the UK and at present its populations appear to be limited primarily by cold winter temperatures. A rise in average winter temperatures in the UK is considered likely to lead to higher aphid populations and more frequent and intense defoliation[29] (Figure 8.1). However, the relationship between *E. abietinum* and its host plant is more complex than this simple picture might suggest, and details of the relationship illustrate several other features of the interaction between insects and their host plants that influence how pest populations may respond to climate change.

Figure 8.1 The green spruce aphid, and an example of typical defoliation in Norway spruce.

Green spruce aphid in the UK

E. abietinum is distributed throughout the UK and feeds exclusively on one-year-old and older needles of spruce, especially Sitka spruce. Feeding leads to chlorosis of the needle tissues, followed by needle death and premature abscission. Defoliation can be extensive in years of high aphid density. In the mild, oceanic climate of northwest Europe, the aphid occurs on spruce throughout the year and reproduces continuously as wingless, parthenogenetic females, even during the winter months. Peak numbers occur in late spring–early summer (May–July), after which time numbers decline rapidly in response to a decrease in the nutritional quality of the phloem sap[30] (see Figure 8.2). A small number of aphids persist through the summer, but populations increase again in the autumn following an improvement in host plant quality after the trees stop growing and enter dormancy. There is a short flight period at the time of the population peak in the spring.

The size of the spring population peak is closely related to the number of aphids that over-winter[30]. This is turn depends on the numbers of aphids present in the autumn and survival rates over the winter period. Cold temperatures below −7°C, especially sudden frosts, kill most individuals and prevent damaging populations developing in the following spring[31]. Extended periods of low temperatures, e.g. below +6°C, also reduce aphid survival through torpor and starvation.

The dramatic effect of low winter temperatures means that years with high *E. abietinum* populations and severe defoliation tend to occur only after mild winters, although not after every mild winter. The population dynamics of *E. abietinum* also show a strong 2-year cycle in which years of high peak density are followed by a year of much lower density[32]. The reasons for this short-term fluctuation in population numbers are not entirely clear, but cold winter temperatures act to disrupt the cycle and reduce the frequency of years with damaging aphid populations.

Figure 8.2 Fluctuations in E. abietinum *populations on 22-year-old Sitka spruce at three sites in Radnor Forest, Wales. Site 1 is at 315 m above sea-level, Site 3 is at 510 m and Site 5 is at 610 m. The aphid population index is the total (uncalibrated) number of aphids counted at each site using a standardised protocol. Meteorological data are provided by an automatic weather station at each site.*

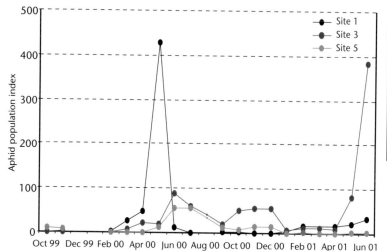

Mean temperature (°C)

	Site 1	Site 3	Site 5
Mar 00	5.9	4.8	3.9
Apr 00	6.0	4.8	3.9
May 00	10.5	9.2	8.2
Jun 00	13.4	12	11.1
Mar 01	3.0	2	1.2
Apr 01	5.5	4.5	3.7
May 01	10.5	9.9	8.8

Direct effects of higher temperatures on the green spruce aphid

Temperatures are generally below the optimum for *E. abietinum* for most of the year. Consequently, in common with many other aphid pest species, warmer temperatures will lead to an increase in development rates and reproduction of *E. abietinum* through direct effects on physiological processes[33]. In turn, higher growth rates and fecundity will lead to shorter generation times and, potentially, higher population densities. Direct effects of temperature on the performance of *E. abietinum* will be most pronounced in the autumn and early spring when development is not limited by poor nutritional quality of the host.

Higher mean temperatures will also allow more aphids to survive the winter. At present, average winter temperatures in the UK are close to freezing, and any warming due to climate change is likely to produce a marked decrease in the occurrence of frosts. Accumulated day-degrees below freezing are

expected to decrease by up to 40% by 2020 and by 60–70% by 2050[34]. Under current climatic conditions, winter temperatures limit years of severe defoliation by *E. abietinum* to one in every 3–6 years[35]. Warmer winter temperatures will increase the frequency of outbreaks and increase the severity of defoliation in peak years.

Changes in the phenological relationship between spruce and *E. abietinum*

Spruce is nutritionally most suitable for *E. abietinum* before budburst in the spring. Once the trees have flushed, the total nitrogen content and amino-acid balance of the phloem sap declines and aphid development and fecundity decrease. Warmer spring temperatures will allow the aphid population to increase earlier and more quickly. In contrast, warmer temperatures are not expected to advance the date of budburst in Sitka spruce by more than a few days[36,37]. As a result, spruce will remain suitable for the rapid development of *E. abietinum* for a relatively longer period in warm springs, which will facilitate increases in the aphid population. The frequency of very hot summers is expected to increase in the future, and this may also influence *E. abietinum* populations. The build-up of aphid numbers in the autumn is related to an improvement in host quality associated with bud-set and the start of dormancy. In years with exceptionally hot and dry summers, spruce enters dormancy early and provides the aphid with a longer period favourable for development before the winter. When such conditions are combined with a mild autumn, large numbers of aphids may develop and over-winter[38].

High densities of *E. abietinum* and severe defoliation reduces the growth of spruce[39]. The greater frequency and intensity of defoliation caused by *E. abietinum* under a warmer climate is expected to lead to a progressive decline in the productivity of Sitka spruce, despite the direct positive effects of higher temperatures and [CO_2] on tree growth[29]. However, there are good reasons to suspect that the increase in the impact of *E. abietinum* will not be linearly related to rises in temperatures. Spruce trees are killed by repeated defoliation in successive years. As the frequency of severe defoliation increases, tree mortality is likely to supersede the effects of the aphid on increment[29].

Response of natural enemies

Populations of *E. abietinum* certainly appear to be very responsive to small differences in current climate (Figure 8.2), but natural enemies also appear to drive aspects of the population dynamics. Predators and parasites are important in reducing *E. abietinum* numbers during late summer and autumn, and they probably help maintain low aphid numbers in the year after an outbreak.

At Radnor Forest in Wales, *E. abietinum* populations reached higher densities and peaked earlier in Sitka spruce stands at low elevation (site 1) in 2000, but numbers in the same stands were much reduced in 2001 (Figure 8.2). The smaller numbers of aphids at low elevations in the second year follows the pattern of low numbers after a year of high numbers. The reverse was seen at mid-elevation (site 3), where a relatively low population was present in 2000, followed by a population increase in 2001. Aphid populations at high elevation (site 5) were limited by temperature in both years. However, further research is required to determine to what extent the wide range of natural enemies, including pathogens, parasitoids and predators, are able to suppress the aphid population.

Aphids on spruce are exposed and vulnerable to a wide range of generalist parasites and predators throughout the year, and increases in the abundance of enemies, partly in response to increased supplies of aphids, might be expected to have a significant impact on the aphid's population. For other univoltine insect species, such as winter moth, faster development in response to warmer temperatures may reduce the period when they are vulnerable to attack by parasites and predators and reduce mortality[40]. In this sense, populations of many pest insects might be able to escape control by their natural enemies more often under a warmer climate.

Pinewood nematode *Bursaphelenchus xylophilus*, and its vectors in the genus *Monochamus*

Pinewood nematode (PWN) (*Bursaphelenchus xylophilus*) is a native of North America where it develops on a range of pine species and over most of its range lives as a saprophyte on recently dead trees[41]. The nematode feeds on the remaining intact wood cells at the time of tree mortality and completes its life cycle on various fungi that are inevitably present on wood[42]. Significantly, the nematode is not regarded as a dangerous pathogen in its native range, including the southern USA where temperature and drought stress are component parts of the forest system[43]. The nematode is carried from tree to tree by longhorn beetles in the genus *Monochamus* and there is considerable evidence to indicate that this genus of beetle is the only effective vector, even in situations where the nematode has been introduced[44,45].

Pathology of pinewood nematode

Taking account of the innocuous nature of PWN in its native range, it was not surprising that it was not initially recognised as the causal agent of pine wilt disease in Japan and, indeed, was originally described as a new species, *B. lignicolus*[46]. Later studies revealed that the agent was *B. xylophilus* and that it had originated in the USA and been introduced into Japan, probably during the 19th century[45]. In contrast to the normal saprophytic mode of *B. xylophilus* in North America, the nematode is able to survive and breed in the living tree and, by a combination of increased density and production of a toxin, causes rapid blockage of the xylem, thus preventing water transport within the stem. Mortality occurs quickly and is characterised by a sharp decline in resin production, followed by reddening of foliage (see Figure 8.3). Millions of trees have been killed in Japan since the arrival of the nematode and it has also become established in China, Korea and, more recently, Portugal. A Pest Risk Analysis of the risks to Europe from PWN concluded that availability of susceptible tree species, especially Scots pine, was high but that expression of wilt disease in living trees was likely to be restricted to areas where the July or August isotherm was >20°C and that epidemic wilt was only likely at >24°C[47]. A further risk factor was the presence or absence of potential vectors in the genus *Monochamus*. A number of *Monochamus* species are present throughout mainland Europe, but as the genus is absent in the UK and Ireland, there is a considerably lower risk for these countries.

The potential effects of climate change on the pinewood nematode *Monochamus* interaction

As indicated above, pine wilt disease is a syndrome that is heavily dependent on a combination of four principal factors: the nematode, the vector, the host tree and environmental conditions, especially temperature. This can be illustrated by reference to Figure 8.4 where the cycles of both nematode and vector are shown. The saprophytic cycle relies on opportunistic selection of dying or recently dead trees for oviposition by a *Monochamus* female. It is only if a female is carrying sufficient nematodes to establish a population that the cycle can be completed so that, when the vector pupates, there are nematodes in the vicinity ready to migrate to the adult when it emerges. All *Monochamus* carry out feeding in the crowns of standing trees and it is possible for nematodes to be introduced to the tree during this process. It is during this phase that the susceptibility–temperature interaction with the host tree is critical.

Figure 8.3 Typical reddening of foliage followed by necrosis as a result of pinewood nemotode infestation in Pinus *sp. in Japan.*

Figure 8.4 *Schematic diagram of the biological interactions between PWN, its vectors, the host tree and climate. Tinted boxes represent activity on living trees, and untinted boxes on dying or recently dead trees.*

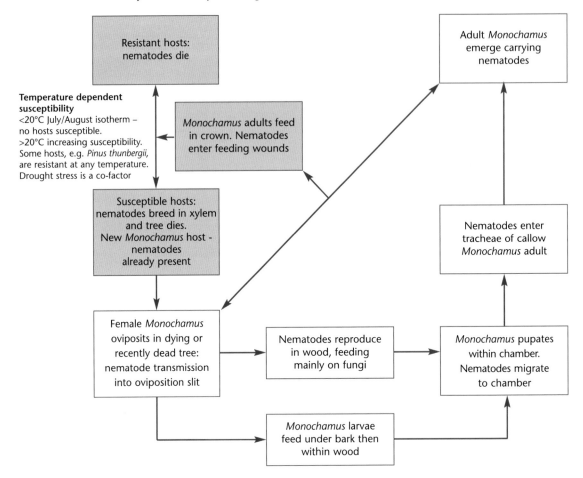

Although there is a range of intrinsic susceptibility between pine species, nematodes will not survive unless temperatures are high enough to sustain rapid development and, in parallel, some stress to the host tree from local environmental factors such as drought. Thus, expression of wilt is strongly dependent on temperature and, in Japan, no disease has been expressed in areas where August isotherms are below 24°C, even though both susceptible pine species and *Monochamus alternatus*, the known vector in Japan, are present. In assessing future risk from PWN, it is important to consider average temperature increases that will take the July/August isotherms beyond the

minimum 20°C. Figure 8.5 shows the distribution of current August isotherms for Europe and also indicates where the current infestations and expression of wilt disease are located in Portugal.

From the map in Figure 8.5, it is possible to assess where shifts in average temperature are likely to lead to expression of wilt symptoms; this is shown as the shaded area that covers a shift of 5°C in the August isotherm, even though current projections are for smaller shifts. In Portugal, this would lead to a northward shift in expression of wilt symptoms into the southern end of the major *Pinus pinaster* forests in the north of the

Figure 8.5 Risk area for expression of pine wilt disease arising from infection by pine wood nematode, *Bursaphelenchus xylophilus*, in Europe, defined by August isotherms. Climate change is likely to affect the shaded area in the main map. The inset shows the current distribution of pinewood nematode in the Setubal region of Portugal. This is the only known area of infestation in Europe and is within the area predicted in previous Pest Risk Analysis[47].

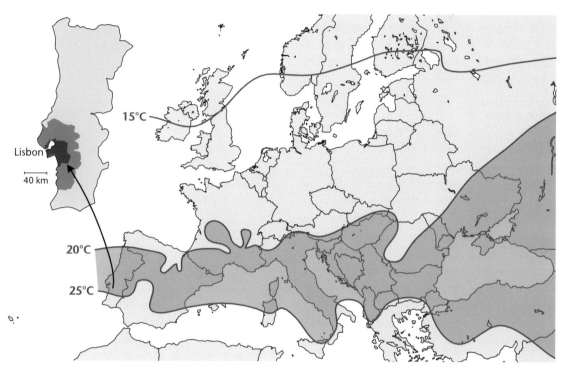

country. The rate of wilt expression might also be increased because of the reduction in generation time for the local vector species, *M. galloprovincialis*, and the greatly increased availability of suitable breeding resources for the vector. Such positive feedback loops have been observed in Japan, where populations of *M. alternatus* have increased from low secondary levels to high densities, thus further increasing the rates of transmission of *B. xylophilus*[48].

It is important to realise that establishment of *B. xylophilus* is possible across most of Europe where it would be likely to exist in the saprophytic mode typical in its native range in North America[47]. Thus, risk assessment of the potential effects of climate change must take account of predictions of summer temperature increases. For trees in the UK, the temperature aspects will also need to be combined with the need for *Monochamus* spp. to establish as well as the nematode itself, thus moderating the overall risk.

Southern pine beetle *Dendroctonus frontalis* in the USA

Southern pine beetle (*Dendroctonus frontalis*) is one of the most damaging pests in southeast USA where it causes extensive mortality to native pines, *Pinus taeda* and *Pinus echinata*[49] (Figure 8.7). It is a mass attack bark beetle that overcomes tree defences, expressed mainly in quantity and constitution of resin, by a combination of beetle density and parallel introduction of several fungi including

Ophiostoma minus (=minor) and *Ceratocystiopsis ranaculosus*[50]. Severity of attack depends partly on the state of health of the host trees and partly on the number of beetle generations per year, which can vary from 2 to 7, in relation to average summer temperatures over the north to south range of the beetle[51]. Damage and tree losses are extensive and result in both economic and severe environmental impacts.

Recent analysis of the temperature requirements of *D. frontalis* has provided information on which to base predictions of climate change effects on the range of establishment of the beetle, and of destructive outbreaks[1]. The western limits of *D. frontalis* extend to the edge of distribution of pines on the Great Plains, while northerly distribution is dependent on minimum winter temperatures. Analysis indicated that a 90% probability of winter temperatures declining to –16°C was the key mortality factor determining northerly distribution (Figure 8.6). The limit of regular destructive outbreaks is approximately 300 km south where the probability of winter

temperature reaching less than –16°C is 50% (at 35.4° N). In assessing the potential effect of climate change, the key predictor will, therefore, be winter temperature, so that any northerly shift in the probability of winter temperatures dropping to –16°C or less will affect both distribution and likelihood of reaching outbreak status. Projected temperature rises of 3–4°C in both summer and winter for the eastern USA are predicted by the Hadley Centre HADCM2 model. This would push the predicted range and outbreak probability northwards.

A recent study of the risks to Europe posed by *D. frontalis* was carried out by Evans and co-workers[52] using the CLIMEX programme[53] to predict the likelihood of establishment and damage. CLIMEX calculates an Ecoclimatic Index (EI) which integrates Annual Growth Index, a measure of potential population growth, with other factors such as low overwinter temperatures that might limit survival during unfavourable periods. This places constraints on the EI, which provides a measure of the potential of the selected

Figure 8.6 Distribution of southern pine beetle in North America. The northern limits of distribution and destructive outbreaks are defined by probability of winter temperatures dropping below –16°C [1].

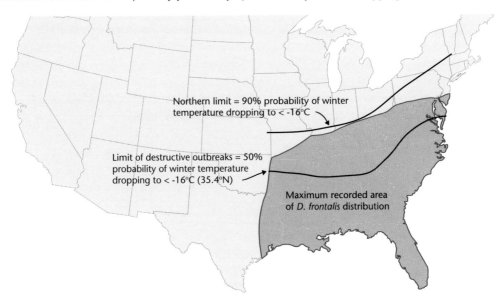

Figure 8.7 Widespread damage to a crop of loblolly pine caused by southern pine beetle in southeast USA. [Source: R.F. Billings, USA].

location to support a permanent population of the test organism. The EI is scaled from 0 to 100 such that values close to 0 indicate that populations would not survive in the long term. EI values over 30, for example, indicate a very favourable climate for a species, but do not necessarily imply that pest outbreaks will occur. EI values should, therefore, be used with caution in predicting population performance in new locations, as is the case in the current analysis of the pest risk to Europe from *D. frontalis*.

Figure 8.8 shows the predicted EI values for *D. frontalis* in Europe. In some ways, these predictions are surprising because the view has tended to be that the beetle does not pose a threat to Europe. Assuming that the predictions from CLIMEX are correct, then climate and availability of pine species in Europe would suggest that it could establish successfully. Taking a direct interpolation of the latitudinal range of outbreak potential from the USA (35.4° N), the likelihood of damaging outbreaks is low and limited to southern Europe. However, the Mediterranean and mild oceanic climates of Europe would suggest that cold winter temperatures are not

likely to be limiting, as is the case in the USA. Attack patterns in Europe are, therefore, more likely to be driven by the number of generations that the beetle can achieve per year. At the outbreak limit in the USA, the beetle is still achieving five generations per year, driven by the high average summer temperatures. A further factor in risk assessment is whether the spectrum of fungal associates normally carried by *D. frontalis* adults would be present if the beetle established in Europe.

Climate change predictions for the UK include increased annual mean temperatures by 2–3°C with warming slightly more in winter than in summer. Warming is slightly higher for continental and Mediterranean Europe (see Chapter 2). These data suggest that the risk from *D. frontalis* would rise considerably from the present CLIMEX predictions. Further analysis of risk within a full Pest Risk Analysis is being carried out and will provide more detailed predictions of future risk.

D. frontalis has been used to illustrate that pests that initially would appear to offer low risk may need to be considered under future climate change scenarios. Other bark beetles, such as *Ips typographus*, already pose

Figure 8.8 CLIMEX® *predictions of climatic suitability for establishment of southern pine beetle in Europe*[52]. *An ecoclimatic index >30 indicates that the insect could establish damaging populations. The limit of destructive outbreaks in North America is at 35°N. Climate change predictions would push the limit towards 40°N.*

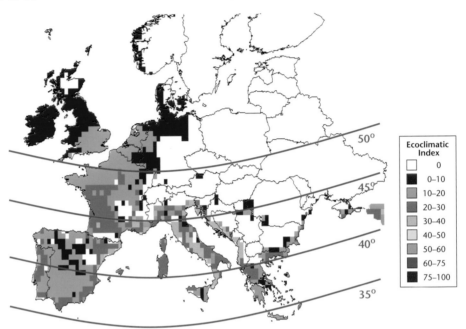

considerable threats and would undoubtedly respond positively to higher average temperature, compounded by tree stress[54].

Conclusions

It is extremely difficult to predict the impact of climate change on forest pests, particularly its impact on the abundance of pests. The direct effect of increasing temperatures may tend to benefit insect pests, whereas the indirect effect of climate change through the host plant may be neutral or negative. The overall impact of the indirect effect on forest pests through natural enemies is impossible to predict, such is the diversity and complexity of the interactions involved.

Perhaps the only certain prediction is that the distribution of forest pests will change. Already it has been observed that many European butterfly species with a southerly

distribution have spread further north during the last few decades, and species with a northern distribution have tended to retreat further north from the southern edge of their range[55]. Forest insects would be expected to show similar shifts in geographic distribution, with a northward movement of southern species and a contraction in range of north temperate and boreal species. The establishment of Asian longhorn beetle (*Anoplophora glabripennis*) in New York and Chicago[56] and the recent finding of the beetle breeding on trees in Austria serve to emphasise that changes in distributions of important pests are occurring in widely separated regions of the world. Although there is clearly a strong link with movements of these pests in international trade, the potential role of climate change in aiding establishment and in determining impacts of pests must also be taken into consideration.

In conclusion, climate change will have an unpredictable impact on forest pests in the UK and elsewhere. Some of our existing pests will become more important, some less so. Most significantly new pests will emerge, including some species that have been shown to be devastating elsewhere. Clearly, there is a need to remain vigilant to the threat of the emergence of new pests.

References

1. UNGERER, M.J., AYRES, M.P. and LOMBARDERO, M.J. (1999). Climate and the northern distribution limits of *Dendroctonus frontalis* Zimmermann (Coleoptera: Scolytidae). *Journal of Biogeography* **26**, 1133–1145.

2. VIRTANEN, T. and NEUVONEN, S. (1999). Climate change and macrolepidopteran biodiversity in Finland. *Chemosphere: Global Change Science* **1**, 439–448.

3. WILLIAMS, D.W. and LIEBHOLD, A.M. (1995). Forest defoliators and climatic change: Potential changes in spatial distribution of outbreaks of Western spruce budworm (Lepidoptera: Tortricidae) and gypsy moth (Lepidoptera: Lymantriidae). *Environmental Entomology* **24**, 1–9.

4. WILLIAMS, D.W. and LIEBHOLD, A.M. (1997). Latitudinal shifts in spruce budworm (Lepidoptera: Tortricidae) outbreaks and spruce-fir forest distributions with climate change. *Acta Phytopathologica et Entomologica Hungarica* **32**, 205–215.

5. SOUTHWOOD, T.R.E. (1961). The number of species of insect associated with various trees. *Journal of Animal Ecology* **30**, 1–8.

6. KENNEDY, C.E.J. and SOUTHWOOD, T.R.E. (1984). The number of species of insects associated with British trees: a re-analysis. *Journal of Animal Ecology* **53**, 455–478.

7. MACARTHUR, R.H. and WILSON, E.O. (1967). *The theory of island biogeography.* Princeton University Press, Princeton, USA.

8. PATOCKA, J. (1976). Influence of low temperatures on the mortality of eggs of some moths (Lepidoptera). *Vestnik Ceskoslovenske Spolecnosti Zoologicke* **40**, 107–117.

9. FEENY, P. (1976). Plant apparency and chemical defence. *Recent Advances in Phytochemistry* **10**, 1–40.

10. HUNTER, M.D. (1997). Incorporating variation in plant chemistry into a spatially explicit ecology of phytophagous insects. In: *Forests and insects*, eds A.D. Watt, N. Stork and M.D. Hunter. Chapman & Hall, London, 81–96.

11. DEWAR, R.C. and WATT, A.D. (1992). Predicted changes in the synchrony of larval emergence and budburst under climatic warming. *Oecologia* **89**, 557–559.

12. HUNTER, M.D. (1992). A variable insect–plant interaction: the relationship between tree budburst phenology and population levels of insect herbivores among trees. *Ecological Entomology* **17**, 91–95.

13. BUSE, A. and GOOD, J.E.G. (1996). Synchronisation of larval emergence in winter moth (*Operophtera brumata* L.) and budburst in pedunculate oak (*Quercus robur* L.) under simulated climate change. *Ecological Entomology* **21**, 335–343.

14. BUSE, A., GOOD, J.E.G., DURY, S. and PERRINS, C.M. (1998). Effects of elevated temperature and carbon dioxide on the nutritional quality of leaves of oak (*Quercus robur* L.) as food for the winter moth (*Operophtera brumata* L.). *Functional Ecology* **12**, 742–749.

15. WATT, A.D. and McFARLANE, A.M. (1991). Winter moth on Sitka spruce: synchrony of egg hatch and budburst, and its effect on larval survival. *Ecological Entomology* **16**, 387–390.

16. DOCHERTY, M., SALT, D.T. and HOLOPAINEN, J.K. (1997). The impacts of climate change and pollution on forest pests. In: *Forests and insects*, eds A.D. Watt, N. Stork and M.D. Hunter. Chapman & Hall, London, 229–247.

17. DURY, S.J., GOOD, J.E.G., PERRINS, C.M., BUSE, A. and KAYE, T. (1998). The effects of increasing CO_2 and temperature on oak leaf palatability and the implications for herbivorous

insects. *Global Change Biology* **4**, 55–61.

18. WATT, A.D., LINDSAY, E., LEITH, I.D., FRASER, S.M., DOCHERTY, M., HURST, D.K., HARTLEY, S.E. and KERSLAKE, J. (1996). The effects of climate change on the winter moth, *Operophtera brumata*, and its status as a pest of broadleaved trees, Sitka spruce and heather. *Aspects of Applied Biology* **45**, 307–316.

19. VIRTANEN, T., NEUVONEN, S., NIKULA, A., VARAMA, M. and NIEMELA, P. (1996). Climate change and the risks of *Neodiprion sertifer* outbreaks on Scots pine. *Silva Fennica* **30**, 169–177.

20. BALTENSWEILER, W. (1993). A contribution to the explanation of the larch budmoth cycle, the polymorphic fitness hypothesis. *Oecologia* **93**, 251–255.

21. BALTENSWEILER, W. (1993). Why the larch budmoth cycle collapsed in the subalpine larch-cembran pine forests in the year 1990 for the first time since 1850. *Oecologia* **94**, 62–66.

22. DAY, K.R. (1984). Phenology, polymorphism and insect–plant relationships of the larch budmoth, *Zeiraphera diniana* (Guenée) (Lepidoptera: Tortricidae) on alternative conifer hosts in Britain. *Bulletin of Entomological Research* **74**, 47–64.

23. FOX, J.W. and MORIN, P.J. (2001). Effects of intra- and interspecific interactions on species responses to environmental change. *Journal of Animal Ecology* **70**, 80–90.

24. DOCHERTY, M., WADE, F.A., HURST, D.K., WHITTAKER, J.B. and LEA, P.J. (1997). Responses of tree sap-feeding herbivores to elevated CO_2. *Global Change Biology* **3**, 51–59.

25. AWMACK, C.S., WOODCOCK, C.M. and HARRINGTON, R. (1997). Climate change may increase vulnerability of aphids to natural enemies. *Ecological Entomology* **22**, 366–368.

26. DU MERLE, P. (1983). Comparative phenology of pubescent oak, holly oak and *Tortrix viridana* L. (Lep., Tortricidae). Evidence for two sympatric populations of the insect each adapted to one of the oaks. *Acta Oecologica, Oecologia Applicata* **4**, 55–74.

27. LARSSON, S. (1989). Stressful times for the plant stress–insect performance hypothesis. *Oikos* **56**, 277–283.

28. WATT, A.D. (1994). The relevance of the stress hypothesis to insects feeding on tree foliage. In: *Individuals, populations and patterns in ecology*, eds S.R. Leather, A.D. Watt, N.J. Mills and K.F.A. Walters. Intercept, Andover, 73–85.

29. STRAW, N.A. (1995). Climate change and the impact of the green spruce aphid, *Elatobium abietinum* (Walker), in the UK. *Scottish Forestry* **49**, 134–145.

30. DAY, K.R. and KIDD, N.A.C. (1998). Green spruce aphid population dynamics: effects of climate, weather and regulation. In: *The green spruce aphid in western Europe: ecology, status, impacts and prospects for management*, eds. K.R. Day, G. Halldorsson, S. Harding and N.A. Straw. Technical Paper 24. Forestry Commission, Edinburgh, 41–52.

31. POWELL, W. and PARRY, W.H. (1976). Effects of temperature on overwintering populations of the green spruce aphid *Elatobium abietinum*. *Annals of Applied Biology* **82**, 209–219.

32. ZHOU, X., PERRY, J.N., WOIWOOD, I.P., HARRINGTON, R., BALE, J.S. and CLARK, S.J. (1997). Detecting chaotic dynamics of insect populations from long-term survey data. *Ecological Entomology* **22**, 231–241.

33. HARRINGTON, R., BALE, J.S. and TATCHELL, G.M. (1995). Aphids in a changing climate. In: *Insects in a changing environment*, eds R. Harrington and N.E. Stork. Academic Press, London, 126–155.

34. HULME, M. and JENKINS, G.J. (1998). *Climate change scenarios for the UK*. UKCIP Technical Report No. 1. Climatic Research Unit, University of East Anglia, Norwich.

35. CARTER, C.I. (1977). *Impact of green spruce aphid on growth: can a tree forget its past?* Research and Development Paper 116. Forestry Commission, Edinburgh

36. CANNELL, M.G.R. and SMITH, R.I. (1986). Climatic warming, spring budburst and frost damage on trees. *Journal of Applied Ecology* **23**, 177–191.

37. MURRAY, M.B., SMITH, R.I., LEITH, I.D., FOWLER, D., LEE, H.S.J., FRIEND, A.D. and JARVIS, P.G. (1994). Effects of elevated CO_2, nutrition and climatic warming on bud phenology in Sitka spruce (*Picea sitchensis*) and their impact on the risk of frost damage. *Tree Physiology* **14**, 691–706.

38. CARTER, C.I. (1989). *The 1989 outbreak of the green spruce aphid*, Elatobium abietinum. Research Information Note 161. Forestry Commission, Edinburgh.

39. STRAW, N.A., FIELDING, N.J., GREEN, G. and PRICE, J. (2000). The impact of green spruce aphid, *Elatobium abietinum* (Walker), and root aphids on the growth of young Sitka spruce in Hafren Forest, Wales: effect on height, diameter and volume. *Forest Ecology and Management* **134**, 97–109.

40. BUSE, A., DURY, S.J., WOODBURN, R.J.W., PERRINS, C.M. and GOOD, J.E.G. (1999). Effects of elevated temperature on multi-species interactions: the case of pedunculate oak, winter moth and tits. *Functional Ecology* **13**, 74–82.

41. BERGDAHL, D.R. (1988). Impact of pinewood nematode in North America: present and future. *Journal of Nematology* **20**, 260–265.

42. WINGFIELD, M.J. (1987). A comparison of the mycophagous and the phytophagous phases of the pine wood nematode. In: *Pathogenicity of the pine wood nematode*, ed. M. Wingfield. APS Press, St Paul, USA, 81–90.

43. DWINELL, L.D. and NICKLE, W.R. (1989). *An overview of the pine wood nematode ban in North America*. USDA Forest Service General Technical Report SE-55. USDA, Ashville, USA, 1–13.

44. LINIT, M.J. (1988). Nematode-vector relationships in the pine wilt disease system. *Journal of Nematology* **20**, 227–235.

45. MAMIYA, Y. (1988). History of pine wilt disease in Japan. *Journal of Nematology* **20**, 219–226.

46. MAMIYA, Y. and KIYOHARA, T. (1972). Description of *Bursaphelenchus lignicolus* n.sp. (Nematoda : Aphelenchoididae) from pine wood and histopathology of nematode-infested trees. *Nematologica* **18**, 120–124.

47. EVANS, H.F., McNAMARA, D.G., BRAASCH, H., CHADOEUF, J. and MAGNUSSON, C. (1996). Pest Risk Analysis (PRA) for the territories of the European Union (as PRA area) on *Bursaphelenchus xylophilus* and its vectors in the genus *Monochamus*. *EPPO Bulletin* **26**, 199–249.

48. KOBAYASHI, F. (1988). The Japanese pine sawyer. In: *Dynamics of forest insect populations*, ed. A.A. Berryman. Plenum, New York, 431–454.

49. McNULTY, S.G., LORIO, P.L., AYRES, M.P. and REEVE, J.D. (1997). Predictions of southern pine beetle populations under historic and projected climate using a forest ecosystem model. In: *The productivity and sustainability of southern forest ecosystems in a changing environment*, eds R.A. Mickler and S. Fox. Springer-Verlag, New York, 617–634.

50. STEPHEN, F.M. and PAINE, T.D. (1985). Seasonal patterns of host tree resistance to fungal associates of the southern pine beetle. *Zeitschrift für angewandte Entomologie* **99**, 113–122.

51. THATCHER, R.C. and PICKARD, L.S. (1967). Seasonal development of the southern pine beetle in East Texas. *Journal of Economic Entomology* **60**, 556–568.

52. EVANS, H.F., BAKER, R.H.A. and MCLEOD, A. (2001). Evaluating the risk of invasion by potential forest pests. In: *Protection of world forests from insect pests: advances in research*, eds R.I. Alfaro *et al*. IUFRO World Series, vol. II. IUFRO Secretariat, Vienna, 55–67.

53. SUTHERST, R.W., MAYWALD, G.F. and SKARRATT, D.B. (1995). Predicting insect distributions in a changed climate. In: *Insects in a changing environment*, eds R. Harrington and N. Stork. Academic Press, London, 59–91.

54. ANDERBRANT, O. (1986). A model for the temperature and density dependent reemergence of the bark beetle Ips typographus. *Entomologia Experimentalis et Applicata* **40**, 81–88.

55. PARMESAN, C., RYRHOLM, N., STEFANESCU, C., HILL, J.K., THOMAS, C.D.,

DESCIMON, H., HUNTLEY, B., KAILA, L., KULLBERG, J., TAMMARU, T., TENNENT, W.J., THOMAS, J.A. and WARREN, M.S. (1999). Poleward shifts in geographical ranges of butterfly species associated with regional warming. *Nature* **399**, 579–583.

56. HAACK, R.A., LAW, K.R., MASTRO, V.C., OSSENBRUGGEN, H.S. and RAIMO, B.J. (1997). New York's battle with the Asian long-horned beetle. *Journal of Forestry* **95**, 11–15.

CHAPTER NINE   Mark Broadmeadow and Tim Randle

9

The Impacts of Increased CO₂ Concentrations on Tree Growth and Function

KEY FINDINGS

- Research into the direct effects of rising carbon dioxide concentrations ($[CO_2]$) on trees presents problems as a result of the size of facility required, and also the timeframe over which the experiments must be conducted; a number of approaches are, however, available.

- Rates of carbon uptake will increase because the primary enzyme of photosynthesis is not saturated at current ambient $[CO_2]$; at the same time, higher $[CO_2]$ will inhibit photorespiration; the temperature optimum of photosynthesis will rise.

- In impact studies, faster growth rates have been shown to result in nutrient deficiencies or imbalances, often manifested as a 'down-regulation' of photosynthesis.

- The effect of $[CO_2]$ on respiration has been variable, and no consensus has been arrived at.

- Stomatal conductance and thus water use on a leaf area basis are generally reduced at enhanced $[CO_2]$; an increase in leaf area is often observed in impact studies, and thus, water use on a ground area or individual tree basis may not decrease at elevated $[CO_2]$.

- If the increase in leaf area observed in impact studies is borne out in mature forest stands, there would be a number of important implications over and above changes in transpiration: increased precipitation interception losses; increased wind resistance and potential snow loading; altered forest floor microclimate as a result of increased light interception; increased litter input to the soil.

- Over a range of impact studies, mostly on saplings and young trees, a doubling of atmospheric $[CO_2]$ resulted in an average biomass increment of 50% over the course of the experiments; however, there are concerns that this may not be borne out in mature forest stands.

- Timber quality has been affected in some studies, although the current view is that this impact is largely a result of faster growth rates.

- Rising $[CO_2]$ and climate change are predicted to result in General Yield Class (GYC) increases of 2 (6 to 8 for oak, 14 to 16 for Sitka spruce) comparing rotations approaching harvest now with new plantings.

- Current forest yield models are likely to require modification if they are to provide accurate yield forecasts in the future.

Introduction

The atmospheric carbon dioxide concentration ([CO_2]) has increased from ~270 ppm prior to the industrial revolution to a current value of ~370 ppm, largely as a result of the burning of fossil fuels and widespread vegetation clearance. The concentration is expected to continue rising to between 550 and 1000 ppm by the end of this century[1]. The large uncertainty in the magnitude of this increase is because we do not know how policy initiatives such as the Kyoto Protocol will impact on CO_2 emissions and we are not certain how the global carbon cycle may feed back on atmospheric [CO_2]. This rise in [CO_2] has a number of important implications for tree growth.

In addition to the indirect effects of enhanced atmospheric [CO_2] acting through radiative forcing of the global climate (see Chapter 2), higher [CO_2] also has a direct effect on some of the physiological processes of plants, including photosynthesis and respiration. A wealth of information is available on the physiological impact of elevated [CO_2], particularly on annual crop species. Short generation times, relatively small growth forms, and the lack of long-lived woody material means that there is consensus and a degree of certainty over these effects. It is more difficult to manipulate the atmosphere within which trees are growing as a result of their large size and long generation/rotation time, and there is therefore less certainty over the effects of rising [CO_2] on woody species, particularly in the long term. In general, research conducted on seedlings, saplings and young trees has shown that the direct effects of elevated [CO_2] result in increased growth rates[2-4], together with other impacts related to water use, carbon and nutrient allocation and timber quality. There is, however, some concern that the responses to elevated [CO_2] observed in experiments on young trees and saplings may not be replicated in mature forest trees. Putting these concerns aside, there is evidence

that the productivity of UK and European forests has increased over the last 50 years[5-8], at the same time as [CO_2] has risen from ~310 ppm to 370 ppm. However, it is difficult to attribute this to a single factor as, over this same period, management practice, silviculture and genetic stock have all improved, nitrogen deposition from the atmosphere has increased, weather patterns have altered, and the changing age structure of UK forests may also have contributed to an apparent increase in productivity (see Chapter 10).

This chapter assesses the most likely implications of the rise in atmospheric [CO_2] for UK forestry, including interactions with the other aspects of climate and environmental change that are outlined in Chapters 3, 4 and 5. These interactions are not restricted to effects on tree growth, but also relate to sensitive areas such as water use at a landscape level, and nutrient sustainability of forest soils. The impacts of elevated [CO_2] on tree growth will be demonstrated by results of research carried out at the Forestry Commission open-top chamber facilities at Headley (Hampshire) and Glendevon (Perthshire), together with summary data from the EU 4th framework ECOCRAFT project[9] (Predicted Impacts of Rising Carbon Dioxide and Temperature on Forests in Europe at Stand Scale). Because of the complex nature of interactions between climate, atmospheric [CO_2] and site factors, an assessment of the impacts of rising [CO_2] cannot be made using these experimental results alone, and needs to draw heavily on the modelling activities described in Chapter 11.

Experimental approaches

Research into the effects of climate on tree growth can exploit natural spatial variation in factors such as rainfall and temperature. In contrast, spatial variation in atmospheric [CO_2] is too limited for a similar approach to be used for investigating the effects of [CO_2] on tree growth. Analysis of growth responses

Figure 9.1 *A range of facilities used for elevated CO_2 impact studies on free rooted trees: (a) branch bag on Sitka spruce (Glencorse, Scotland – University of Edinburgh); (b) free air carbon enrichment (FACE) (north Carolina, USA – Duke University); (c) whole tree chamber on Scots pine (Mekrijarvi Research Station, Finland – University of Joensuu); (d) biosphere (Beskydy mountains, Czech Republic – University of Brno); (e) open-top chambers (Headley Nursery, UK – Forest Research). [Sources: (a) C. Barton, (b) J. Heath].*

Table 9.1 Comparison of different approaches to elevated $[CO_2]$ impact studies. Costs given are approximate, and dependent on the nature of monitoring equipment installed. The estimates are only intended to give an indication of the general range of costs and are representative of individual chambers (except for FACE).

Approach	Time-frame	Use	Advantages	Limitations	Costs (£) installation	running (annual)
Growth chamber	< 1 year	Individual process studies for seedlings/ saplings	• Low cost (for limited number of chambers); • control of environmental conditions; • intensive care of plants; • enables gas exchange to be measured continuously.	• Environmental conditions; • rooting volume; • physical space and tree size; • maximum age of trees.	20 000 (each)	1 000
Open-top chamber	1–8 years	Acclimated long-term responses of small trees/ saplings	• Open top to chambers – limits modification to environment.	• Limit to size (and age) of trees; • some experiments use potted plants with restricted rooting volumes; • water supply cannot be adequately controlled.	> 5 000	2 000
Branch bag	1–3 years	Responses of mature plant tissue	• Enables impact studies on mature plant tissue at low cost; • allows continuous gas exchange measurements to be made.	• Tissue may not have developed at elevated CO_2; • heating of branch bag by sunlight; • humidity rise in branch bag.	1 000	1 000
Whole tree chamber	< 10 years	Whole tree responses	• Enables studies on mature trees *in situ*; • control of water supply possible.	• Limited (individual) replication.	> 10 000	2 000
Biosphere	< 10 years	Responses of whole trees/ ecosystems	• Enables whole ecosystem to be studied; • enables studies on larger trees; • control of water supply possible.	• Limited air movement in large chamber; • large physical size of structure; • limited 'plot' replication.	> 50 000	20 000
FACE (free air carbon enrichment)	< 1 rotation	Ecosystem responses	• Natural conditions; • enables whole ecosystem to be studied.	• Cost (both at installation and during running); • plot replication; limited material available as large numbers of research teams generally involved.	> 5 000 000	> 1 000 000

using temporal changes in [CO$_2$] can be undertaken, but this approach is complicated by the changes in confounding factors such as management and environmental variables that have occurred over the same period (see Chapter 10). Research into the effects of elevated [CO$_2$] can therefore only be undertaken in the form of impact studies, where the environment within which the tree is growing is artificially manipulated. There are a number of approaches that can be used, and these vary in scale, cost and the time-frame over which they operate[10] (see Figure 9.1).

All these approaches have limitations, but nevertheless, they are important for providing data which enable predictions of the impacts of changing [CO$_2$] on forest growth and function to be made. Potential limitations of impact studies relate to the presence of artefacts in experimental procedures including the following:

- Acclimation of the photosynthetic apparatus to elevated [CO$_2$] may take more than one month; short-term studies are therefore of limited value.
- Studies of allocation may be compromised if potted plants are used, since rooting space is often limited; the natural thermal environment of roots is also difficult to replicate.
- Artificial soils may produce experimental results that are not replicated in 'forest soils'.
- Nutrient supply should be considered – fertilised experiments may not be representative of forest conditions; faster growth rates that are often observed under experimental conditions may lead to nutrient deficiencies developing where they might not in the field.
- Experiments on seedlings and saplings may not be representative of mature forest trees.
- Because experiments of this nature are often harvested at the time of canopy closure, the results may not be representative of a closed forest.

A comparison of the different experimental systems that are available is shown in Table 9.1. Despite the limitations of these experimental systems, impact studies have provided a wealth of data that describe tree responses to elevated [CO$_2$] and interactions with other environmental variables. Such studies also provide data for parameterising process models of forest growth which can be applied to predicting the impact of global climate change on forest growth and health.

Carbon balance

Tree growth is the result of net carbon availability – the difference between photosynthesis and respiration. The carbon fluxes attributable to both photosynthesis (GPP – gross photosynthetic productivity) and respiration (R) are large, leaving net carbon uptake as a relatively small fraction of overall carbon turnover, generally in the range of 25–30%[11]. For example (see Figure 9.2), in an oak plot in Alice Holt forest (Hampshire, UK; [a]GYC6), GPP has been estimated as 14 tC ha^{-1} yr^{-1}, and R as 10.3 tC ha^{-1} yr^{-1} using the process model ForestFlux[12] while annual carbon exchange (NEF – net ecosystem flux) has been measured by eddy correlation[13] as 3.8 tC ha^{-1} yr^{-1}. Traditional mensuration measurements indicate that over the period 1994–2000, timber increment accounted for 3.02 tC ha^{-1}yr^{-1} while carbon converted into branch and root wood can be calculated as 0.54 and 0.50 tC ha^{-1}yr^{-1} respectively, based on expansion factors given by Dewar and Cannell[14]. Any climatic or environmental factor which changes one of the two large fluxes – GPP or R – can thus have a disproportionally large effect on the much smaller annual carbon balance, and thus on forest productivity. Furthermore, changes to the availability of carbon may affect other processes, including the susceptibility to pest and pathogen attack through a change in

[a]General Yield Class – site index defined as mean annual volume increment (m^3).

Figure 9.2 Typical values of annual carbon fluxes (tonnes carbon per hectare) for GYC6 oak. GPP and R are estimated as 14 tC ha^{-1} yr^{-1} and 10.3 tC ha^{-1} yr^{-1}, respectively, and net ecosystem flux (NEF) was measured as 3.8 tC ha^{-1} yr^{-1}. It is assumed that there is no change in soil carbon, and thus all NEF is represented by wood increment. The increase in standing carbon is based upon mensuration assessments made in 1994 and 2001, and the allocation of carbon to branch and root wood is estimated from Dewar and Cannell[14]. Note that measured NEF is the difference between GPP and R, and in this example, does not agree exactly with estimates of carbon conversion into woody biomass.

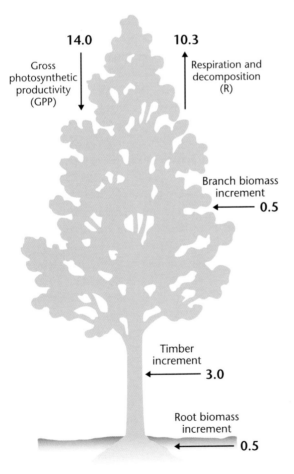

14.0

Gross photosynthetic productivity (GPP)

10.3

Respiration and decomposition (R)

Branch biomass increment
0.5

Timber increment
3.0

Root biomass increment
0.5

allocation of carbon to defence strategies, and the ability to withstand extended periods of drought. The impact of elevated [CO_2] on photosynthesis and respiration are discussed in detail in the sections that follow, together with assessments of how other environmental variables may influence these responses.

Carbon fixation

Carbon dioxide is the substrate for RuBisCO (ribulose-bis-phosphate carboxylase oxygenase), the main enzyme involved in the fixation of carbon (see explanatory box on leaf gas exchange). An increase in CO_2 concentration will enhance the rate of photosynthesis because RuBisCO is not saturated at current ambient [CO_2]. RuBisCO also has the capacity to react with oxygen, a process known as photorespiration, and which reduces net carbon uptake. This 'oxygenase' function of RuBisCO increases with rising temperature at a faster rate than the 'carboxylase' function, such that at 38–40°C, photorespiratory and photosynthetic carbon fluxes are equal, and no net photosynthesis occurs. As a consequence, enhanced [CO_2] has two further impacts on photosynthesis: first, higher concentrations of CO_2 compete with oxygen for the active sites on RuBisCO, promoting photosynthesis by reducing its oxygenase function, and, secondly, as the oxygenase function is reduced, the temperature optimum of photosynthesis rises, as shown in Figure 9.3.

The increase in the temperature optimum of photosynthesis is of limited importance in the UK as a result of the temperate climate that is experienced here. However, in the tropics, it is more significant because ambient temperatures are much closer to the point (38–40°C) at which photosynthesis is balanced by photorespiration. As shown in Figure 9.3, the relationship between net photosynthesis and temperature is steeper at these higher temperatures and thus a shift in the temperature optimum of photosynthesis has a larger effect.

Leaf gas exchange

Photosynthesis is the process by which carbon dioxide (CO$_2$) from the atmosphere and light energy from the sun is converted or 'fixed' into sugar molecules (CHO) which are eventually transformed into cellulose, lignin and other carbon containing compounds which constitute wood. The rate of photosynthesis is dependent on environmental variables including light and temperature, and the concentration of CO$_2$ in the sub-stomatal cavity ([CO$_2$]$_i$). In turn, the concentration of CO$_2$ within the leaf is dependent on ambient CO$_2$ levels ([CO$_2$]$_a$, the rate of photosynthesis itself, and the degree to which the stomatal guard cells are open (stomatal conductance, g_s). The stomatal guard cells themselves respond to light, temperature, humidity and CO$_2$ concentration.

Light energy from the sun is 'harvested' by chlorophyll molecules within the chloroplasts (in the form of adenosine triphosphate, ATP), where CO$_2$ is then converted to small sugar molecules by the enzyme RuBisCO (ribulose-bis-phosphate carboxylase oxygenase), with the production of oxygen. This enzyme can also react with oxygen, converting sugar molecules back to CO$_2$ – a process known as photorespiration. Most biological systems consume fixed carbon to provide energy (the process of respiration), which occurs mainly in the mitochondria, and its rate is largely a function of temperature. At any point in time, net carbon exchange between the leaf and the atmosphere is thus a product of the individual rates of respiration, photorespiration and photosynthesis. The stomatal guard cells also control the rate of water loss from the leaves (transpiration), with the result that photosynthesis and transpiration are closely linked.

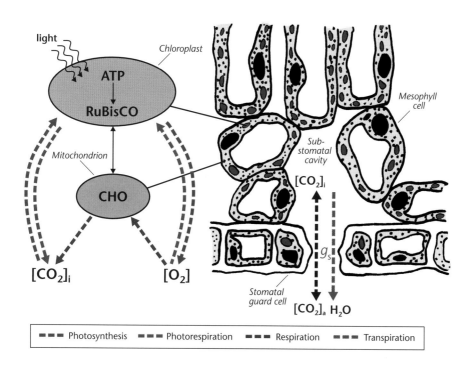

Figure 9.3 Temperature response of photosynthesis in oak at ambient (grey line: 360 ppm) and elevated (green line: 700 ppm) CO₂. Third order polynomials were fitted by least squares and average eight response curves for each treatment. Arrows indicate the temperature optimum of photosynthesis for each treatment.

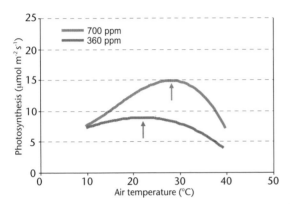

Two parameters are commonly used to describe the activity of the photosynthetic apparatus: V_{cmax} is the maximum (theoretical) rate of RuBisCO activity and J_{max} is the maximum rate of electron transport to RuBisCO. The complex expressions which have been developed to describe photosynthesis are outside the scope of this publication, but the brief definitions given above are provided, as experimental results are commonly reported using them and, furthermore, they are required as inputs for many process models (see Chapter 11).

Since RuBisCO generally contains about half of the total foliar nitrogen content, a close relationship exists between V_{cmax} and leaf nitrogen concentration, as shown in Figure 9.4. Photosynthesis is also a function of stomatal conductance, and the relationships between photosynthesis, photosynthetic capacity and stomatal conductance, together with other parameters are explored in detail by von Caemmerer and Farquhar[15] and Ball and co-workers[16].

A number of studies have indicated long-term down-regulation of the photosynthetic apparatus in response to elevated [CO₂], which may be related to nitrogen availability as demonstrated by the results of two experiments on oak at the Headley open-top chamber facility (Figure 9.5). In the first experiment, no additional nutrients were supplied, and V_{cmax} of plants grown at elevated [CO₂] was significantly lower (17%) than that of plants at ambient [CO₂]. In contrast, nutrient supplements were supplied in the second experiment in the form of a slow release fertiliser, and no reduction in V_{cmax} was observed in response to elevated [CO₂]. It is also apparent that values of V_{cmax} were generally higher in the latter experiment.

The ECOCRAFT project assessed the impact of elevated CO₂ on a number of photosynthetic parameters. A small, significant reduction of approximately 10% was apparent in both V_{cmax} and J_{max} across 16 experimental studies and 19 tree species[18] (Table 9.2). It should be borne in mind that all of these studies were undertaken on free-rooted trees, generally in native forest soils, and thus are likely to be representative of future forest

Figure 9.4 Relationship between the photosynthetic parameters Jmax (open symbols) and Vcmax (filled symbols) (maximum light and RuBisCO limited rates of photosynthesis, respectively) and foliar nitrogen content expressed on an area basis in a mature oak tree[17]. Linear regressions were fitted by least squares.

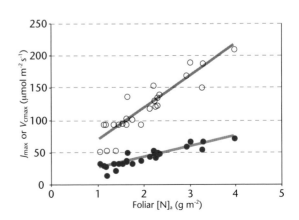

Table 9.2 *Meta-analysis of the effects of enhanced CO_2 concentrations on photosynthetic parameters across 16 experimental studies in the ECOCRAFT project[18]. The mean effect size is expressed as the ratio of each parameter at elevated CO_2 to that at ambient CO_2 concentrations. A_{max} is the light and CO_2 saturated rate of photosynthesis; A_{360} and A_{700} are measured rates of photosynthesis at ambient and 700 ppm CO_2, respectively; J_{max} and V_{cmax} are as defined in the text; $[N]_m$ is leaf nitrogen concentration expressed as a function of weight. A mean effect size of less than one indicates a reduction, or down-regulation in that parameter.*

Parameter	Mean effect size	95% Confidence interval	Number of studies
A_{max}	1.51	1.39–1.63	28
A_{360}	0.81	0.75–0.87	17
A_{700}	0.91	0.87–0.96	14
J_{max}	0.88	0.80–0.98	19
V_{cmax}	0.91	0.85–0.98	19
$[N]_m$	0.85	0.79–0.92	27

Figure 9.5 *The response of V_{cmax} to elevated $[CO_2]$ under high and low nutrient regimes. Error bars represent SEMs with individual open-top chambers as the experimental unit.*

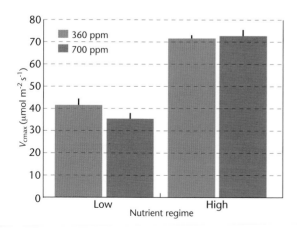

responses. In contrast, the review of Curtis and Wang[4] identified a much larger down-regulation (~30% across all experiments) but in their meta-analysis, this was reduced to 10% for free-rooted trees, indicating the importance of experimental conditions when interpreting responses to elevated $[CO_2]$.

The role of foliar nitrogen content (N_m: Table 9.2) in photosynthesis is evident, with a 15% reduction observed in elevated $[CO_2]$ grown trees, and it is likely that it is responsible for the reduction in V_{cmax} and J_{max}, and thus the observed down-regulation of photosynthesis at both 360 ppm and 700 ppm CO_2. Notwithstanding the small down-regulation of the photosynthetic apparatus, elevated $[CO_2]$ still increased photosynthesis by approximately 50% (A_{max}: Table 9.2). The key question that remains to be answered, is how far compensatory mechanisms both within plants and within ecosystems will counteract any potential increase in biomass accumulation as a result of rising $[CO_2]$.

Respiration

Although respiration is as important as photosynthesis to carbon balance (see above), this process is under-represented in the scientific literature, and the results that have been reported are more variable than for photosynthesis, both in magnitude and direction[2–4,19]. The overriding tendency is for elevated $[CO_2]$ to result in a reduction in respiration and, indeed, a direct, reversible inhibition of the enzymes of dark respiration has been demonstrated[20]. There is good evidence that tissue respiration rates are linearly related to nitrogen concentration[21] (see Figure 9.6), and this relationship is generally used in long-term models of tree growth (e.g. Hybrid[22]). Any reduction in tissue nitrogen concentrations would thus be expected to lead to a reduction in respiration rates, thus affecting carbon balance. Alternatively, greater substrate availability resulting from enhanced

Figure 9.6 Relationship between respiration rate and nitrogen content for a combined data-set of root, wood and leaf tissue of three species of oak, grown at ambient and elevated CO_2 concentrations during both summer and winter. The slope of the 20°C relationship is 2.01 times that of the 10°C relationship, indicating a doubling of respiration rate for a 10°C rise in temperature (i.e. Q_{10}=2.0). Linear regressions were fitted by least squares.

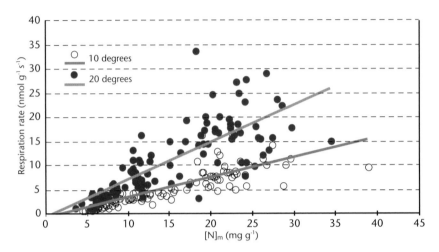

Table 9.3 The effect of elevated $[CO_2]$ on leaf respiration rate expressed as a function of nitrogen content, area and weight for all experiments within the ECOCRAFT project. [Source: Ecocraft, 1999[9]].

Experiment	Species	Mean effect size		
		Nitrogen	Area	Weight
Bily Kriz	*Picea abies*			
Flakaliden BB	*Picea abies* (control)	1.20	1.13*	1.09*
	Picea abies (fertilised)	1.17	1.19*	1.06*
Glencorse	*Betula pendula*	0.89	0.78	0.75
Glencorse BB	*Picea sitchensis*		0.87	0.83
Headley II	*Quercus petraea*	1.11	0.94	0.87
	Pinus sylvestris	0.97		1.00
Headley III	*Quercus petraea*	0.80	0.91*	0.73*
	Quercus robur			
	Quercus rubra	1.09	1.22*	1.10*
Mekrijarvi	*Pinus sylvestris*	1.07	0.74*	1.10*
Orsay	*Fagus sylvatica*			
TUB I	*Fagus sylvatica*		1.03*	1.09*
UIA pine	*Pinus sylvestris*	0.73	0.93*	0.73
UIA poplar II	*Populus* 'Beaupré'		0.27*	
	Populus 'Robusta'		1.00*	
Gembloux	*Picea abies*		0.80	
	Picea abies		1.80	
	Picea abies		1.04	
Mean		**0.98**	**0.96**	**0.93**

*Denotes experiments included within the meta-analysis, which yielded mean effect sizes of 0.91 and 1.01 for area and weight respectively.

[CO_2] has been shown to lead to higher rates of maintenance respiration.

Work in the open-top chambers at Headley identified no consistent effects on root, branch or foliage respiration during either summer or winter in a fertilised experiment[9] although a small reduction had been observed in a previous experiment when nutrients were limiting[23].

When all experiments conducted as part of the ECOCRAFT project were analysed together, no consistent effect of elevated [CO_2] on respiration was evident (mean effect size of 1.01: Table 9.3). However, this does not mean that respiration is unaffected by [CO_2], but that the direction of any effect is highly dependent on growth conditions, or on the balance between nitrogen content driven reductions in respiration, and increases in respiration linked to substrate availability.

Stomatal conductance, transpiration and water use

Stomata close in response to elevated [CO_2], and it has been postulated that this is driven through the sensing of [CO_2] in the sub-stomatal cavity[16]. This well-documented short-term response reduces stomatal conductance by ~20% at twice current ambient [CO_2][2,24]. The data presented for three species of oak in Figure 9.7 are at the higher end of reported responses to [CO_2] (36% reduction for all three species at 700 ppm CO_2), and contrast with some studies in which no response was observed. It is also uncertain whether the relatively large reductions in conductance, which are commonplace in studies on seedlings and young trees, will be observed in mature forest stands[25]. Some of the variation in the magnitude of the response of stomatal conductance to [CO_2] can be explained by age, experimental methodology and growth form, and these differences have been explored by Curtis and Wang[4] and Medlyn and co-workers[24].

In a total of 48 experiments, Curtis and Wang[4] only found an average (non-significant) 11% reduction in stomatal conductance at enhanced [CO_2]. However, many of the experiments analysed by Curtis and Wang assessed the response of pot-grown plants, which in many cases may have had restricted rooting volumes, thus interfering with the direct effects of [CO_2] alone. Many of the experiments were also of relatively short

Figure 9.7 The effect of growth at enhanced CO_2 concentrations on stomatal conductance in three species of oak. Error bars represent SEM with individual open-top chambers treated as the experimental unit.

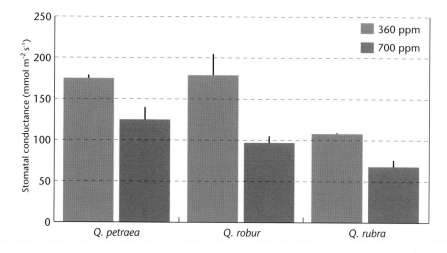

duration. In contrast, Medlyn and co-workers[24] assessed the response of only free-rooted trees and reported a mean [CO_2] effect of a 20% reduction in conductance. Further analysis revealed that conifer species responded less than deciduous species, the reduction was greater in experiments of more than one-year duration, young trees were more responsive than mature trees, water stress increased the magnitude of CO_2-induced stomatal closure and nutrient stress had the opposite effect.

The general consensus is that growth at 700 ppm CO_2 will lead to reduced water use by trees, but there is also evidence that elevated [CO_2] may also alter the response of stomatal conductance to other environmental variables, including reductions in the sensitivity to both leaf–air vapour pressure deficit (LAVPD)[26,27] and soil moisture deficit[28]. If growth at elevated [CO_2] does result in desensitised stomatal responses to these two environmental variables, then there is potential for an enhanced susceptibility to drought-related mortality.

The reduction in stomatal conductance that is expected as a result of any rise in atmospheric CO_2 concentrations will provide an additional protective benefit to plants. Damage to foliage from ground level (tropospheric) ozone pollution is mediated through the stomata, and hence any reduction in stomatal conductance will act to ameliorate ozone pollution. Figure 9.8 demonstrates this beneficial side-effect using foliar chlorophyll content as an indicator of ozone damage, with higher levels of chlorophyll observed in those treatments which exhibit lower stomatal conductance as a function of either elevated CO_2, or drought treatments. The lack of a relationship between chlorophyll content and conductance in the ambient ozone treatments indicates that current levels of ozone do not elicit a degradation of chlorophyll, although reductions in productivity are thought likely[29,30]. Ambient background concentrations of ozone are also predicted to increase

Figure 9.8 Relationship between foliar chlorophyll content and stomatal conductance in oak for ambient and elevated ozone treatments. Stomatal conductance is expressed as the (open-top) chamber mean of measurements made on seven occasions during the 1995 growing season. Differences in stomatal conductance within each ozone treatment are a function of the other factorial treatment combinations of ambient or elevated CO_2, and irrigation or drought[32].

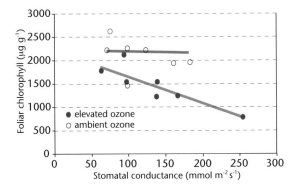

considerably over the 21st century[31], which would raise the significance of this side-effect.

In addition to the physiological response of reduced stomatal conductance at enhanced [CO_2], there is also evidence of a structural response to changing atmospheric [CO_2]. Analysis of both herbarium specimens grown under sub-ambient [CO_2], and recent experimental material from impact studies grown at enhanced [CO_2] has revealed a reduction in stomatal density of some 14%[33,34]. The trend towards greater acclimation in longer term impact studies[24] may therefore be, at least in part, a result of reduced stomatal density, alongside the reduction in conductance.

Although the above discussion suggests that the water use of woodland may reduce on a leaf area basis and, indeed, water use efficiency (defined as unit carbon assimilated per unit water transpired) at enhanced [CO_2] generally shows a considerable increase[35], this is not necessarily the case for a forest stand. As Table

9.4 indicates, most impact studies on young trees suggest an increase in leaf area. If this is borne out, transpiration may actually increase on an individual tree or ground area basis, while canopy water use would also increase as a result of increased interception losses from incident rainfall (see Chapter 5). Furthermore, although stomatal conductance may show a small decrease at enhanced $[CO_2]$, the associated increase in leaf temperature as a result of reduced evaporative cooling may limit the reduction in transpiration by increasing LAVPD. Outside the direct impacts of rising $[CO_2]$, transpiration will also increase as a result of the predicted rise in potential evapo-transpiration (see Chapter 2). It is thus apparent that while the direction of the impact of rising $[CO_2]$ on stomatal conductance can be predicted, its magnitude cannot, and moreover, not even the direction of the impact on canopy water use can be predicted with certainty. As is the case with many of the potential impacts of rising $[CO_2]$, FACE experiments and work in natural CO_2 springs will provide the key to future research in this area.

Figure 9.9 The effect of elevated [CO₂] on the growth of three species of oak after two-years exposure. Seedlings were raised in a glasshouse in ambient or elevated [CO₂] and transferred to open-top chambers after one-year. The upper chamber is the ambient control (360 ppm CO₂), and the lower is the 700 ppm CO₂ treatment.

Observed growth effects

The growth response of woody plants varies greatly in the scientific literature, with reported CO_2 fertilisation effects (CFE[b]) ranging from 0 to +225% (Figure 9.9). Much of this variation can be accounted for by age of plant, experimental conditions and other limiting factors.

At Headley, when three species of oak were grown from seed in open-top chambers at 350 or 700 ppm CO_2, and supplied with adequate nutrients and water, growth rates more than doubled for the duration of this three-year experiment, as is clearly illustrated in Figure 9.9. In contrast, in a previous experiment, the growth of ash showed no enhancement at 700 ppm CO_2 when no additional nutrients were

supplied. Furthermore, in the final year of this three year experiment, the relative growth rate (RGR: biomass increment per unit biomass) of ash was reduced in elevated $[CO_2]$ compared to the ambient control. This response of ash contrasted with that of oak grown in the same experiment, which generally has a lower nitrogen requirement than ash, and maintained its enhancement of RGR at 700 ppm CO_2[32]. Further evidence of the interaction between the CFE and nutrient supply is given in Figure 9.10, which presents growth data from the open-top chamber site at Glendevon. Here, nutrient supply was imposed as a treatment in a factorial experiment together with elevated $[CO_2]$. The response to both nutrient supply

[b]CFE – CO_2 fertilisation effect; ratio of growth at elevated $[CO_2]$ to that at ambient $[CO_2]$.

and [CO$_2$] was highly variable, with Scots pine responding to both treatments, Sitka spruce responding to [CO$_2$] in the supplementary nutrient treatment only, and alder showing a smaller CO$_2$ response than the other two species.

When all 19 experiments which contributed to the ECOCRAFT project are analysed together (Table 9.4), a mean CFE for total biomass of 49% is evident. Above- and below-ground responses were similar (Table 9.4), suggesting that in these experiments allocation was unaffected by [CO$_2$] treatment. There was also no difference in the response of different plant functional groups (conifer or broadleaf species), but where a stress treatment was included within an experiment (e.g. drought, nutrient deficiency), the stress treatment generally had a lower CFE (mean effect size 1.39) than the unstressed treatment (mean effect size 1.66)[9].

Many studies have suggested a change in carbon allocation in response to enhanced [CO$_2$], manifested as an increased root:shoot ratio. However, many of the early studies were conducted on potted trees with restricted rooting volume. More recent studies on free-rooted trees which included complete destructive harvests have shown little evidence of a change in the root:shoot ratio[23]. However, although fine roots (less than 2 mm in diameter) contribute little to total below-ground biomass, their density in the soil generally increases[25], and this does appear to be a specific response to enhanced [CO$_2$], particularly under conditions of drought or nutrient deficiency[37]. This response is important in two respects. First, the turnover of fine root biomass is one of the main routes through which carbon enters the soil, and is thus important in terms of carbon sequestration. Secondly, since water and nutrient uptake is through the fine roots, growth in elevated [CO$_2$] is likely to confer an advantage when resources are limited.

There is a considerable body of evidence which suggests that leaf area is increased in

Figure 9.10 Interaction between nutrition and CO$_2$ supply in three tree species. Additional nutrients (+nut) were supplied on the basis of demand, according to the method developed by Ingestad and Lund[36].

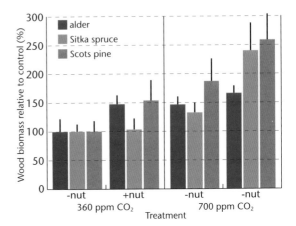

elevated [CO$_2$], as is self-evident in Figure 9.9. An analysis of the 12 ECOCRAFT project studies in which leaf area was measured indicated an increase of 34%. It is unlikely that the magnitude of this response will be replicated in a mature, closed canopy, as at least some of this apparent CO$_2$ driven effect is likely to be a result of different rates of development – larger trees would be expected to have larger leaf areas. However, evidence of

Table 9.4 Results of a meta-analysis of the impact of elevated [CO$_2$]on tree growth within the ECOCRAFT project[9].

	Mean effect size	95% Confidence interval	Number of studies
Above-ground biomass	1.51	1.34–1.69	21
Below-ground biomass	1.56	1.38–1.77	20
Total biomass	1.54	1.37–1.73	19
Leaf area	1.34	1.05–1.72	12

increased litter production in the FACE study (see below) points towards an increase in leaf area in this instance. If an increase in leaf area index is a consequence of rising atmospheric $[CO_2]$, the implications are far reaching:

- both interception of incident rainfall and transpiration losses from forest canopies will increase, leading to smaller throughfall volumes and reduced water availability for both ground vegetation and tree species;
- an increased aerodynamic resistance would result in an increased vulnerability to storm damage;
- an increased vulnerability to snow damage in evergreen species would ensue because of increased snow loading;
- reduced light transmission to the forest floor would potentially impact upon the composition of ground vegetation communities;
- increased litter input could affect soil carbon and nutrient cycles.

There is evidence that the CFE is larger in seedlings and young trees than in mature trees[4,25,38], and it is uncertain whether the magnitude of the CFE observed in the majority of experiments on young trees will be carried forward beyond the juvenile stage. Experiments in FACE systems and in whole tree chambers will provide answers to these questions, and it is encouraging that results are beginning to appear from these experiments, as described in the following section.

Results from FACE

Recent results from the free air carbon enrichment (FACE: see Figure 9.1) experiment in south Carolina, USA, suggest that the beneficial effects of elevated $[CO_2]$ on tree biomass increment may be short-lived, and disappear after 2–3 years exposure, particularly on nutritionally poor sites[39]. This corroborates the significant interaction with nutrient supply,

particularly nitrogen, evident in the experiments on young trees described previously. In the 'prototype,' unreplicated experiment ($FACE_P$), a transitory enhancement of growth was observed over the first 2–3 years, followed by a period when no significant impact on growth was evident. However, when additional nitrogen was supplied at an annual rate of 111 kg ha⁻¹ (together with a balanced supply of other macronutrients), a growth enhancement of 74% was observed in the 600 ppm CO_2 plot, compared to only 37% in the fertilised, ambient CO_2 plot. Similar results have been observed to date in the replicated main FACE experiment, although it is impossible at this stage to project these limited results forward. In addition, there was an apparent correlation between soil water availability in spring, and the magnitude of the growth enhancement.

The experiment has also made an important contribution to identifying future trends in an ecosystem-based carbon cycle – litter production was enhanced after only three years exposure, as might be anticipated on the basis of the results from experiments on young trees (Table 9.4). However, in the limited period over which the experiment has been running, only a minimal increase in the carbon content of the organic horizon was observed, with no change in the carbon content of the lower mineral horizons[40]. Ellsworth[41] has also demonstrated reduced stomatal sensitivity to drought in a number of understorey species, again corroborating the results of Heath and Kerstiens[28] and Tognetti and co-workers[27], from chamber and natural CO_2 spring studies, respectively.

It is clear that this important experiment will continue to provide invaluable information on the long-term responses of forest ecosystems to rising atmospheric $[CO_2]$. However, it should be borne in mind that these results are for a single species, loblolly pine (*Pinus taeda*), growing on a moderately fertile site with warm summers and plentiful precipitation throughout the year. The interactions that have been demonstrated between CO_2 enrichment and both fertility and water supply highlight the fact that these results should not be applied globally in a simplistic approach; they shed light on some of the many complex interactions that are present within any forest ecosystem but the response to elevated $[CO_2]$ will not be the same for all forests.

Another FACE system has recently been established in Italy, assessing the impact of elevated $[CO_2]$ on *Populus* clones grown as short rotation coppice[42]. Although this experiment does not address long-term effects on conventional high forest, it is providing evidence of the impact of elevated $[CO_2]$ on the functioning and growth of a woody species, free of the problems associated with other manipulative systems. Early results corroborate the observed increase in leaf production in loblolly pine[42].

Timber quality

A number of effects of elevated $[CO_2]$ on timber quality have been observed, mostly resulting from enhanced growth rates. That wood quality could be affected by changing climate and $[CO_2]$ is supported by the following observations: rapid growth may increase compression wood production in some species[43]; late flushing may be correlated with shake in oak – earlier flushing dates could counteract this effect[44]; wood density has been shown to be higher at elevated $[CO_2]$[45]; vessel element size and number has also been shown to increase in response to elevated $[CO_2]$[45].

Soil carbon balance

Although not directly relevant to forest growth or condition, soil carbon balance is important to long-term carbon fluxes and carbon sequestration, and the potential effects of rising $[CO_2]$ are discussed here. Any perturbation to

the soil carbon cycle has the potential to alter the carbon content of the soil, which can be much higher than the carbon content of the vegetation (see Chapter 5). Possible causes include changes in the micro-climate of the soil (temperature and moisture content), changes in litter quality, particularly the nitrogen content of the litter, and changes in the quantity of litter being added. Plants grown at enhanced $[CO_2]$ have been shown to attain larger total leaf areas (see Table 9.4), resulting in increased litter input, and for those leaves to have lower nutrient concentrations as a result of dilution, particularly on nutrient limited sites. In addition, root exudation of sugars is often enhanced at elevated $[CO_2]$ and has been shown to lead to increased activity of mycorrhizae. The response of soil systems is far slower than the response of individual plants, or above-ground ecosystems, and as such, overall responses to rising atmospheric $[CO_2]$ are difficult to assess or predict.

Modelling the impacts of rising CO_2 concentrations

Modelling of forest growth responses to changing environmental conditions is discussed in Chapter 11, but it is valuable here to explore current expectations of the likely effects of elevated $[CO_2]$ on forest growth in the UK. The simulations presented here include both estimates of annual carbon fluxes drawing out the relative effects of climate change and rising atmospheric $[CO_2]$ and long-term growth trends, based on recent climate simulations from the Hadley Centre[46] (see Chapter 2), together with CO_2 concentration scenarios published by IPCC[47] (IS92a). Model simulations have been performed using the Forest Research process model ForestFlux (formerly GROMIT[12]) operating at an hourly time-step. Conventional process representations are utilised throughout (photosynthesis: von Caemmerer and Farquhar[15]; stomatal conductance: Jarvis[48]; light interception: Goudriaan[49]).

Annual carbon fluxes

The doubling of $[CO_2]$ to 700 ppm in isolation has an overriding effect on annual carbon exchange in oak, more than doubling simulated NEF (Table 9.5). In contrast, when the predicted climate of the 2080s is simulated using current atmospheric $[CO_2]$, a dramatic reduction in NEF is predicted, resulting from a combination of increased respiratory CO_2 losses and increasingly severe soil moisture deficits due to increased evapo-transpiration and lower summer rainfall (see Chapter 2).

The simulation representing the most likely scenario for the 2080s (700 ppm CO_2 and modified climate) results in a large increase in NEF compared to the current scenario, largely as a result of the combination of a longer growing season, and higher rates of net canopy assimilation during the early part of the summer, when water is not limiting (Figure 9.11).

Although these simulations are useful for exploring possible scenarios, they are theoretical, and represent a static system which is unable to respond to any environmental

Table 9.5 Simulated annual carbon exchange of pedunculate oak in southern England under four scenarios of climate and $[CO_2]$. Results are expressed as mean annual fluxes based on four year-long simulations (1995–1998 baseline) using the model ForestFlux.

Climate scenario	$[CO_2]$ (ppm)	Predicted NEF (tC ha⁻¹ yr⁻¹)	% Change in NEF
Current	360	3.37	–
Current	700	7.03	+108.8
2080s	360	1.09	-67.7
2080s	700	5.31	57.7

perturbation as would happen in the real world; they are included purely to demonstrate the relative impact of changes in climate and atmospheric composition in isolation, based upon the results from the impact studies described in this chapter. However, when linked to a suitable long-term growth model,

Figure 9.11 Simulated annual course of NEF of pedunculate oak in southern England, representing current conditions of climate and $[CO_2]$ (grey line) and the predicted scenario for the 2080s, with 700 ppm $[CO_2]$ and modified climate (green line). Note the extended growing season in the 2080s simulation.

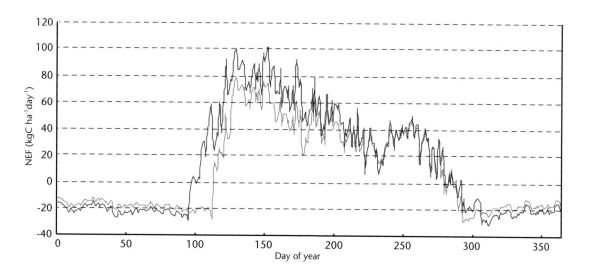

feedbacks at the level of both the tree and the ecosystem provide more realistic simulations, enabling generalised predictions to be made.

Long-term growth

The model outputs described in the preceding section have been extended and used as inputs to long-term growth models through the implementation of allocation and height and diameter growth routines. As discussed in Chapter 11, the modelling of long-term growth using this mechanistic approach is generally good at simulating relative change, but unless the model is constrained by sophisticated empirical yield models, the absolute estimates of forest growth may be less realistic. Furthermore, since forest mensuration data are not available for modified atmospheric composition, the growth constraints may not be representative of future conditions. The deviation of model output from current Yield Tables[j] is evident in Figure 9.12. Nevertheless, the impact of both predicted climate change (UKCIP98 scenarios[46]) and rising atmospheric [CO$_2$] (IS92a from[47]) on volume growth of oak and Sitka spruce are explored in Figure 9.12. In both cases, a significant improvement in site index is predicted; in the examples given, GYC rises from 6 to 8 for oak, and from 14 to 16 or 18 in the case of Sitka spruce. The predicted rise in productivity in the UK is primarily a result of rising [CO$_2$], and has already been observed (see Chapter 10), but lengthening of the growing season in response to climatic warming also plays a part (see Chapter 3 and Figure 6.4). It should be borne in mind that these simulations do not account for insect or pathogen damage, the impact of which may change as a result of climate change, as discussed in Chapters 7 and 8. In addition, tree mortality resulting from catastrophic events such as storms (Chapter 4), unseasonal frosts and extreme winter cold (Chapter 3) and extreme drought (Chapters 3 and 5) are also not included in the model.

Figure 9.12 Growth simulations of (a) Sitka spruce in southwest Scotland for rotations planted in 1968, 2010 and 2050, and (b) oak in southern England planted in 1930 and 2010[51]. Climate data are for Alice Holt, Hampshire and Clatteringshaws, Dumfries and Galloway (courtesy of British Atmospheric Data Centre) respectively, climate change predictions are for the UKCIP98 Medium-high scenario[46] (see Chapter 2), and [CO$_2$] is assumed to rise according to the IPCC IS92a scenario[47].

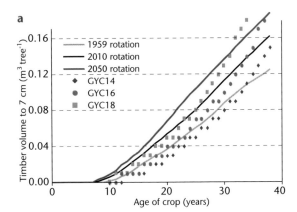

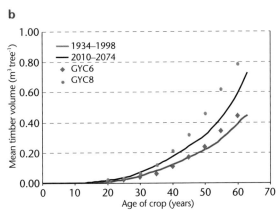

Although there are limitations to the applicability of these predictions, they do provide an indication of the likely direction and magnitude of the combined effects of climate change and rising atmospheric [CO$_2$]. Furthermore, they provide an opportunity to compare predictions with those made by knowledge-based models derived from spatial variability of current species distributions such as those presented in Chapters 11 and 12. These models do not account for rising $[CO_2]$ levels, and it is interesting to compare Figure 9.12 with predicted changes in species suitability for beech, for example, as shown in Figure 11.9. As suggested in Table 9.5, climate change impacts alone may well result in reduced productivity as predicted by ESC (Chapter 11). However, rising $[CO_2]$ has the potential to modify this response, resulting in a predicted increase in productivity, highlighting the key role that $[CO_2]$ levels could play in determining the response of forest ecosystems to climate change.

In contrast to the perceived beneficial effects of rising $[CO_2]$ in the UK, recent work at the Hadley Centre for Climate Change Research, in which a dynamic vegetation model has been actively linked to a Global Climate Model (HadCM3), predicts that rising $[CO_2]$ will not compensate for climatic warming and changes in rainfall patterns in all regions of the world. There is also a suggestion that the loss of some tropical forests may accelerate the rate of $[CO_2]$ increase, and thus global warming[52]. We must therefore be aware that the predicted increases in forest productivity resulting from climate change are not universal. Indeed, in the UK, if the magnitude of global warming has been underestimated, then this predicted increase in forest productivity may be short-lived.

Conclusions

It is clear that in general terms, enhanced atmospheric $[CO_2]$ is likely to be beneficial to tree and forest growth throughout the UK, through its fertilisation effect on photosynthesis. Higher $[CO_2]$ may also ameliorate ozone pollution to a small extent, and lead to lower rates of transpiration through the well-documented response of stomatal closure. In a world where only $[CO_2]$ rises, and there is no climatic change, budburst might be delayed,

wood quality could change, both for the better and for the worse, soil carbon might increase as a result of lower foliar nitrogen levels, while increased foliage production could lead to understorey community changes. Furthermore, the balance between host plants and insect pests could be altered by changing nutritional quality of sap, or the availability of additional carbohydrate to invest in defence mechanisms (see Chapter 8). However, it is the interactions between these responses that have been observed in experimental systems and a changing global climate that will determine exactly how UK forests will respond to global climate change over the coming decades.

Acknowledgements

The authors thank the Forest Research staff at Headley nursery and in the Environmental Research chemical analysis laboratory for their hard work in making the open-top chamber experiments a success. We are indebted to Paul Jarvis for his leadership of the ECOCRAFT project, to Belinda Medlyn for developing the database and carrying out the meta-analyses, and to all other colleagues within the ECOCRAFT consortium. The ECOCRAFT project was supported by the European Commission through contract ENV4-CT95-0077.Helpful comments on this chapter were provided by Andy Moffat and Richard Jinks. Finally, thanks must go to Meg Crookshanks, Samantha Broadmeadow, Rona Pitman, Sue Benham and Dave Durrant for their contributions to the work.

References

1. IPCC (2001). *Climate change 2001: the scientific basis*, eds J.T. Houghton, Y. Ding, D.J. Griggs, M. Noguer, P.J. van der Linden and D. Xiaosu. WGI Report to the IPCC Third Assessment. Cambridge University Press, Cambridge.

2. CEULEMANS, R. and MOUSSEAU, M. (1994). Tansley Review No. 71. Effects of elevated

atmospheric CO_2 on woody plants. *New Phytologist* **127**, 425–446.

3. DRAKE, B.G., GONZÀLEZ-MELER, M.A. and LONG, S.P. (1997). More efficient plants: a consequence of rising atmospheric CO_2? *Annual Review of Plant Physiology and Plant Molecular Biology* **48**, 609–639.

4. CURTIS, P.S. and WANG, X. (1998). A meta-analysis of elevated CO_2 effects on woody plant mass, form and physiology. *Oecologia* **113**, 299–313.

5. WORRELL, R. and MALCOLM, D.C. (1990). Productivity of Sitka spruce in northern Britain. 2. Prediction from site factors. *Forestry* **63**, 119–128.

6. BRIFFA, K.R. (1991). Detection of any widespread and unprecedented changes in the growth of European conifers. Final Report to the UK Forestry Commission. Climatic Research Unit, University of East Anglia, Norwich.

7. SPIECKER, H., MIELIKAINEN, K., KOHL, M. and SKOVSGAARD, J., eds (1996). *Growth trends in European forests*. Springer-Verlag, Berlin.

8. CANNELL, M.G.R., THORNLEY, J.H.M., MOBBS, D.C. and FRIEND, A.D. (1998). UK conifer forests may be growing faster in response to increased N deposition, atmospheric CO_2 and temperature. *Forestry* **71**, 277–296.

9. ECOCRAFT (1999). Predicted impacts of rising carbon dioxide and temperature on forests in Europe at stand scale. Final project report (ENV4-CT95-0077). IERM, University of Edinburgh, Edinburgh.

10. PONTAILLER, J.-Y., BARTON, C.V.M., DURRANT, D. AND FORSTREUTER, M. (1998). How do we study CO_2 impacts on trees and forests? In: *European forests and global change – the likely impacts of rising CO_2 and temperature*, ed. P.G. Jarvis. Cambridge University Press, Cambridge, 1–28.

11. WANG, Y.-P., REY, A. and JARVIS, P.G. (1998). Carbon balance of young birch trees grown in ambient and elevated atmospheric CO_2 concentrations. *Global Change Biology* **4**, 797–807.

12. BROADMEADOW, M.S.J., HEATH, J. and RANDLE, T.J. (1999). Environmental limitations to physiologically effective O_3 exposure. *Water, Air and Soil Pollution* **116**, 299–310.

13. AUBINET, M., GRELLE, A., IBROM, A., RANNIK, Ü., MONCRIEFF, J., FOKEN, T., KOWALSKI, A.S., MARTIN, P.H., BERBIGIER, P., BERNHOFER, C., CLEMENT, R., ELBERS, J., GRANIER, A., GRÜNWALD, T., MORGENSTERN, K., PILEGAARD, K., REBMANN, C., SNIJDERS, W., VALENTINI, R., and VESALA, T. (2000). Estimates of the annual net carbon and water exchange of forests: the EUROFLUX methodology. *Advances in Ecological Research* **30**, 113–175.

14. DEWAR, R.C. and CANNELL, M.G.R. (1992). Carbon sequestration in the trees, products and soils of forest plantations: an analysis using UK examples. *Tree Physiology* **11**, 49–71.

15. VON CAEMMERER, S. and FARQUHAR, G.D. (1981). Some relationships between the biochemistry of photosynthesis and the gas exchange of leaves. *Planta* **153**, 376–387.

16. BALL, J.T., WOODROW, I.E. and BERRY, J.A. (1987). A model predicting stomatal conductance to the control of photosynthesis under different environment conditions. In: *Progress in photosynthesis research,* Vol. IV, *Proceedings of the VII International Congress on Photosynthesis*, ed. I. Biggins. Martinus Nijhoff, Dordrecht, 221–224.

17. BROADMEADOW, M.S.J., PITMAN, R.M., JACKSON, S.B., RANDLE, T.J., and DURRANT, D.W.H. (2000). Upgrading the level II protocol for physiological modelling of cause–effect relationships: a pilot study. Final report for EC project No. 98.60.UK.003.0. Forest Research, Farnham.

18. MEDLYN, B.E., BADECK, F.W., DE PURY, D.G.G., BARTON, C.V.M., BROADMEADOW, M., CEULEMANS, R., DE ANGELIS, P., FORSTREUTER, M., JACH, M.E., KELLOMÄKI, S., LAITAT, E., MAREK, M., PHILIPPOT, S., REY, A., STRASSEMEYER, J., LAITINEN, K., LIOZON, R., POITER, B., ROBERNTZ, P., WANG, K. and JARVIS, P.G.

(1999). Effects of elevated [CO_2] on photosynthesis in European forest species: a meta-analysis of model parameters. *Plant, Cell and Environment* **22**, 1475–1495.

19. GONZÀLEZ-MELER, M.A., DRAKE, B.G. and AZCON-BIETO, J. (1996). Rising atmospheric carbon dioxide and plant respiration. In: *Global change: effects on coniferous forests and grasslands,* eds A.I. Breymeyer, D.O. Hall, J.M. Melillo and G.I. Ågren. Wiley, Chichester, 161–181.

20. GONZÀLEZ-MELER, M.A., RIBAS-CARBO, M., SIEDOW, J.N. and DRAKE, B.G. (1996). Direct inhibition of plant mitochondrial respiration by elevated CO_2. *Plant Physiology* **112**, 1349–1355.

21. RYAN, M.G. (1991). Effects of climate change on plant respiration. *Ecological Applications* **1**, 157–167.

22. FRIEND, A.D., STEVENS, A.K., KNOX, R.G. and CANNELL, M.G.R. (1997). A process-based, terrestrial biosphere model of ecosystem dynamics (Hybrid v3.0). *Ecological Modelling* **95**, 249–287.

23. CROOKSHANKS, M., BROADMEADOW, M.S.J. and TAYLOR, G. (1998). Elevated CO_2 and tree growth: contrasting responses in *Fraxinus excelsior, Quercus petraea* and *Pinus sylvestris. New Phytologist* **138**, 241–250.

24. MEDLYN, B.E., BARTON, C.V.M., BROADMEADOW, M., CEULEMANS, R., DE ANGELIS, P., FORSTREUTER, M., FREEMAN, M., JACKSON, S.B., KELLOMÄKI, S., LAITAT, E., REY, A., ROBERNTZ, P., SIGURDSSON, B., STRASSEMEYER, J., WANG, K., CURTIS, P.S., and JARVIS, P.G. (2001). Elevated [CO_2] effects on stomatal conductance in European forest species: a synthesis of experimental data. *New Phytologist* **149**, 247–264.

25. NORBY, R.J., WULLSCHLEGER, S.D., GUNDERSON, C.A., JOHNSON, D.W. and CEULEMANS, R. (1999). Tree responses to rising CO_2 in field experiments: implications for the future forest. *Plant, Cell and Environment* **22**, 683–714.

26. HEATH, J. (1998). Stomata of trees growing in CO_2-enriched air show reduced sensitivity to vapour pressure deficit and drought. *Plant, Cell and Environment* **21**, 1077–1088.

27. TOGNETTI, R., LONGOBUCCO, A., MIGLETTA, F. and RASCHI, A. (1998). Transpiration and stomatal behaviour of *Quercus ilex* plants during the summer in a Mediterranean carbon dioxide spring. *Plant, Cell and Environment* **21**, 613–622.

28. HEATH, J. and KERSTIENS, G. (1997). Effects of elevated CO_2 on leaf gas exchange in beech and oak at two levels of nutrient supply: consequences for sensitivity to drought in beech. *Plant, Cell and Environment* **20**, 57–67.

29. DURRANT, D.W.H., WADDELL, D.A., BENHAM, S.E. and HOUSTON, T.J. (1992). *Air quality and tree growth: results of the open-top chamber experiments 1991.* Research Information Note 221. Forestry Commission, Edinburgh.

30. SEMENOV, S. and KOUKHTA, B. (1996). Ozone influence on tree and crop growth: modelling the effects and estimating critical loads. In: *Critical levels for ozone in Europe: testing and finalizing the concepts,* eds L. Karenlampi and L. Skarby. UN-ECE Workshop Report. University of Kuopio, Finland, 96–107.

31. NEGTAP (2001). *Transboundary air pollution: acidification, eutrophication and ground-level ozone in the UK.* Report of the National Group on Transboundary Air Pollution. DEFRA, London.

32. BROADMEADOW, M.S.J. and JACKSON, S.B. (2000). Growth responses of *Quercus petraea, Fraxinus excelsior* and *Pinus sylvestris* to elevated carbon dioxide, ozone and water supply. *New Phytologist* **146**, 437–451.

33. WOODWARD, F.I. (1987). Stomatal numbers are sensitive to increases in CO_2 from pre-industrial levels. *Nature* **327**, 617–618.

34. WOODWARD, F.I. and KELLY, C.K. (1995). The influence of CO_2 concentration on stomatal density. *New Phytologist* **131**, 311–327.

35. BROADMEADOW, M.S.J., FREER-SMITH, P.H. and JACKSON, S.B. (1999). Climate

change – the evidence so far and predictions for tree growth. *Irish Forestry* **55**, 122–132.

36. INGESTAD, T. and LUND, A.-B. (1986). Theory and techniques for steady state mineral nutrition and growth of plants. *Scandinavian Journal of Forest Research* **1**, 439–453.

37. EAMUS, D. and JARVIS, P.G. (1989). The direct effects of increase in the global atmospheric CO_2 concentration on natural and commercial temperate trees and forests. *Advances in Ecological Research* **19**, 1–55.

38. JARVIS, P.G. (1995). Scaling processes and problems. *Plant, Cell and Environment* **18**, 1079–1089.

39. OREN, R., ELLSWORTH, D.S., JOHNSEN, K.H., PHILLIPS, N., EWERS, B.E., MAIER, C., SCHÄFER, K.V.R., McCARTHY, H., HENDREY, G., McNULTY, S.G. and KATUL, G.G. (2001). Soil fertility limits carbon sequestration by forest ecosystems in a CO_2-enriched atmosphere. *Nature* **411**, 469–472.

40. SCHLESINGER, W.H. and LICHTER, J. (2001). Limited carbon storage in soil and litter of experimental plots under increased atmospheric CO_2. *Nature* **411**, 466–469.

41. ELLSWORTH, D.S. (1999). CO_2 enrichment in a maturing pine forest: are CO_2 exchange and water status in the canopy affected? *Plant, Cell and Environment* **22**, 461–472.

42. FERRIS, R., SABATTI, M., MIGLIETTA, F., MILLS, R.F. and TAYLOR, G. (2001). Leaf area is stimulated in *Populus* by free air CO_2 enrichment (POPFACE), through increased cell expansion and production. *Plant, Cell and Environment* **24**, 305–315.

43. DONALDSON, L.A., HOLLINGER, D., MIDDLETON, T.M. and SOUTER, E.D. (1987). Effect of CO_2 enrichment on wood structure in *Pinus radiata* (D. Don). *IAWA Bulletins* **8**, 285–289.

44. SAVILL, P.S. and MATHER, R.A. (1990). A possible indicator of shake in oak: relationship between flushing dates and vessel sizes. *Forestry* **63**, 355–362.

45. HATTENSCHWILER, S., SCHWEINGRUBER, F.H. and KORNER, Ch. (1996). Tree ring responses to elevated CO_2 and increased N deposition in *Picea abies*. *Plant Cell and Environment* **19**, 1369–1378.

46. HULME, M. and JENKINS, G.J. (1998). *Climate change scenarios for the UK: scientific report*. UKCIP Technical Report No. 1. Climatic Research Unit, University of East Anglia, Norwich.

47. IPCC (1995). *Climate change 1994: radiative forcing of climate change and an evaluation of the IPCC IS92 emission scenarios*, eds J.T. Houghton, L.G. Meira Filho, J. Bruce, H. Lee, B.A. Callander, E. Haites, N. Harris and K. Maskell. Cambridge University Press, Cambridge.

48. JARVIS, P.G. (1976). The interpretation of the variations in leaf water potential and stomatal conductance found in canopies in the field. *Philosophical Transactions of the Royal Society of London, Series B* **273**, 593–610.

49. GOUDRIAAN, J. (1988). The bare bones of leaf angle distribution in radiation models for canopy photosynthesis and energy exchange. *Agricultural and Forest Meteorology* **43**, 155–169.

50. EDWARDS, P.N. and CHRISTIE, J.M. (1981). *Yield models for forest management*. Booklet 48. Forestry Commission, Edinburgh.

51. BROADMEADOW, M.S.J. (2000). *Climate change – implications for UK forestry*. Information Note 31. Forestry Commission, Edinburgh.

52. COX, P.M., BETTS, R.A., JONES, C.D., SPALL, S.A. and TOTTERDELL, I.J. (2000). Acceleration of global warming due to carbon-cycle feedbacks in a coupled climate model. *Nature* **408**, 184–187.

CHAPTER TEN: Melvin Cannell

10 Impacts of Climate Change on Forest Growth

KEY FINDINGS

- In much of continental Europe, the majority of forests are growing faster now than they did in the early 20th century, although in some areas, they may be showing symptoms of decline.

- It is likely that forests in much of Britain are also growing faster now than they did several decades ago.

- Much of the increase in forest growth rates can be attributed to advances in silvicultural practice, genetic improvement and, in central Europe, the cessation of site-degrading practices such as litter collection for fuel.

- It is also likely that increasing CO_2 concentrations, N deposition and temperatures have had a positive, non-zero effect on forest growth, both in Britain and across much of Europe. At present, it is not possible to quantify the relative contributions of these three environmental drivers.

- Given that CO_2 levels and temperatures are set to rise above current levels in the coming decades, it may be expected that forest growth rates in Britain will continue to rise, except perhaps in areas prone to summer droughts or nutritional limitations.

Introduction

Assessments of the impacts of climate change on forestry in the UK were made by Cannell and co-workers[1] and by the Climate Change Impacts Review Group, set up by the then Department of Environment, Transport and the Regions[2]. An important conclusion of these reviews was that forestry was one sector in the UK that was likely to benefit from climate change. In particular, climate change would enable a range of new species to thrive in the UK, and, in areas not suffering increased summer droughts, forests may grow faster. These positive effects will occur in response to increasing carbon dioxide concentration ($[CO_2]$) and the warming trend, which are the most robust of the global change predictions. By contrast, the potential negative effects of climate change on forestry are associated with extreme events, such as storms and unseasonal frosts, which are more uncertain.

In this chapter, an outline is given of the evidence that forests in Europe, including the UK, might already be growing faster than they did early in the 20th century, and that this is, in part, a response to a combination of increasing $[CO_2]$, nitrogen (N) deposition and temperature. If this is so, then further positive growth responses can be expected in response to the further increases in $[CO_2]$ and temperature predicted for this century.

Forests and global change

Trees may already be growing faster in response to climate change

There is observational and circumstantial evidence that many of our forests are more productive than hitherto. There are three sources of evidence: the existence of a terrestrial carbon 'sink', increasing forest growth trends in Europe, and the predictions of mathematical models which formalise what we know about forest growth processes.

The global terrestrial carbon sink – forests are a significant part of it

One of the strongest indications that forests are growing faster comes from analyses of the global carbon budget. Worldwide, the land seems to taking up and storing 0.5–2.5 GtC yr[-1] – otherwise it is impossible to balance the perturbed global carbon budget[3]. This means that vegetation, and particularly forests, are fixing more carbon and that carbon is accumulating in biomass and soils.

The land between 30 and 60 degrees north has been identified as a strong contributor to this sink, regardless of land use change, based on forest inventories[4], 'forward' modelling of global $[CO_2]$[5], variations in atmospheric $[CO_2]$ and $^{13}CO_2$[6,7] and O_2/N_2 ratios[8]. Forests must account for a large part of this sink because of their large biomass and high C:N ratios[3]. Although arguments have been put forward that the terrestrial sink is greatest in particular regions, the reality is that it changes over time and that, averaged over decades, the forests in all continents make a contribution, including Europe and presumably the UK[7,9].

Studies of forest productivity trends

The 'forest growth trends' study in Europe

During the 1980s, when concern about forest decline in Europe was initially raised, a significant number of forest studies were showing that forest growth rates had actually increased during the 20th century. During the early 1990s, the European Forest Institute initiated an EU-funded project to bring together the results of 22 studies in 12 countries, using data from research plots, forest inventories (permanent sample plots) and tree ring and stem analyses. The results were clear in some regions: site productivity had increased in southern areas of northern

Europe, in most regions of central Europe and in some parts of southern Europe. However, in the boreal zone of northern Europe, and drier areas of southern Europe, the results were more variable. In central Europe, the increases were commonly 20–30% and exceptionally 100–200%[10], while those areas where forest growth rates were declining due to nutrient supply, pollution or climate limitation, were in restricted localities. The main conclusion of the study was that the majority of forests were growing faster than expected, often requiring the revision of old growth and yield tables.

Forest productivity studies in the UK

Neither the UK nor Ireland were part of the EU study described above, but the expectation might be that any general European forest growth trend would apply here too. In fact, in Britain, studies on relationships between site factors and the General Yield Class (GYC) of conifer forests have invariably revealed negative correlations between stand age and GYC. If taken at face value, young forests seem to have higher GYCs than older forests on the same site types[11-13]. There appears to have been a mean increase in GYC of Sitka spruce (*Picea sitchensis*) of about 1.0 m^3 ha^{-1} yr^{-1} every decade, comparing forests planted in the 1930s and 1970s in northern Britain and an increase of 1.2–1.6 m^3 ha^{-1} yr^{-1} per decade in GYC of many conifers planted on better quality land in Scotland. This observation implies that growth rates have increased by 20–40%. Of course, some of this increase can be attributed to improved silvicultural practices and genetic improvement, but some may be due to climate change. A further possibility is that the observed correlation between GYC and stand age is due in part to survey design: correlations are much weaker if the analysis is restricted to data from long-term monitoring plots assessed over many decades[14].

An EU study was initiated in 2000 to identify the causes of increased forest growth rates in Europe – to which the UK is contributing. Nitrogen deposition, which increased two-to-four-fold during the 20th century[15,16] is one strong candidate, but other possible causes include increasing [CO_2], rising temperatures and recovery from previous practices that reduced soil fertility, such as litter collection for fuel and exploitative agriculture.

Model simulations of forest growth

The photosynthetic enzyme in leaves, RuBisCO (ribulose-bis-phosphate carboxylase oxygenase), is only one-third saturated at current atmospheric [CO_2]. Consequently, all process-based, mathematical models of forest growth which represent photosynthesis and the carbon, nitrogen and water cycles within forest ecosystems, predict that rising [CO_2], without climatic change, increases forest growth, net primary productivity and total carbon storage[9,16-19]. Kellomaki and co-workers[20] estimated that timber production in Scots pine (*Pinus sylvestris*) forests in southern Finland could increase by 20% within a rotation in which [CO_2] increased by 3.3 ppm yr^{-1}. Atmospheric [CO_2] increased by 28% during the 20th century and is currently rising by about 1.5 ppm yr^{-1}.

In a recent study, using two very different process-based forest growth models, it was suggested that increases in N deposition and [CO_2] have each promoted the growth rates of conifer forests in northern Britain by 7–14% since the 1930s[21]. In the models, the combined effects of N deposition and [CO_2] were approximately additive.

It is possible, of course, that all the models are wrong. They all have uncertainties associated with parameter values, model structure and process omission, so the accumulated errors associated with predictions of growth are potentially very large[22]. Indeed, forest and crop model intercomparisons have revealed large discrepancies indicating the high level of uncertainty[23]. However, the current consensus is that forest growth rates have increased over the course of the 20th century for the reasons given above, and that although the magnitude of the increase is uncertain, current models of forest growth are capable of correctly representing the processes involved in the observed increase.

What factors are accelerating forest growth rates?

If forests are, indeed, growing faster than hitherto, it is important to know the causes. If increased growth is solely or mainly due to silvicultural practices and genetic improvement, then it will continue only as long as improvements can be identified and implemented. If N deposition is a major driver, the acceleration in growth will vary across the UK and will stabilise, because N deposition levels are not expected to rise greatly. If increasing [CO$_2$] is an important driver, then growth rates may be increasing almost everywhere and may continue for the next 50–100 years.

Increasing CO$_2$ levels

There are basically two main sources of observational evidence that tree growth is accelerated by elevated [CO$_2$]. First, there are the CO$_2$-exposure experiments (see Chapter 9). Over 70 experiments world-wide have shown that young, pot-grown trees usually grow faster in elevated [CO$_2$] and these experiments are assessed in a number of review papers[24-26]. Doubling current [CO$_2$] commonly increases net photosynthesis by 40–60% and growth by 10–80%. There is, however, persistent doubt about whether mature trees respond in the same way as seedlings, although there is also some supportive evience that they do: bagged branches on mature trees photosynthise faster at elevated [CO$_2$][27]; semi-mature pines exposed to 550 ppm CO$_2$ in the open air have

photosynthesised faster for 2 years[28]; Holm oak (*Quercus ilex*) trees continuously exposed to about 650 ppm CO$_2$ for 30 years near natural CO$_2$ vents in Italy grow about 12% faster than trees growing in ambient [CO$_2$] nearby[29]. Secondly, there is evidence for increasing forest growth rates in areas of the world where there is little N deposition and where increasing [CO$_2$] seems a plausible explanation. Perhaps the most persuasive observation is that, across northern latitudes, tree rings show that forests started growing faster after 1850, when N deposition levels were low, before the 20th century warming, but when [CO$_2$] first started to increase[30].

Increasing nitrogen deposition from the atmosphere

The evidence that N deposition may be accelerating forest growth in the UK is equivocal. There has been no consistent or predictable response of Sitka spruce plantations in Britain to N fertilisation after canopy closure[31]. Most of the N required for growth after canopy closure, is met by recycling from senescing foliage and by mineralisation of litter, which recycles much of the N with a turnover time of 3–6 years[32-35]. Consequently, in the latter half of a forest rotation, relatively little of the N deposited from the atmosphere may be taken up by the trees, more is lost by leaching and the level of N deposition required to cause leaching is less than in the early years[36].

In this respect, plantations in Britain are different from many long-established forests in continental Europe, especially those which grow on poor soils or have deep humus layers. For instance, in much of Sweden, forests respond positively to N-fertilisation[37,38].

However, in Europe, it is commonly necessary to apply very large amounts of N to obtain a 30–50% increase in productivity. Thus, applications of 150 kgN ha^{-1} *per year* are needed to increase growth by 30–50% in much of Sweden[39]. Very large amounts of N (500–2000 kgN ha[-1] yr[-1]) must be applied to bring about substantial *long-term* increases in N mineralisation at most sites, because there has to be an appreciable fractional increase in soil N. For instance, a moderately poor soil which has 2000 kgN ha[-1] of soil N 'capital' and a mineralisation rate of 3%, mineralises 60 kgN ha[-1] yr[-1]. If 300 kgN ha[-1] is added – and only half of this remains in the soil after a period of years – then the soil N capital rises to 2150 kgN ha[-1] and annual mineralisation to 64.5 kgN ha[-1] yr[-1], a rise of only 7.5%. We should note that annual deposition of 15 kgN ha[-1] yr[-1] which is typical for the UK, amounts to a total of only 300 kgN ha[-1] over a 20-year period.

Expectations of large responses to increased N deposition may arise from the extraordinary growth responses obtained in 'optimum nutrition experiments' conducted in Sweden on Scots pine in the SWECON project[39] and Norway spruce (*Picea abies*) in the Skogaby experiment[40], in Australia on radiata pine (*Pinus radiata*)[41] and in Portugal on *Eucalyptus globulus*[42]. In all cases, either nitrogen or all nutrients were supplied according to demand, usually with and without irrigation. In many of the experiments, growth rates have been doubled, but only *with irrigation* and an optimum supply of *all* nutrients, including at least 100 kgN ha[-1]yr[-1] for several years. At Skogaby, an increase in above-ground productivity of 31% was obtained without irrigation, but required 300 kgN ha[-1] in six small applications over three years[43]. The growth response over six years to 600 kgN ha[-1] *with irrigation* was equivalent to about 300 kg stemwood ha[-1] per kg N applied[41]. Thus, deposition enhanced by 15 kgN ha[-1]yr[-1] over 20 years (300 kgN ha[-1], without irrigation: a typical value for the UK) is likely to have increased growth by considerably less than half that observed at Skogaby. However, it should be borne in mind that N deposition of 10–40 kgN ha[-1] yr[-1], typical for the UK[44], may have a larger impact at establishment and prior to canopy closure when N-demand is high, particularly on some of the impoverished soils that have been used for commercial forestry in the UK.

Increasing temperatures

At a regional scale, the growth of forests in northern Europe is positively related to temperature, or more precisely to temperature sum above a threshold[45]. Even at the scale of northern Britain, there are strong positive relationships between temperature and the General Yield Class of conifer plantations, equivalent to an increase of 2–4 m[3] ha[-1] yr[-1] per 1°C[11,46,47]. It is tempting to apply these relationships to predict effects of warming over time. However, spatially-derived correlations may not apply over time. First, other spatially-variable quantities are likely to be correlated with temperature, such as solar radiation, soil characteristics, 'exposure' and vapour pressure deficit. Vapour pressure deficits and evaporation rates increase with temperature, increasing periods of stomatal closure and the likelihood of plant water stress. Secondly, tree responses to rising temperatures over time may be constrained by adaptations to photoperiod and temperature–response functions adapted to cooler conditions. The application of the observed correlations between temperature and growth rate to predict likely impacts of climate change is therefore not a valid approach. Robust predictions of forest growth in the future can only be made using some of the more complex modelling approaches outlined in Chapter 11, particularly those that are capable of addressing the key drivers of forest productivity described in this chapter.

Conclusions

In much of continental Europe, the majority of forests are growing faster now than they did in the early 20th century, although in some localities, forests may be showing symptoms of decline as a result of other factors including air pollution. It is likely that forests in much of Britain are also growing faster now than they did some decades ago. Much of the increase in forest growth rates can be attributed to improvements in silvicultural practices, genetic improvement and, in central Europe, the cessation of site-degrading practices such as litter collection for fuel. In the UK, survey design and the age structure of the forest estate may also have contributed to the observed correlation between stand age and productivity. However, it is likely that increasing [CO_2], N deposition and temperatures have had a positive effect on forest growth, both in Britain and across much of Europe. At present, it is not possible to quantify the relative contributions of these three environmental drivers. Given that [CO_2] and temperatures are set to rise above current levels in the coming decades, it may be expected that forest growth rates in Britain will continue to rise, except perhaps in areas prone to summer droughts, nutritional limitations or prolonged soil waterlogging.

References

1. CANNELL, M.G.R., GRACE, J. and BOOTH, M.A. (1989). Possible impacts of climatic warming on trees and forests in the United Kingdom: a review. *Forestry* **62**, 337–364.

2. PARRY, M.L., ed. (1996). *Review of the potential effects of climate change in the United Kingdom*. The Stationery Office, London.

3. HOUGHTON, R.A., DAVIDSON, E.A. and WOODWELL, G.M. (1998). Missing sinks, feedbacks and understanding the role of terrestrial ecosystems in the global carbon balance. *Global Biogeochemical Cycles* **12**, 25–34.

4. HOUGHTON, R.A. (1996). Terrestrial sources and sinks of carbon inferred from terrestrial data. *Tellus Series B* **48**, 420–432.

5. DENNING, A.S., FUNG, I.Y. and RANDALL, D. (1995). Latitudinal gradient of atmospheric CO_2 due to seasonal exchange with land biota. *Nature* **376**, 240–243.

6. CIAIS, P., TANS, P.P., TROLIER, M., WHITE, J.W.C. and FRANCEY, R.J. (1995). A large northern hemisphere terrestrial CO_2 sink indicated by the $^{13}C/^{12}C$ ratio of atmospheric CO_2. *Science* **269**, 1098–1102.

7. BOUSQUET, P., PEYLIN, P., CIAIS, P., le QUERE, C., FRIEDLINGSTEIN, P. and TANS, P.P. (2000). Regional changes in carbon dioxide fluxes of land and oceans since 1980. *Science* **290**, 1342–1346.

8. KEELING, R.F., PIPER, S.C. and HEIMANN, M. (1996). Global and hemispheric CO_2 sinks deduced from changes in atmospheric O_2 concentration. *Nature* **381**, 218–221.

9. WHITE, A., CANNELL, M.G.R. and FRIEND, A.D. (2000). CO_2 stabilization, climate change and the terrestrial carbon sink. *Global Change Biology* **6**, 1–17.

10. SPIECKER, H., MIELIKAINEN, K., KOHL, M. and SKOVSGAARD, J., eds (1996). *Growth trends in European forests*. European Forest Institute Report No. 5. Springer-Verlag, Berlin.

11. WORRELL, R. and MALCOLM, D.C. (1990). Productivity of Sitka spruce in northern Britain. 2. Prediction from site factors. *Forestry* **63**, 119–128.

12. MACMILLAN, D.C. (1991). Predicting the General Yield Class of Sitka spruce on better quality land in Scotland. *Forestry* **64**, 359–372.

13. TYLER, A.L., MACMILLAN, D.C. and DUTCH, J. (1996). Models to predict the General Yield Class of Douglas fir, Japanese larch and Scots pine on better quality land in Scotland. *Forestry* **69**, 13–24.

14. MATTHEWS, R., METHLEY, J., ALEXANDER, M., JOKIEL, P. and SALISBURY, I. (1996). Site classification and yield prediction for lowland sites in England and Wales. Final report for FC and MAFF joint contract CSA 2119. Forestry Commission, Farnham.

15. PITCAIRN, C.E.R., FOWLER, D. and GRACE, J. (1995). Deposition of fixed atmospheric nitrogen and foliar nitrogen content of bryophytes and *Calluna vulgaris* (L.) Hull.

Environmental Pollution **88**, 193–205.

16. MYLONA, S. (1996). Sulphur dioxide emissions in Europe 1880–1991 and their effects on sulphur concentrations and deposition. *Tellus Series B* **48**, 662–689.

17. MELILLO, J.M., PRENTICE, I.C., FARQUHAR, G.D., SCHULZE, E-D. and SALA, O.E. (1996). Terrestrial biotic responses to environmental change and feedbacks to climate. In: *Climate change 1995. The science of climate change*, eds J.T. Houghton, L.G. Meira Filho, B.A. Callander, N. Harris and K. Maskell. Contribution of Working Group I, IPCC. Cambridge University Press, Cambridge, 448–481.

18. THORNLEY J.H.M. and CANNELL, M.G.R. (1996). Temperate forest responses to carbon dioxide, temperature and nitrogen: a model analysis. *Plant, Cell and Environment* **19**, 1331–1348.

19. McMURTRIE, R.E. and COMINS, H.N. (1996). The temporal response of forest ecosystems to doubled atmospheric CO_2 concentration. *Global Change Biology* **2**, 49–57.

20. McGUIRE, A.D., MELILLO, J.M., KICKLIGHTER, D.W., PAN, Y., XIAO, X., HELFRICH, J., MOORE III, B., VOROSMARTY, C.J. and SCHLOSS, A.L. (1997). Equilibrium responses of global net primary production and carbon storage to doubled atmospheric carbon dioxide: sensitivity to changes in vegetation nitrogen concentration. *Global Biogeochemical Cycles* **11**, 173–189.

21. KELLOMAKI, S., KARJALAINEN, T. and VAISANEN, H. (1997). More timber from boreal forests under changing climate? *Forest Ecology and Management* **94**, 195–208.

22. CANNELL, M.G.R., THORNLEY, J.H.M., MOBBS, D.C. and FRIEND, A.D. (1998). UK conifer forests may be growing faster in response to increased N deposition, atmospheric CO_2 and temperature. *Forestry* **71**, 277–296.

23. MONTEITH, J.L. (1996). The quest for balance in crop modelling. *Agronomy Journal* **88**, 695–697.

24. RYAN, M.G., McMURTRIE, R.E., HUNT, E.R., FRIEND, A.D., PULLIAM, W.M., AGREN, G.I., ABER, J.D. and RASTETTER, E.B. (1993). Comparing models of ecosystem function for temperate conifer forests. II Simulation of the effect of climate change. In: *Effect of climate change on forests and grasslands*, eds J.M. Melillo, G.I. Agren and A. Breymeyer. Wiley, Chichester.

25. WULLSCHLEGER, S.D., POST, W.M. and KING, A.W. (1995). On the potential for a CO_2 fertilization effect in forests: estimates of the biotic growth factor based on 58 controlled-exposure studies. In: *Biotic feedbacks in the global climatic system*, eds G.M. Woodwell and F.T. McKenzie. Oxford University Press, Oxford, 85–107.

26. CURTIS, P.S. and WANG, X. (1998). A meta-analysis of elevated CO_2 effects on woody plant mass, form and physiology. *Oecologia* **113**, 299–313.

27. JARVIS, P.G., ed. (1998). *European forests and global change: the likely impacts of rising CO_2 and temperature*. Cambridge University Press, Cambridge.

28. TESKEY, R.O. (1995). A field study of the effects of elevated CO_2 on carbon assimilation, stomatal conductance and leaf and branch growth of *Pinus taeda* trees. *Plant, Cell and Environment* **18**, 565–573.

29. ELLSWORTH, D.S. (1999). CO_2 enrichment in a maturing pine forest: are CO_2 exchange and water status in the canopy affected? *Plant, Cell and Environment* **22**, 461–472.

30. HATTENSCHWILER, S., MIGLIETTA, F., RACHI, A. and KORNER, C.H. (1997). Thirty years of *in situ* tree growth under elevated CO_2: a model for future forest responses? *Global Change Biology* **3**, 463–471.

31. BRIFFA, K.R., SCHWEINGRUBER, F.H., JONES, P.D., OSBORN, T.J., HARRIS, I.C., SHIYATOV, S.G., VAGANOV, E.A. and GRUDD, H. (1998). Trees tell of past climates: but are they speaking less clearly today? *Philosophical Transactions of the Royal Society of London* **B353**, 65–73.

32. McINTOSH, R. (1984). *Fertilizer experiments in*

established conifer stands. Forestry Commission Forest Record 127. HMSO, London.

33. MILLER, H.G. (1981). Forest fertilization: some guiding concepts. *Forestry* **54**, 157–167.

34. MILLER, H.G. (1986). Carbon x nutrient interactions – the limitations to productivity. *Tree Physiology* **2**, 373–385.

35. MILLER, H.G., COOPER, J.M. and MILLER, J.D. (1992). Response of pole-stage Sitka spruce to applications of fertilizer nitrogen, phosphorus and potassium in upland Britain. *Forestry* **65**, 15–33.

36. THORNLEY, J.H.M. and CANNELL, M.G.R. (1992). Nitrogen relations in a forest plantation-soil organic matter ecosystem model. *Annals of Botany* **70**, 137–151.

37. EMMETT, B.A., REYNOLDS, B., STEVENS, P.A., NORRIS, D.A., HUGHES, S., GORRES, J. and LUBRECHT, I. (1993). Nitrate leaching from afforested Welsh catchments – interactions between stand age and nitrogen deposition. *Ambio* **22**, 386–394.

38. TAMM, C-O. (1991). *Nitrogen in terrestrial ecosystems*. Springer-Verlag, Berlin.

39. BINKLEY, D. and HOGBERG, P. (1997). Does atmospheric deposition of nitrogen threaten Swedish forests? *Forest Ecology and Management* **92**, 119–152.

40. LINDER, S. (1987). Responses to water and nutrition in coniferous ecosystems. In: *Potential and limitations of ecosystem analysis*, eds E-D. Schulze and H. Zwolfer. Ecological Studies No. 61. Springer-Verlag, Berlin, 180–202.

41. NILSSON, L-O. (1997). Manipulation of conventional forest management practices to increase forest growth – results from the Skogaby project. *Forest Ecology and Management* **91**, 53–60.

42. LINDER, S., BENSON, M.L., MYERS, B.J. and RAISON, R.J. (1987). Canopy dynamics and growth of *Pinus radiata*. I. Effects of irrigation and fertilization during a drought. *Canadian Journal of Forest Research* **10**, 1157–1165.

43. PEREIRA, J.S., LINDER, S., ARAUJO, M.C., PEREIRA, H., ERICSSON, T., BORRALHO, N. and LEAL, L.C. (1989). Optimization of biomass production in *Eucalyptus globulus* plantations – a case study. In: *Biomass production by fast-growing trees*, eds J.S. Pereira and J.J. Landsberg, Kluwer, Dordrecht. 101–121.

44. NILSSON, L-O. and WIKLUND, K. (1992). Influence of nutrient and water stress on Norway spruce production in south Sweden – the role of air pollutants. *Plant and Soil* **147**, 251–265.

45. FOWLER, D., SUTTON, M.A., SMITH, R.I., PITCAIRN, C.E.R., COYLE, M., CAMPBELL, G. and STEDMAN, J. (1998). Regional mass budgets of oxidised and reduced nitrogen and their relative contribution to the N inputs of sensitive ecosystems. *Environmental Pollution* **102**, S1, 337–342.

46. BEUKER, E. (1994). Long-term effects of temperature on the wood production of *Pinus sylvestris* L. and *Picea abies* (L.) Karst. in old provenance experiments. *Scandinavian Journal for Forestry Research* **9**, 34–45.

47. ALLISON, S.M., PROE, M.F. and MATTHEWS, K.B. (1994). The prediction and distribution of general yield classes of Sitka spruce in Scotland by empirical analysis of site factors using a geographic information system. *Canadian Journal for Forest Research* **24**, 2166–2171.

48. PROE, M.F., ALLISON, S.M. and MATTHEWS, K.B. (1996). Assessment of the impact of climate change on the growth of Sitka spruce in Scotland. *Canadian Journal of Forest Research* **26**, 1914–1921.

Predictions and Responses

11. Modelling the future climatic suitability of plantation forest tree species   151

12. Impacts on the distribution of plant species found in native beech woodland   169

13. Challenges ahead: how should the forestry sector respond?   181

11

Modelling the Future Climatic Suitability of Plantation Forest Tree Species

KEY FINDINGS
- Existing empirical yield models are unable to account for the effects of climate change and rising carbon dioxide concentration ($[CO_2]$).
- Mechanistic, process-based models can account for the effects of both rising $[CO_2]$ and climate change; however, they are generally 'data hungry' and, although they are good at simulating relative changes to productivity, their ability to make absolute predictions of forest yield is limited.
- Knowledge-based modelling approaches such as Ecological Site Classification (ESC) are good in absolute terms because they are based on observed distributions of yield or presence, and require only climate and soil information in addition to the distribution data.
- The drawback of knowledge-based models is their inability to account for the predicted rise in $[CO_2]$; they therefore represent worst case scenarios, in that the beneficial effects of rising $[CO_2]$ to water use and yield are not taken into account.
- The application of the UKCIP98 scenarios in the ESC model results in a number of tentative predictions for UK plantation forest species as listed. These predictions show commercial suitability.
  - Sitka spruce will become more suitable across the cooler uplands of Scotland and northern England, and also the eastern side of Scotland; the Suitable area in parts of lowland England may become Unsuitable; the southwest peninsula and Wales should, at least, remain Suitable.
  - Corsican pine will become Very Suitable in eastern Scotland where it is currently Suitable, while growth rates will increase across southern England.
  - Douglas fir will remain, at least, Suitable across most of south and east England, and Very Suitable in the West Midlands and much of the southwest and east Wales; the climate is predicted to become more suitable for Douglas fir across the whole of Scotland, but particularly in the east.
  - Beech is likely to become Very Suitable across much of eastern Scotland, where it is currently marginally Suitable; in England, the areas where it is currently Suitable and Very Suitable are likely to contract northwards, and in areas of southern England, beech may no longer be Suitable as a timber crop.
- The character and composition of native woodland ecosystems is also likely to change, possibly with the formation of new communities and sub-communities.

Introduction

Models of one form or another have been used to predict forest yield in the UK since the 1920s[1,2], and are now essential for forest management, particularly in the area of production forecasting. Today's models incorporate data from sample plots going back to the inception of the Forestry Commission. They are consequently highly developed, giving accurate predictions of timber yield, but are static and unable to account for changes in climate or atmospheric composition at a given site. A different modelling approach is now required, not just for assessing the impacts of climate change, but for many other reasons which include the prediction of canopy and forest structure, landscape visualisation for planning and predictions of the ecological and hydrological impacts of forest management. As climate change progresses, a new set of environmental conditions will develop for which there are currently no data on which to base inferences of how forests will respond. As outlined in Chapter 1, the extensive interactions that should be expected for any ecosystem response to climate change, require that a number of complex models are developed and integrated with one another.

This chapter describes the progression of modelling development that has been undertaken in the UK, and which will need to continue, in order to improve the accuracy of our predictions of the likely impacts of climate change. The main body of the chapter presents an extensive case study of the application of one modelling approach, Ecological Site Classification (ESC), to this problem area, giving examples of the changing suitability of plantation tree species. It does not profess to provide answers but, in a developmental role, indicates how species suitability may change spatially in response to climate alone.

Modelling approaches

Stand-based empirical models

Empirical production forecast models are based upon mensurational variables (top height, basal area and diameter at breast height) recorded for single-species, even-aged stands under specific management options, including different spacing and thinning histories. They are therefore only available where specific sample plot data have been collected. Examples include the UK Forest yield tables[3], and the STANDPAK modelling system developed in New Zealand[4]. Yield models of this type are only valid for projecting forward under constant environmental conditions (climatic and nutritional). This type of model is therefore unsuitable for the projection of the impacts of climate change on forest yield, and cannot be applied to mixed species stands, or to management intervention which is not included in the sample plot network. Although traditional yield models of this type are unable to assess climate change impacts properly, they provide a foundation to the more complex modelling approaches described in the following sections. Models of this type have been further developed through the use of expansion factors for non-merchantable fractions (branch, bark, root) to provide an estimate of carbon stocks in biomass (see, for example Carbine[5] and C-FLOW[6]).

State–space-based empirical models

State–space models of stand growth are based on empirical data, but represent the canopy in the form of space occupied by individual crowns (e.g. M3)[7]. They can therefore be applied to uneven aged stands, mixed species stands, and novel silvicultural treatments, including extended rotation stands. These models are based on empirical data and require productivity or yield class as an input, rather than productivity being generated as an output. They are therefore unsuitable for climate change research, although as described in the preceding section, the allocation routines are necessary growth/architectural constraints for more complex models of forest growth.

Physiological process-based models

The two approaches described in preceeding sections rely on empirical mensuration data to provide the information on which the models are based. In contrast, process-based models only use empirical yield data to constrain outputs, and to provide allocation parameters. Most of these models rely on documented relationships between climate, nutrient supply, other site factors and physiological processes, including photosynthesis and evapo-transpiration to provide detailed information on the potential for tree growth (see Figure 11.1). The time-frame of input variables can vary between one year and 30 minutes, while the model itself can operate at the individual tree, stand or regional level. Because these models are based on physiological processes, they provide the opportunity to incorporate the results from impact studies, where changes in model parameters have been observed in response to enhanced $[CO_2]$ (see Chapter 9). Process-based models can also be linked to soil modules which include nutrient pools. The resultant ecosystem model can then be self-perpetuating and able to model the impacts of climate change in the long term. However, the fact that environmental conditions will differ from those currently experienced by UK forests means that the range of climate combinations of the future cannot, in many cases, be validated against existing data.

Sample plot data can only provide validation of these models under current atmospheric conditions, as the predicted rise in atmospheric $[CO_2]$ cannot be replicated. There is, however, the potential to validate at the level of sub-ambient $[CO_2]$ (270–370 ppm) through modelling the growth of rotations currently coming to maturity, therefore having developed under changing atmospheric composition (see Chapter 10).

Other modelling approaches

A number of other approaches have been used to model ecosystem function, including the analysis of light use efficiency[8], nutrient cycling (FORECAST[9]), water availability (GOTILWA[10]), and the dynamics of resource utilisation through the concept of plant functional type[11].

There are limitations to process-based models and, currently, they are not widely available for British forest conditions, because of the difficulties and uncertainties of parameterising for the environmental variables and tree species grown in Britain. More seriously, the data required for running process-based models are unavailable at the national scale. These limitations therefore strengthen the case for an alternative approach, such as the knowledge-based modelling methodologies described for ESC in this chapter, and for SPECIES in Chapter 12. In ESC and SPECIES, spatial distribution patterns are related to key climatic variables, thus providing the opportunity to model the impacts of predicted climate change. Both have two drawbacks. Firstly, they do not account for the predicted rise in atmospheric $[CO_2]$ or for the effect that this variable may have on tree physiology (see Chapter 9). Secondly, as for any predictive model, ESC and SPECIES are reliant on the availability of productivity or distribution data for the climatic conditions predicted for the UK in the future. Putting these two drawbacks aside, they are valuable in providing a spatial representation of how species suitability or distribution may change as a result of changing climate variables in isolation. Furthermore, in the case of ESC, this is likely to represent a worst case scenario since, in general terms, the effects of rising $[CO_2]$ alone will be beneficial (see Chapters 9 and 10).

Figure 11.1 *Basic structure of a typical process-based model of tree/forest growth.*

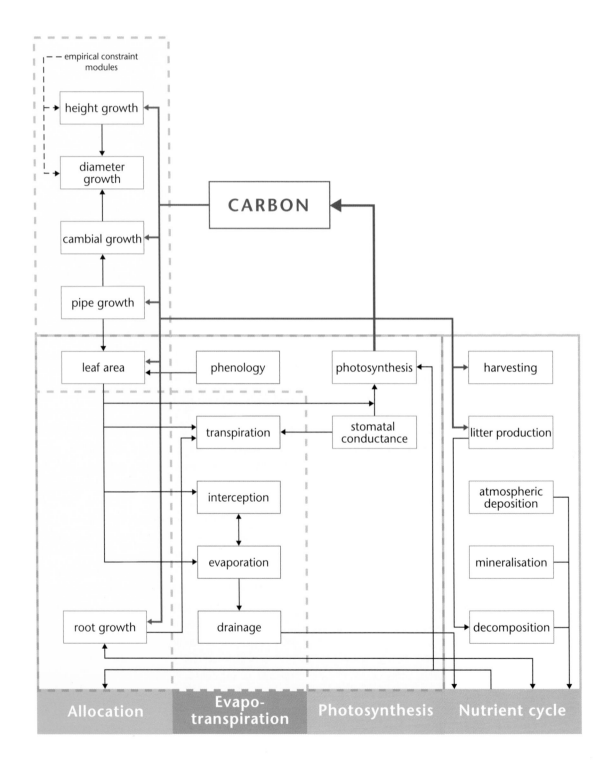

Overview of ESC

Ecological Site Classification (ESC)[12,13] assesses the suitability of tree species and National Vegetation Classification (NVC) woodland communities to climatic and edaphic site factors. The methodology was designed for use at the stand scale, but has been developed on a Geographical Information System (GIS) to provide a spatial forest planning tool at the forest landscape and regional scale[14]. ESC provides an objective methodology linked at differing scales by evaluation of common factors. Users of ESC should also be aware that it is designed as a decision support tool, providing a 'rule of thumb' approach to tree species suitability and yield estimates, and can be refined by local knowledge. The examples given here are of plantation species, and suitability is defined in terms of commercial productivity. Where a species becomes 'unsuitable', this does not mean that widespread mortality will occur, but that growth rates are likely to fall below those considered as commercially viable, and in extreme cases may reduce establishment success.

Description of ESC

Environmental factors assessed by ESC

In ESC, four climatic and two edaphic factors are assessed: accumulated temperature (AT: day-degrees above 5°C)[15,16]; moisture deficit (MD: mm); windiness (DAMS – Detailed Aspect Method of Scoring)[17]; continentality[18]; soil moisture regime (SMR) and soil nutrient regime (SNR). SMR defines the availability of water for tree growth in eight classes ranging from Very Dry to Very Wet. SNR specifies the availability of nitrogen and other nutrients in relation to pH[19]. The spatial distribution of the two soil quality factors are ignored for the purpose of this analysis, which concentrates on the spatial distribution of the climatic factors in the Medium-high climatic predictions from the UKCIP98 scenarios[20] (see Chapter 2).

ESC suitability models

Suitability models for each tree species and native woodland community have been developed as continuous functions and operate in a similar way to fuzzy membership functions[21,22]. The method assumes that the 'degree of truth' that a species is suitable varies between 0 and 1; 0 is completely unsuitable and 1 is completely suitable. An assumption is made that the most limiting factor determines the overall suitability for the species, and that a combination of suitable factors cannot compensate for any unsuitable factor. A group of forest scientists met to discuss the limits of suitability of the species in a Delphi analysis. The results were published as tables of tree species suitability for each of the six ESC factors in Forestry Commission Bulletin 124[23]. In the ESC decision support system[13] the tables have been smoothed into continuous functions in which the Suitable class is defined as having a score equal to or more than 0.5 and less than 0.75, and Very Suitable sites have a score equal to or more than 0.75. Figure 11.2 shows an example for Sitka spruce (*Picea sitchensis*). The ESC decision support system also indicates the likely general yield class (GYC) for a given species on a particular site. ESC assumes the primary factor controlling the rate of growth is climatic warmth. The top panel of Figure 11.2 shows the potential yield of Sitka spruce for a given value of accumulated temperature. The product of potential yield and the next most limiting factor provides the ESC predicted yield for the species on the site. Recent work has shown that the ESC-predicted yield for Sitka spruce is somewhat conservative, underestimating good sites by a small amount[13]. A worked example of the calculation of suitability is given in the caption to Figure 11.2.

Figure 11.2 Suitability criteria for Sitka spruce. The top panel represents the relationship between yield class and AT (accumulated temperature >5°C) for Sitka spruce in the UK. For the other five panels, the x-axis represents the individual climatic and edaphic factors (MD: moisture deficit; windiness; continentality; SMR: soil moisture regime; SNR: soil nutrient regime), and the y-axis, the suitability function of each of those factors (MDf; Df; Of; SMf; SNf).

Worked example: On a site where AT =1600 day-degrees >5°C; MD = 120 mm; windiness = 10; continentality = 4; SMR = Fresh and SNR = Medium, the potential yield of Sitka spruce from AT is about 24 m³ ha⁻¹ yr⁻¹, reduced by the limiting factor of MD to about 20 m³ ha⁻¹ yr⁻¹ (24 x 0.8 = 19.2). For this example, Sitka spruce would have a suitability score of 19.2/28 = 0.61, where 28 is taken to be the maximum yield of Sitka spruce in Britain[3], and would thus be classed as Suitable (i.e. 0.5>Suitable>0.75).

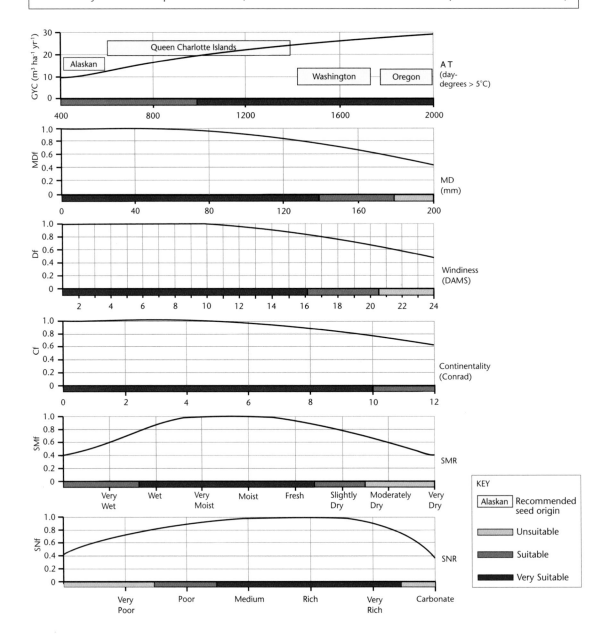

The impact of climate scenarios on ESC climatic factors

Accumulated temperature (AT) provides a climatic warmth index, and moisture deficit (MD) provides a climatic wetness or droughtiness index. Both factors have been interpolated for any grid reference in Britain using multiple linear regression models to predict AT and MD for the 30-year recording period 1961–1990, using the variables latitude, longitude and elevation. AT is calculated by accumulating the number of degrees over the threshold temperature (5°C – above which plant growth is stimulated) for each day of the year, and averaging for 1961–1990. Moisture deficit (MD) is defined as the annual maximum accumulated excess of actual evapo-transpiration for short grass (AET – supplied by MORECS[24]) over rainfall, averaged for 1961–1990. The MD for ESC thus differs from the potential water deficit defined by Birse and Dry[15] and the maximum potential soil moisture deficit of Hodgson[25]. ESC makes use of the arbitrary units of the DAMS windiness model[17], and this has been calculated on a geographical information system for Britain at different resolutions.

Accumulated temperature

The Medium-high climate scenario predictions of AT for 30-year periods centred on the 2020s, 2050s and 2080s[20] are calculated in the same way as the AT baseline map (Figure 11.3). It would, however, be naïve to consider the fine detail of AT (or any other ESC climate factor) in the predicted future climates.

There is evidence of earlier budburst for several tree species over the last five decades of the 20th century (see Chapter 6), and it is likely that the earlier growth described in the phenological record is related to an advance of the climatic warmth factor, AT. The sequence of maps from the baseline to 2080s shows AT increasing throughout the century across Britain. The increased AT reflects warmer summers but also longer growing seasons. The extent of montane climates below about 600 day-degrees is reduced to a few 10 km squares covering the central Grampian mountains. Eastern and central Scotland, northern England and central Wales are likely to experience an increase of 600 day-degrees over the next century, whereas in central and southern England and southwest Wales an AT of over 3000 day-degrees is predicted, which represents almost a 50% increase of the baseline value.

Moisture deficit

Since the climate change scenarios include predictions for potential evapo-transpiration (PET), the future MD scenarios for ESC have been estimated using an approximate relationship between PET and AET for short grass. In reality, AET and PET are very similar when soil moisture is plentiful. However, as the soil dries, the suction required to extract water from the soil increases, plants become less able to satisfy their water demand, and respond by closing stomata to reduce transpiration and thereby avoid desiccation. Using the baseline period data for each 10 km grid square, the difference between MD using PET and MD using AET was plotted against MD using PET, and a quadratic function fitted (r^2 = 0.77). MD using AET was then estimated by applying the difference to MD using PET in the future climate data-sets.

Figure 11.4 shows the predicted MD for the Medium-high climate scenario in the 2020s, 2050s and 2080s. In the north and east of Scotland a decrease in MD reflects the predicted slightly wetter summers, whereas in southern Scotland and northern England there is very little change in MD. In central and southern England, in west Wales and the western peninsula, however, where summers are predicted to be drier, MD increases substantially.

Figure 11.3 *Accumulated temperature (day-degrees above 5°C) for the baseline (1961–90; current) and predicted climates of the 21st century.*

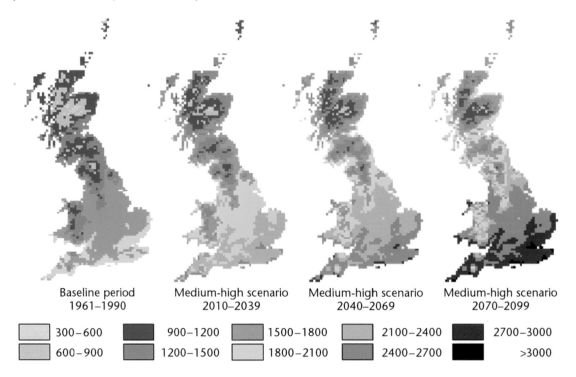

Baseline period 1961–1990	Medium-high scenario 2010–2039	Medium-high scenario 2040–2069	Medium-high scenario 2070–2099

300–600   900–1200   1500–1800   2100–2400   2700–3000
600–900   1200–1500   1800–2100   2400–2700   >3000

Figure 11.4 *Moisture deficit (mm) for the baseline (1961–90; current) and predicted climates of the 21st century.*

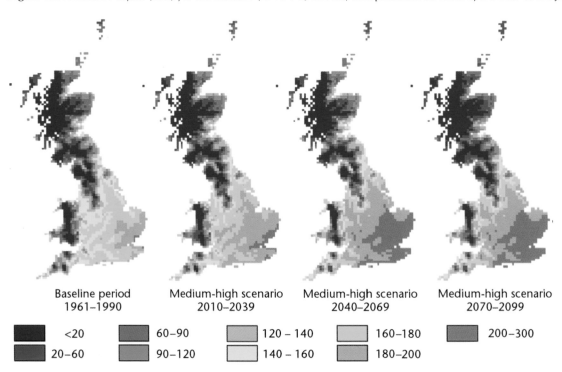

Baseline period 1961–1990	Medium-high scenario 2010–2039	Medium-high scenario 2040–2069	Medium-high scenario 2070–2099

<20   60–90   120–140   160–180   200–300
20–60   90–120   140–160   180–200

Wind exposure

Quine[26] has provided a method of converting mean wind speed to DAMS. However there is an additional problem of scale, because, in relative terms, the mean wind speed data for 10 km squares are low because of bias created by averaging the dominant sheltered sites and few exposed sites. In this analysis, the mean DAMS score for each 10 km square for the baseline period has been adjusted by the proportional change in mean wind speed for each future climate scenario. The result in Figure 11.5 shows little change in the mean wind speed and its effect on DAMS. However, this is not to say the damaging effect of winds will remain the same, since this analysis does not include, for example, changes in the frequency of damaging gusts. A more detailed discussion of the impacts of changing wind climate is given in Chapter 4.

Continentality

The fourth climate factor, used in ESC but not shown here, is continentality. This factor is related to the length of the growing season and the extremes of warmth in summer and cold in winter. The Conrad Index[18] adjusted to sea level is used in ESC. Continentality varies between 1 in the Outer Hebrides and 11 or 12 in Bedfordshire. It is interpolated using latitude, longitude and distance from the sea. It is not known if the index will remain valid in future climates. It is possible that the climate of southeast and central England will move slightly more towards Mediterranean than Continental, with milder winters and increased seasonal differences in precipitation, whereas the west of Britain will continue to be oceanic.

Figure 11.5 *Windiness (DAMS units) for the baseline (1961–90; current) and predicted climates of the 21st century.*

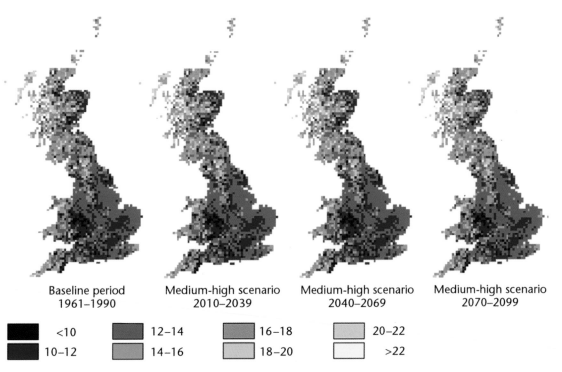

| | Baseline period 1961–1990 | Medium-high scenario 2010–2039 | Medium-high scenario 2040–2069 | Medium-high scenario 2070–2099 |

| <10 | 12–14 | 16–18 | 20–22 |
| 10–12 | 14–16 | 18–20 | >22 |

Species-specific climatic suitability: the role of climate change

The four climate factors were inserted into the continuous functions for a range of species (see Figure 11.2). The climatic suitability classes: Unsuitable, Suitable or Very Suitable were assessed for the species in each 10 km square. For the purpose of this analysis we assume that the soil quality is Very Suitable for growing the particular species, and that climatic factors impose the only restrictions on the species distribution. According to our definitions, where the climate is Unsuitable for a species, one or more of the climate factors reduces the yield class to less than half the maximum yield for the species in Britain; for example, in the case of Sitka spruce, this would be a yield class of 12 m^3 ha^{-1} yr^{-1} or less. Where the climate is Suitable, the yield class is between a half and three-quarters of the maximum yield (yield class of 14–20 m^3 ha^{-1} yr^{-1} for Sitka spruce). Very Suitable climates enable the species to achieve a yield class in the upper quartile of its yield range, which equates to a yield class of over 22 m^3 ha^{-1} yr^{-1} for Sitka spruce. More detailed information on the natural range, climatic and site requirements of tree species is given by Lines[27] and Evans[28]. It should be noted that this type of analysis must be treated with caution. Aside from the uncertainties in the climate predictions and the lack of soil information, the ESC MD factor has been predicted on the basis of assumptions linking the relative rates of potential and actual evaporation. The resolution of the data also tends to mask the finer detail of the climate distribution, and, inevitably, some sites shown within unfavourable areas will provide a more suitable site than predicted – for example, trees that have rooted into chalk with access to deeper groundwater reserves. Suitability is also assessed without any examination of susceptibility to diseases or insect pests (see Chapters 7 and 8) and assumes that recommended ground preparation[29] and planting practices[30] are employed.

Sitka spruce

Sitka spruce (*Picea sitchensis*) is a native of the moist oceanic climate of the Pacific Northwest, extending from Alaska to northern California in a narrow coastal strip. In the climate of the late 20th century it was best suited to the western regions of Britain (Figure 11.6). Two main provenances, from the Queen Charlotte Islands (QCI) and Washington are planted according to climatic warmth (see Figure 11.2), respectively in the northwest and southwest of Britain. It is regarded as Unsuitable within the drier northeast, East Midlands and the southeastern counties of England, where the moisture deficit exceeds about 180 mm. The extension of a warm dry climate westwards across central and southern England is likely to make the currently Suitable areas of the West Midlands and southwest England Unsuitable by the 2020s. In the southwest peninsula and west Wales, the AT increase is substantial whereas the MD increase is marginal, and here Sitka spruce should remain at least Suitable. In the cooler uplands of Scotland and northern England, land currently Suitable for Sitka spruce will become Very Suitable by the 2080s, as a result of the increase in AT and a decrease in MD. The temptation may be to plant the Washington provenance in areas where the Queen Charlotte Islands provenance is currently recommended, but the incidence of spring and autumn frost damage is likely to continue to be a major constraint (see Chapter 3) and predictions are currently uncertain.

Corsican pine

Corsican pine (*Pinus nigra* var. *maritima*) provenances from the islands of Corsica and Sicily and from southern Italy have been planted in Britain. In Corsica, it is a montane species found between 800 m and 1600 m,

Figure 11.6 Climatic suitability for Sitka spruce.

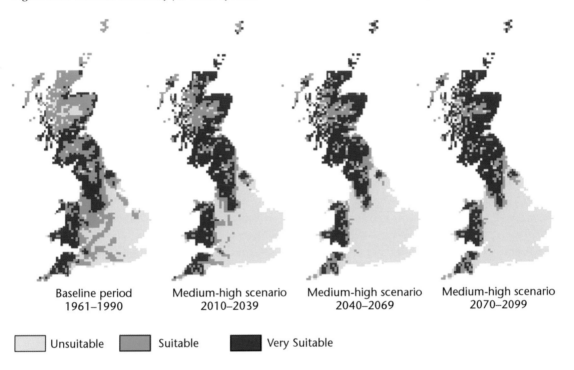

| Baseline period 1961–1990 | Medium-high scenario 2010–2039 | Medium-high scenario 2040–2069 | Medium-high scenario 2070–2099 |

Unsuitable   Suitable   Very Suitable

Figure 11.7 Climatic suitability for Corsican pine.

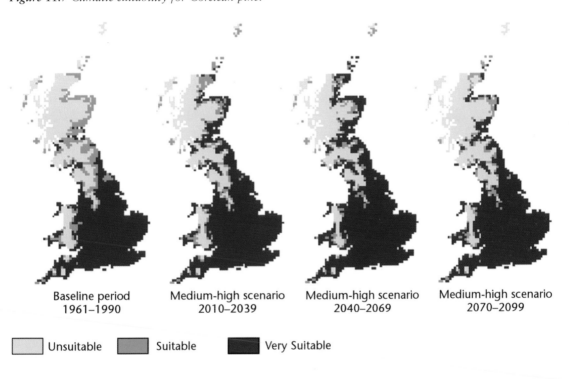

| Baseline period 1961–1990 | Medium-high scenario 2010–2039 | Medium-high scenario 2040–2069 | Medium-high scenario 2070–2099 |

Unsuitable   Suitable   Very Suitable

where winter precipitation is high and the summer drought short. The distribution of Corsican pine in Britain is currently restricted to the warmer southern and eastern lowlands, with an AT of more than 1200 day-degrees (Figure 11.7). The predicted warmer climate of the 21st century will increase the Very Suitable area up the eastern side of northern England and Scotland, and the warmer climate of southern and central England will increase its rate of growth, as the species is Very Suitable up to about 3000 day-degrees. Corsican pine is restricted to areas with a relatively dry climate, where MD is greater than about 90 mm. Therefore the Very Suitable area will be at a maximum between the 2030s and the 2070s. By the 2080s the wetter climate of northeast Scotland will reduce the Very Suitable area, although parts of Caithness may become Very Suitable.

Douglas fir

Douglas fir (*Pseudotsuga menziesii*) occurs along almost the entire length of the western mountain ranges of North America from southern British Columbia to New Mexico. The seed sources of Douglas fir grown commercially in Britain, from Oregon and Washington, are adapted to higher summer temperatures and more severe moisture deficits than currently occur in Britain. The species will therefore tolerate the predicted warmer and drier climate, remaining Suitable in most of southern and eastern England and Very Suitable in the West Midlands and large parts of the west country and eastern Wales (Figure 11.8). The climate is predicted to become more suitable for Douglas fir throughout Scotland, particularly in the east.

Beech

The natural range of beech (*Fagus sylvatica*) extends across southern England, through France and Germany to central Poland and northwards again to southern Sweden. The species is found at higher elevation as far south as the Pyrenees and the mountains bordering the Mediterranean, and as far east as mainland Greece. In England it is particularly associated with chalk and limestone geologies, but also occurs on sands and loams that provide deep rooting and adequate moisture reserves. The species grows well up to an AT of approximately 3000 day-degrees, but is less tolerant of high MD, as evidenced by drought stress in dry summers (a MD of 240 mm is probably the upper limit for Suitable). The warmer and drier climate predicted in southeast England is likely to become Unsuitable for beech due to high MD (Figure 11.9). Northeast Scotland will be a part of Britain where beech becomes Very Suitable rather than marginally Suitable as is the case today. In northern England and the West Midlands beech will become Suitable where it is currently Very Suitable.

Native woodland communities

The character of ancient semi-natural woodland in the UK has evolved over a number of centuries under a relatively stable climate, and is thus representative of that climate. Furthermore, species classed as 'native' are defined as having established themselves in Britain after the most recent glacial period (~11 000 years ago), assuming that we can disentangle human influence from their biogeography[31]. Because of the complex interactions that help to define natural woodland ecosystems, their character is likely to alter when the environment within which they are growing changes, and 'native' species that are currently suited to our climate may no longer be so. The permanency of our current native semi-natural woodland should therefore be debated in the light of probable climate change, while the definition of 'native' species also warrants a re-examination[31,32].

Figure 11.8 Climatic suitability for Douglas fir.

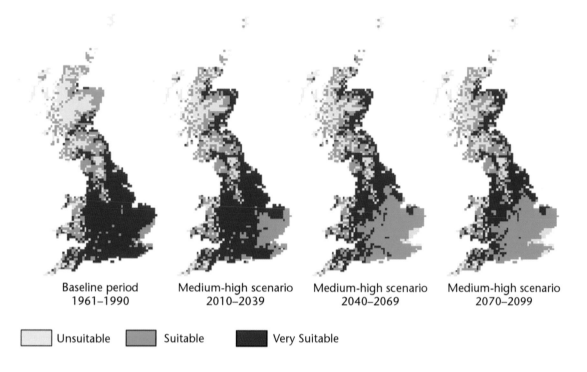

| Baseline period 1961–1990 | Medium-high scenario 2010–2039 | Medium-high scenario 2040–2069 | Medium-high scenario 2070–2099 |

☐ Unsuitable   ▨ Suitable   ■ Very Suitable

Figure 11.9 Climatic suitability for beech.

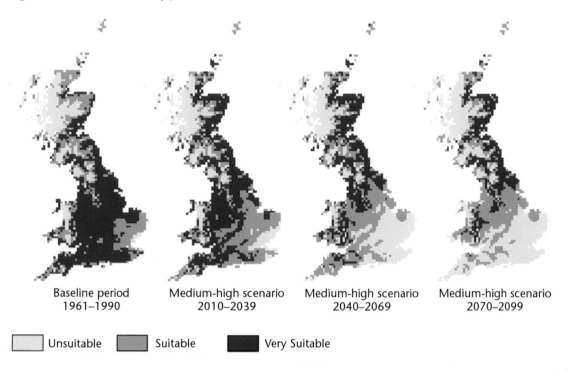

| Baseline period 1961–1990 | Medium-high scenario 2010–2039 | Medium-high scenario 2040–2069 | Medium-high scenario 2070–2099 |

☐ Unsuitable   ▨ Suitable   ■ Very Suitable

As a demonstration of the potential climate-driven changes to the character of semi-natural woodland, six native woodland communities from the National Vegetation Classification (NVC)[33] are discussed in very general terms below, although the distribution maps in future climate scenarios are not shown. This is because there is uncertainty about the suitability of the range of vascular plants and bryophytes considered as community constants, i.e. the plants whose presence helps to define the community. For example, bluebell (*Hyacinthoides non-scripta*) has a preference for soils with a modified Ellenberg value of five[34] which is equivalent to Fresh SMR in ESC. In the drier climate of the 2080s, the SMR of many woodlands of beech and oak in the southern England will become Slightly Dry or Moderately Dry and therefore less suitable for bluebell. Conversely, in parts of northern England, southern and eastern Scotland, the warmer and moister climate might improve for bluebell on some soil types. It is very likely that the nature of many sub-communities will change, and that both new NVC community and sub-community definitions will be required.

The ESC knowledge-based rules used to describe the site suitability of any native woodland community are quite different, and separate, to the rules describing the suitability of the constituent native tree species grown as a crop. The rules for tree species suitability focus on achieving a yield and timber quality consistent with the site suitability description (e.g. Suitable, Very Suitable), whereas yield and timber quality are not a high priority in the assessment of a native woodland type containing that species. For example, on a cold site (i.e. low AT) where, in commercial terms, a tree species (e.g. sessile oak) is assessed as Unsuitable because it will not produce an adequate timber yield, a native woodland analysis might show the site is Suitable for an oak native woodland community. The oak component will grow slowly, and, in the native

woodland assessment, yield and timber quality are less important than survival and regeneration. Consequently, the impacts of climate change are more difficult to predict for native woodland communities than for a species grown as a commercial crop, because conditions for seed production and natural regeneration may be altered, and thus the relative proportions of tree species within the woodland may change with time. If this happens, then by default the woodland has changed to either a new or different type of community.

The W8 community of mixed broadleaved woodland with ash, field maple (*Acer campestre*) and dog's mercury (*Mercuralis perennis*) occurs on Rich and more often Very Rich sites in mild and warm (AT> 1000 day-degrees) climates. It occurs throughout a range of MD (above about 30 mm) but is absent from the wettest regions of Britain. The community is Suitable in the dry warm climates of southern England and is influenced by a more continental flora[33]. It is likely that W8 will remain Suitable in the southern half of England in the 21st century, and will gradually become more suited to northeast England, and eastern Scotland where it currently overlaps with the distribution of the W9 community. W9 mixed broadleaved woodland with dog's mercury is suited to fertile soils in cooler and wetter parts of Britain. Consequently, as the climate becomes warmer, the Suitable area may extend across sheltered upland parts of northern England and Scotland.

Oak and birch are the dominant tree species of the W10 and W11 communities. *Quercus robur* and *Betula pendula* are common, but not exclusive in W10, whereas *Quercus petraea* and *Betula pubescens* are more frequently present in W11. W10 oak–birch with bracken (*Pteridium aquilinum*) and bramble (*Rubus fruticosus*) occurs on Medium to Rich sites in lowland Britain. This gives way to the W11 oak–birch and wood sorrel (*Oxalis acetosella*) community in the cooler and wetter climate of western England, Wales and the uplands of northern England and Scotland. This community has a characteristically sparse continental flora[33], and so higher temperatures in the 21st century will make W11 woodlands more suited to a wider range of plants, changing the character of the W11 woodland community as a result. With an increase in temperature, the W11 community range may encroach into W17 upland oak and birch woodland with blaeberry/bilberry (*Vaccinium myrtillus*). In both W10 and W11 woodlands, the increased warmth will favour the regeneration and growth of oak at the expense of birch.

The warming climate is likely to increase the extent of sites suited to W17 oak/birch woodland found on podzols and podzolic brown earths. Upland sites that are currently Unsuitable by nature of the lack of warmth will benefit. In Scotland, W17 will become increasingly suited to sites in the sub-alpine zone, and climatic warming will allow the tree-line to climb well into the sub-alpine zone. There may be an increase in the area suitable for W18 native Scots pine woodland on Very Poor sites as the tree-line rises, but there could be changes to the field and ground layer composition of W18 sub-communities at lower elevation sites as the climate warms.

Conclusions

ESC uses a knowledge-based model to predict broad classes of suitability for tree species and native woodlands, at the national, regional, landscape or stand scale. The knowledge-base assimilates the experience of a team of forest scientists, and presents this information in a simple and transparent methodology. The approach links tree species distribution, yield and timber quality with climatic (and edaphic) factors. It is a decision support tool that allows the user to question the relationships between environmental factors and tree growth, and conduct sensitivity analyses on the results. At the national scale it has been used with current

and future climate data to suggest tree species suitability. We believe ESC provides a valid, objective and consistent modelling approach and, in the absence of process-based models (or the data to run them), ESC is a useful tool to forecast woodland suitability in the predicted climate of the 21st century. It should be restated at this stage that the predictions of future species suitability given here probably represent a worst case scenario, since the beneficial effects of rising $[CO_2]$ are not accounted for in ESC.

According to the ESC model, the Medium-high scenario prediction for climate change will exert a significant environmental pressure on plantation woodlands in the 21st century. By 2080 the accumulated temperature >5°C in the south and east of England will increase by about 50%. At the same time, a shift to increased seasonality of precipitation in the south and east of England may cause the moisture deficit to increase by as much as 15%. In Scotland, a 30% increase in accumulated temperature is likely, with a reduction in moisture deficit, a result of increased summer precipitation. The change in windiness is less certain, but is predicted to be small (see Chapter 4).

In general terms, it appears that the climate of the south and Midlands of England will become less suitable for many forest species currently planted today, whereas in northern England and eastern Scotland, the climate will become more suitable. The exception will be Corsican pine, for which the climate is likely to become more suitable almost everywhere with higher yields being achieved. The area of southern England currently Unsuitable or marginal for Sitka spruce will extend westwards and northwards. However, in the mountains the species will be able to extend to higher elevations. Beech may be susceptible to drought damage (see Chapter 3) and may well become Unsuitable as a timber crop across parts of southern England, particularly where soil water capacities are low.

Socio-economic factors will play a large part in determining the extent to which increased or decreased productivity will result in changed distributions of plantation species. Current requirements for increased use of native species, of species mixtures and of continuous cover forestry will also influence long-term forest planning. Where native woodland is likely to change character, management could be employed to limit the changes. The conservation of ancient semi-natural woodland is important. However, because of the complex interactions between the many species associated with native woodland ecosystems, it is likely that changes will occur, including movement between NVC woodland classes, and also the possible formation of new communities and sub-communities as a result of climate change.

References

1. MACDONALD, J. (1928). *Growth and yield of conifers in Britain*. Bulletin 10. Forestry Commission, London.

2. HUMMEL, F. and CHRISTIE, J.M. (1953). *Revised yield tables for conifers in Great Britain*. Forest Record 24. Forestry Commission, Edinburgh.

3. EDWARDS, P.N. and CHRISTIE, J.M. (1981). *Yield models for forest management*. Forestry Commission, Edinburgh.

4. WHITESIDE, I.D. (1990). STANDPAK stand modelling system for radiata pine. In: *New approaches to spacing and thinning in plantation forestry*, eds R.N. James and G.L. Tarlton. NZFRI Bulletin No. 151, New Zealand Forest Research Institute, Rotorua, New Zealand.

5. THOMSON, D.A. and MATTHEWS, R.W. (1989). *The storage of carbon in trees and timber*. Research Information Note 160. Forestry Commission, Edinburgh.

6. DEWAR, R.C. (1991). Analytical model of carbon storage in trees, soils and wood products of managed forests. *Tree Physiology* 8, 239–258.

7. MATTHEWS, R.W. and METHLEY, J.M. (1998). Development of interactive yield models for UK conditions. In: *Forest Research Annual Report and Accounts*. The Stationery Office, Edinburgh, 57–61.

8. MEDLYN, B.E. (1998). Physiological basis of the light use efficiency model. *Tree Physiology* 18, 167–176.

9. KIMMINS, J.P., MAILLY, D. and SEELY, B. (2000). Modelling forest ecosystem net primary production: the hybrid simulation approach used in FORECAST. *Ecological Modelling* 122, 195–224.

10. SABATÉ, S., GRACIA, C.A. and SÁNCHEZ, A. (2002). Likely effects of climate change on growth of *Quercus ilex, Pinus halepensis, Pinus pinaster, Pinus sylvestris* and *Fagus sylvatica* forests in the Mediterranean region. *Forest Ecology and Management* (in press).

11. COLASANTI, R.L., HUNT, R. and ASKEW, A.P. (2001). A self-assembling model of resource dynamics and plant growth incorporating plant functional types. *Functional Ecology* 15, 676–687.

12. PYATT, D.G. (2001). Linking the NVC woodlands to the Ecological Site Classification. JNCC Report.

13. RAY, D. (2001). *Ecological Site Classification Decision Support System* V1.7. Forestry Commission, Edinburgh.

14. CLARE, J. and RAY, D. (2001). A spatial model of ecological site classification for forest management in Britain. In: *Proceedings of the 4th AGILE conference on geographic information science in Brno, April 19–21*, ed. M. Konecny.

15. BIRSE, E.L. and DRY F.T. (1970). *Assessment of climatic conditions in Scotland 1: based on accumulated temperature and water deficit*. Macaulay Land Use Research Institute, Aberdeen.

16. BENDELOW, V.C. and HARTNUP, R. (1980). *Climatic classification of England and Wales*. Soil Survey Technical Monograph No. 15. Rothamsted Experimental Station, Harpenden.

17. QUINE, C.P. and WHITE, I.M.S. (1993). *Revised windiness scores for the windthrow hazard classification: the revised scoring method*. Research Information Note 230. Forestry Commission, Edinburgh.

18. CONRAD, V. (1946). Usual formulas of continentality and their limits of validity. *Transactions of the American Geophysical Union* **27**, 663–664.

19. WILSON, S.M., PYATT, D.G., MALCOLM, D.C. and CONNOLLY, T. (2001). The use of ground vegetation and humus type as indicators of soil nutrient regime for an ecological site classification of British forests. *Forest Ecology and Management* **140**, 101–116.

20. HULME, M. and JENKINS, G.J. (1998). *Climate change scenarios for the UK: scientific report*. UKCIP Technical Report No. 1. Climatic Research Unit, University of East Anglia, Norwich.

21. ZADEH, L.A. (1992). Knowledge representation in fuzzy logic. In: *An introduction to fuzzy logic applications in intelligent systems*, eds R.R. Yager and L.A. Zadeh. Kluwer Academic, Boston, 1–25.

22. BEZDEC, J.C. (1993). Fuzzy models : what are they and why? *IEEE Transactions on Fuzzy Systems* **1**, 1–6.

23. PYATT, D.G., RAY, D. and FLETCHER, J. (2001). *An Ecological Site Classification for forestry in Great Britain*. Bulletin 124. Forestry Commission, Edinburgh.

24. THOMPSON, N., BARRIE, J.A. and AYLES, M. (1982*). The Meteorological Office rainfall and evaporation calculation system: MORECS (July 1981)*. Meteorological Office, Bracknell.

25. HODGSON, J.M. (1974). *Soil survey field handbook*. Soil Survey Technical Monograph No. 4. Rothamsted Experimental Station, Harpenden.

26. QUINE, C. (2000). Estimation of mean wind climate and probability of strong winds for wind risk assessment. *Forestry* **73**, 247–258.

27. LINES, R. (1987). *Choice of seed origins for the main forest species in Britain*. Forestry Commission Bulletin 66. HMSO, London.

28. EVANS, J. (1984). *Silviculture of broadleaved woodland*. Forestry Commission Bulletin 62. HMSO, London.

29. PATERSON, D.B. and MASON, W.L. (1999). *Cultivation of soils for forestry*. Bulletin 119. Forestry Commission, Edinburgh.

30. MORGAN, J.L. (1999). *Forest tree seedlings: best practice in supply, treatment and planting*. Bulletin 121. Forestry Commission, Edinburgh.

31. BROWN, N. (1997). Re-defining native woodland. *Forestry* **70**, 191–198.

32. MOFFAT, A.J. (1999). Trees, people and profits – into the next millennium: environmental changes. *Quarterly Journal of Forestry* **93**, 211–220.

33. RODWELL, J.S. (1991). *British plant communities, I: woodlands and scrub*. Cambridge University Press, Cambridge.

34. HILL, M.O., MOUNTFORD, J.O., ROY, D.B. and BUNCE, R.G.H. (1999). *Ellenberg's indicator values for British plants*. ITE, Huntingdon.

CHAPTER TWELVE Pam Berry, Terry Dawson, Paula Harrison
and Richard Pearson

12 Impacts on the Distribution of Plant Species Found in Native Beech Woodland

KEY FINDINGS

- The SPECIES model (Spatial Estimator of the Climate Impacts on the Envelope of Species) is based on a neural network, using processed climate data to simulate the natural distribution of species; the network is 'trained' using European species distribution data, with the result that under future scenarios, it is not required to make predictions outside its range of 'experience'.

- SPECIES has been used to predict the impacts of climate change on the distribution of beech, and the two ground vegetation species, wood anemone and sanicle, which are components of important sub-communities in native beech woodland.

- The observed distribution of beech woodland is wider than predicted using the SPECIES model as a result of planting outside its natural range, which may be limited in Britain due to its relatively recent introduction; the model was trained on the European distribution, which essentially reflects its spread during the Holocene.

- The SPECIES model predicts that climate change is likely to result in climate space for beech disappearing in south and east England by the 2050s, but suitable conditions developing in northern England and east and west Scotland.

- The UK is latitudinally central within wood anemone's range, only being absent from the northern islands of Scotland in its modelled distribution; there is no loss of climate space in any of the scenarios, and the model predicts that the species has the potential to expand into the Hebrides and Shetland Isles by the 2050s.

- The lack of predicted direct effects of climate change on climate space does not mean that there will be no changes to natural vegetation communities; indirect effects acting through changing competition are likely to have impacts on the overstorey and understorey alike.

- Natural woodlands in the UK face a dynamic future, both as a function of natural events leading to changes in the character and composition of woodlands, and because of the influence of man through management, conservation and land use policies.

Introduction

The 21st century is predicted to see a number of changes in the physical environment, driven both directly and indirectly by changes in climate[1]. It is important that the predicted changes are understood and their consequences identified, so that appropriate responses can be devised. No part of the environment will be exempt from such change and past biogeographical research has shown that changes, both in ecosystem and species' distributions and in habitat composition can be expected, resulting from the physiological response of species to changing climatic parameters[2,3].

In southern Britain, beech is a significant forest species comprising some 10% (64 000 ha) of broadleaf woodland in England[4], and is important both as a commercial timber species and in forming a number of native vegetation communities. Lowland beech and yew woodlands are a priority habitat in UK

Biodiversity Action Plans and a number of such woods have been identified as Special Areas of Conservation under the Habitats Directive. In the Habitat Action Plan, climate change is recognised as a factor potentially leading to community change, not only relating to the overstorey species, but also to the many other species which comprise each community. This chapter explores the impact of climate change on three beech woodland species, beech (*Fagus sylvatica*), wood anemone (*Anemone nemorosa*) and sanicle (*Sanicula europaea*) in order that the potential future of this habitat can be explored. The work was largely carried out as part of the MONARCH (Modelling Natural Resources Responses to Climate Change) project, funded by English Nature and a number of other conservation organisations[5].

Beech woodland in the UK

In the UK, beech woodland (Figure 12.1) occurs naturally in southern and eastern

Figure 12.1 Lowland beech woodland with bluebell understorey.

England and in southern Wales, but it grows successfully well outside of this area. Beech woodlands are broadly split into three types representing the range of soils on which they are found and their species composition[6]: *Fagus sylvatica–Mercurialis perennis* woodland (NVC W12)[a] is a calcicolous woodland and represents 40% of the habitat; *Fagus sylvatica–Rubus fruticosus* woodland (NVC W14) is found on brown earths of low base status, often with slightly impeded drainage and forms about 45% of the habitat, while *Fagus sylvatica–Deschampsia flexuosa* woodland (NVC W15) is found on infertile soils where the pH is usually less than 4. The distribution of each woodland type is largely dependent on edaphic factors, although climate may play a part in the absence of natural stands of W15 *Fagus sylvatica–Deschampsia flexuosa* woodland from the drier parts of East Anglia and the cooler and wetter north and west[7].

Modelling changes in beech woodland species' distributions

Although climate is only one factor that affects the distribution of beech woodland, it is thought that as a result of climate change, it may be affected by dieback due to soil moisture stress and by the invasion of more drought tolerant species[8]. In addition to beech, the impact of climate change on two ground flora species is also assessed here, providing an indication of how different species within a single vegetation community may respond, and thus how the composition of these communities may change in the long term. These two species, wood anemone (Figure 12.2) and sanicle, are present throughout the range of beech in the UK, and form important sub-communities.

Overview of the SPECIES model

In order to predict the response of species to climate change a model, SPECIES (Spatial Estimator of the Climate Impacts on the Envelope of Species), was used. This was developed in the RegIS project (Regional Climate Change Impact and Response Studies in East Anglia and North West England) jointly funded by MAFF, DETR and UKWIR (UK Water Industry Research)[9]. SPECIES is based on a neural network, which uses a number of integrated algorithms to pre-process input data on climate (temperature, precipitation and radiation) and soil (available water-holding capacity) to derive bioclimatic variables, such as mean soil water availability for the summer period (May–September), accumulated annual soil water deficit, absolute minimum temperature estimated over a 20-year period, annual maximum temperature and growing day-degrees above 5°C (Figure 12.3). Several of

Figure 12.2 Wood anemone in flower.

---

[a]The National Vegetation Classification (NVC)[6] recognises 19 types of natural and semi-natural climax woodland community, based on geographic/climatic zone and soil type.

Figure 12.3 Schematic representation of the SPECIES model.

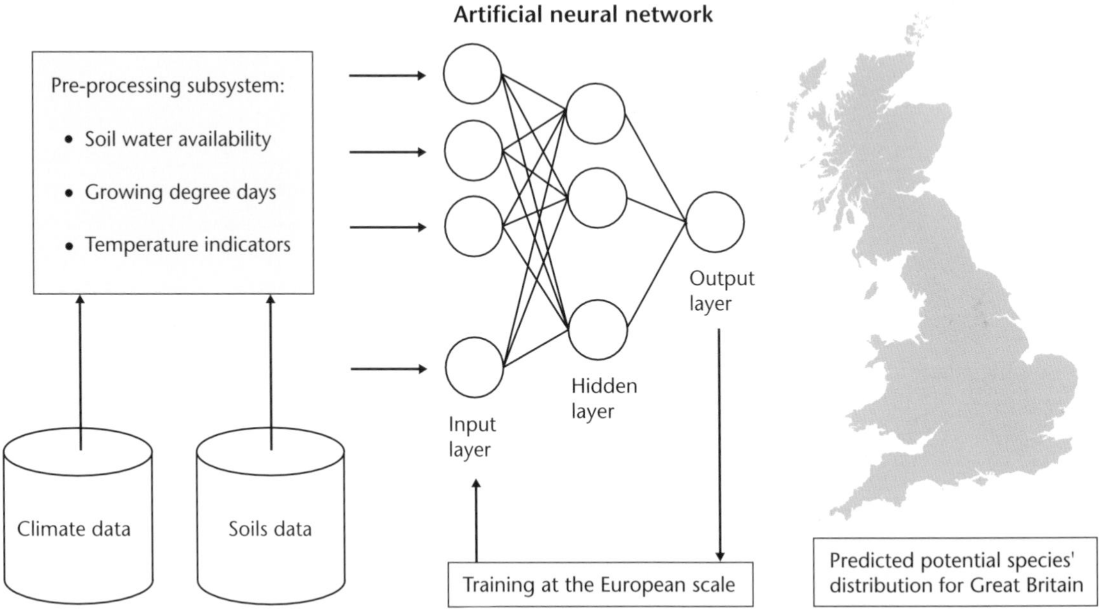

these algorithms are similar to those used in the ESC model described in Chapter 11. The SPECIES model integrates the bioclimatic data to predict the distribution of species through the characterisation of their bioclimatic envelopes. The model is trained using existing empirical data on climate and the European distributions of species with the result that, under future scenarios, it is not required to make predictions beyond its range of experience. It produces a simulated probability distribution map which can be compared with the actual distribution using the kappa coefficient of agreement. The trained model can then be used to estimate the potential redistribution of those species in the British Isles under scenarios of future climate change. Four scenarios from the UK Climate Impacts Programme (UKCIP)[10] were adopted in this study (see Chapter 2): the Low and High scenarios for the 2020s and 2050s, to represent a range of possible responses over short and medium-term time scales.

Modelled distribution of beech

The observed distribution of beech woodland in the British Isles is more widespread than its modelled distribution under current climatic conditions (Figure 12.4). The former includes commercial plantations, while the latter is a result of the model being trained on the natural distribution of beech, essentially representing the historical limit of its spread during the Holocene period which is thought to be a direct response to climate change[11,12]. Due to its late arrival in Britain (8000 years ago) it had difficulty in invading and spreading through closed forest[12], while propagation is limited to mast years, restricting its spread further. Beech therefore has a more limited natural distribution than might otherwise have been the case.

The model trains well under the baseline climate at the European level with observed and simulated distributions showing 81%

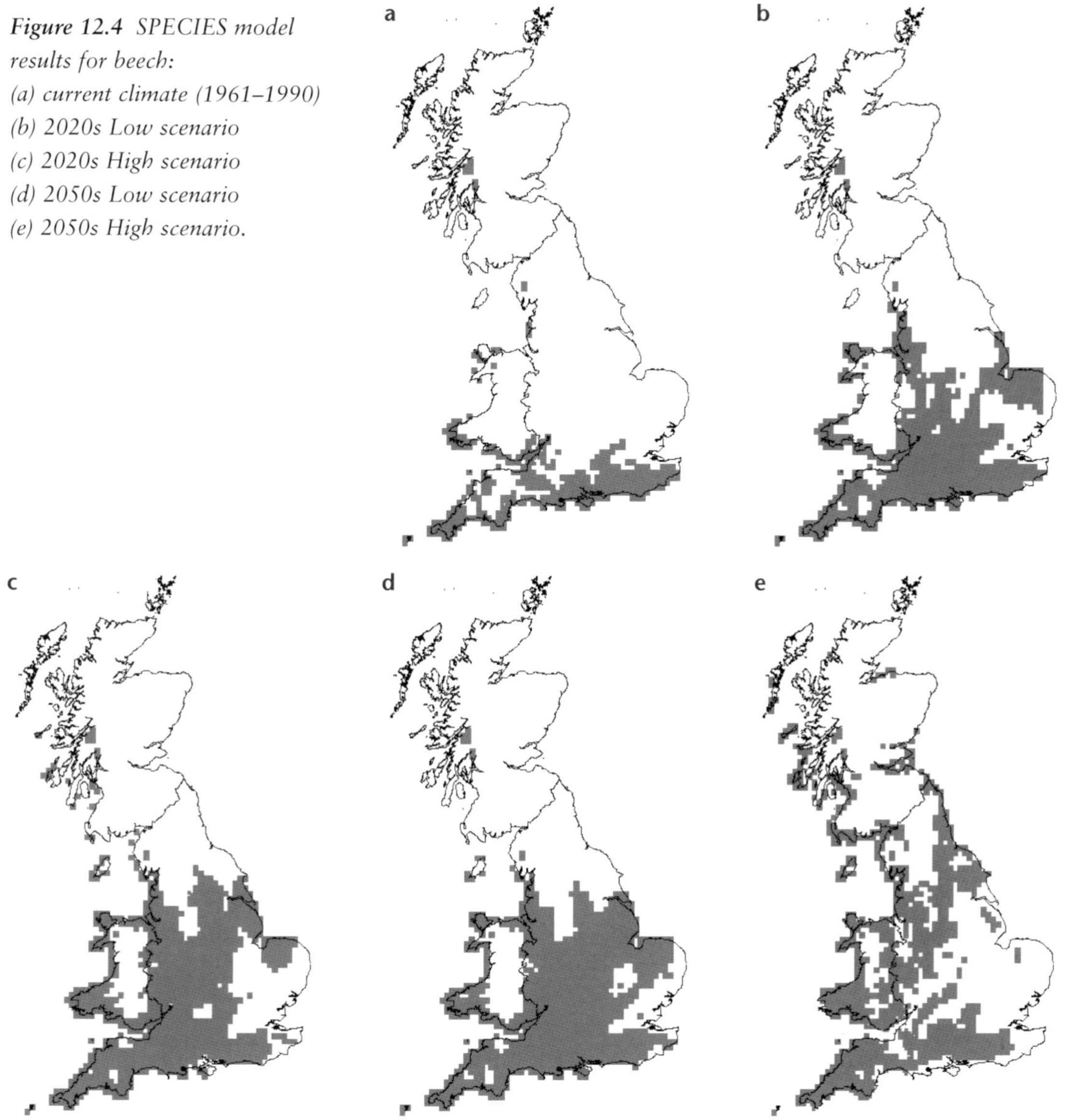

Figure 12.4 SPECIES model
results for beech:
(a) current climate (1961–1990)
(b) 2020s Low scenario
(c) 2020s High scenario
(d) 2050s Low scenario
(e) 2050s High scenario.

agreement[b]. The simulated (natural) distribution for beech shows it in southern and southwestern England, but also in lowland areas of Wales, west Lancashire and the Lake District (Figure 12.4). These last three areas are beyond beech's ob-served natural distribution, but well within its planted limits. It is simulated not to occur in Ireland.

Under the 2020s Low scenario, suitable climate space for beech expands northwards, such that it reaches the southern part of the Lake District on the west coast of Britain and the Humber on the east coast, with two outliers in Scotland near Inveraray and Fort William.

[b]The performance of each network is statistically analysed using the Pearson correlation coefficient and the kappa coefficient of agreement. The kappa statistic is used to test the similarity of spatially mapped data and thus is a measure of the agreement between the actual and simulated distributions.

These two areas in Scotland have higher maximum temperatures than other parts at similar latitude, and their west coast position means that the absolute minimum temperature is also high for the latitude. Similar conditions for maximum temperatures are found around Inverness, but minimum temperatures are lower. Beech also has the potential to spread into those parts of East Anglia where its moisture requirements can be met. Suitable climate space is not found on the higher parts of Exmoor, Dartmoor and Wales or in the Pennines, due to low minimum temperatures. Under the 2020s High scenario, suitable climate space could be found at higher altitudes and further north on the east coast, as winter temperatures become more favourable, with more outliers on the west coast of Scotland. However, parts of East Anglia, the east Midlands and the London area become unsuitable in response to increased moisture deficits.

The 2050s Low scenario is quite similar to the 2020s High, but with suitable climate space in Scotland being reduced back to the two outliers seen under the 2020s Low scenario. The conditions in southern Britain are almost entirely suitable except for a band stretching from Yarmouth to southwest of London. The 2050s High scenario shows suitable climate space in the southern part of the Outer Hebrides and the area around Ullapool and Inverness. In southern Britain, however, parts of Kent, East Anglia and the Midlands are no longer suitable due to decreased soil water availability.

This modelling indicates that the natural distribution of beech could generally be favoured in terms of potential range expansion by the increases in temperature (both absolute minimum and maximum) and rainfall. This corresponds with other research on response surfaces, which suggests that beech has an optimum temperature of around −1°C (January) and 18°C (July), with a particularly steep gradient for January temperatures[2]. It

could, however, lose some of its existing habitat in the southeast of England. This is particularly the case under the High scenarios. Other work supports this response suggesting that drought limits the growth of this species under current climate conditions[13]. In the case of a beech woodland in Wales, repeated droughts over 15 years (1976–1991) caused the decline and death of much of the beech canopy[14,15] and for the majority of beech in the woodland, growth rates slowed down and recruitment was poor for a number of years[16]. Recent work has also highlighted the interannual variability in the impact of both ozone pollution and drought on crown condition in beech[17].

Although the simulations described above indicate that climate change is likely to benefit the distribution of beech over the UK as a whole, its current natural distribution is likely to contract, largely as a result of increased summer water deficits[8]. Furthermore, uncertainty over stomatal responses to soil and atmospheric moisture deficits as a result of rising CO_2 levels[18] (see Chapter 9), together with effects of reduced winter chilling on budburst and seed set, may compound the predicted effects of drought in southern England.

The results from the SPECIES model are quite similar to those for the ESC model (Chapter 11) with a potential loss in the southeast of England. It should be pointed out that the former is dealing with the potential natural distribution of the species, while the latter is concerned with its growth as a commercial forestry crop. This means that the northern range limit is very much further north for the distribution predicted by ESC as humans have artificially extended its range margins. It also means that, given beech is grown north of its natural range, it has the potential, either through natural or artificial means, to continue to form woodland under the climate change scenarios.

Modelled distribution of wood anemone

Wood anemone is found throughout Great Britain, apart from the northern extremities of Scotland, the Hebrides, Orkney and Shetland Islands. Most typically it is found in woodlands where it can form sub-communities in *Fraxinus excelsior–Acer campestre–Mercuralis perennis* (W8), *Quercus robur–Pteridium aquilinum–Rubus fruticosus* (W10) and *Quercus petraea–Betula pubescens–Oxalis acetosella* (W11) woods[6]. Wood anemone in W8 woodland is found in southeastern sub-communities where there is pronounced waterlogging of the soil and in many of the other communities it is associated with damper soils[6]. It is also found in W12 *Fagus sylvatica–Mercurialis perennis* woodland, where it can be locally prominent, and in W14 *Fagus sylvatica–Rubus fruticosus*. It can also be frequent in calcareous grasslands and found locally in acidic grasslands, hedges, heathland, various montane sites and roadside verges. In the northern and western parts of its range it is not confined to woodland and the controlling factors on its distribution are thought to be soil moisture and humidity[19].

The agreement between observed and modelled distributions across Europe is again good (81%), and when the model is applied to Britain it shows a simulated distribution, which is very similar to its actual distribution. However, its absence from the Fenland area is not apparent (Figure 12.5), indicating how human influence, particularly land use, can lead to discrepancies between observed and modelled distributions.

Given that Britain is latitudinally central within wood anemone's range and that it has a wide ecological tolerance, climate is not predicted to limit its distribution under the future (climate change) scenarios. It does, however, have the potential to expand into parts of the Hebrides and Orkneys under the 2020s Low scenario and throughout the Hebrides under the 2020s High scenario. The

situation under the 2050s Low scenario is similar to the equivalent for the 2020s, but under the 2050s High scenario, suitable climate space has reached the southern part of the Shetland Islands. This potential stability in distribution under future climate scenarios does not mean to say that it will not experience changes in abundance – competition from other ground flora species, together with potential changes to the microclimate (light, moisture and nutrient availability) of the woodland floor and associated changes in overlying cover could all contribute to changing community composition.

Modelled distribution of sanicle

Sanicle is a stress-tolerant perennial found throughout the British Isles in woods on moist, richer soils, especially beech woods on lime-rich soils. It is found in W8, *Fraxinus excelsior–Sorbus aucuparia–Mercuralis perennis* (W9), W10 and W12 woodland, forming a sub-community in the latter. Here sanicle may be the vernal dominant, instead of dog's mercury (*Mercuralis perennis*) and there may also be a variety of geophytes, particularly orchids[6]. It has a 90% similarity in habitat requirement with wood anemone[20], but is much less common.

The network trained well at the European scale (85% agreement), and the British Isles simulated distribution corresponds closely with the actual distribution. This species is frequent throughout most of England, Wales and western Scotland, and is common across Ireland. Under all of the climate change scenarios it occurs across the whole of the UK and Ireland with no loss of suitable climate space. Its response, therefore, is very similar to that for wood anemone.

Modelled distribution of other species

The response of a number of other species associated with beech woodland was also modelled as part of the RegIS, MONARCH

Figure 12.5 SPECIES *model*
results for wood anemone:
(a) current climate (1961–1990)
(b) 2020s Low scenario
(c) 2020s High scenario
(d) 2050s Low scenario
(e) 2050s High scenario.

and CHIRP projects[9,21,22]. In all cases, the five species showed comparatively little response to the climate change scenarios, as outlined in Table 12.1. However, birch (*Betula pendula*) did show a similar, but less severe response to beech, losing climate space in south and east England, while expanding its range in Scotland. The lack of a response in the other species suggests that there are some components of beech woodland that have the potential to remain stable in the face of climate change, although it should be borne in mind that if the dominant species (beech) is threatened, the character of the woodland may change.

Table 12.1 Summary of the response of other beech woodland species to climate change. Model simulations were carried out as part of the RegIS, MONARCH and CHIRP projects[9,21,22].

Species	NVC association	Response to climate change
Birch (*Betula pendula*)	W12, W14, W15	Starts to lose climate space in S and E of England under 2020s High and 2050s scenarios.
Pedunculate oak (*Quercus robur*)	W12, W14, W15	No change.
Yew (*Taxus baccata*)	W12, W14, W15	Slight expansion.
Cleavers (*Galium aparine*)	W12	No change.
Hard fern (*Blechnum spicant*)	W15	Little change.

Implications of climate change for native beech woodland

The SPECIES model shows how the climate space available to beech and two ground flora species which are important components of sub-communities found in beech woodland might change under future climate scenarios. However, there are a number of factors, such as land cover changes, habitat availability and management practices that the model does not take into account. Also, in the need to develop a generic model, species-specific variables are not included. In beech, for example, summer drought is more damaging when combined with high temperatures. The response of beech to temperature and drought may be related to competition[23], and is certainly related to the initiation of masting. In addition the model gives no indication of the species' migration abilities and the possibility of these predicted future distributions being realised.

The SPECIES model has shown three examples of possible species' responses. In the case of wood anemone and sanicle there is little apparent change in their likely distribution, while for beech, the area where it may grow naturally is likely to increase. Beech is already planted well to the north of its natural distribution, and these trees could act as centres of propagation thus enabling it to realise these potential future distributions. However, this natural expansion of its range may be a slow process given the high variability in beech mast production[24]. In contrast, the two high scenarios suggest that beech would experience some contraction of available climate space in parts of the southeast and East Anglia where it is already susceptible to summer drought under current conditions. Modelling work of others[25] suggests that *Fagus sylvatica* could be lost from a greater area of southern England and especially the southwest, due to failure for chilling requirements to be met, but that *Quercus robur* should be able to survive. In those areas that are commonly subject to large moisture deficits forest managers need to be planning to plant more drought tolerant species and to be flexible about the possible invasion of other species. This is even more important for those involved in the conservation of beech woodlands. The future of the canopy composition for W12 *Fagus sylvatica–Mercuralis perennis* woodland has been explored by Paterson[26].

Although wood anemone apparently would

not suffer a reduction in its climate space, it could be affected indirectly. It is already thought to be absent from many beech woods because of spring drought[19]. This was not a direct input into the SPECIES model, but other work has suggested that although winter water availability may increase in the future, so will summer deficits and the overall effect in southeast England may be a decrease in water availability[27]. In Central Europe, however, it is quite abundant on soils which dry out in summer[19]. The distribution of wood anemone overlaps considerably with *Hyacinthoides non-scripta* and *Mercuralis perennis* and it is thought that it is found where relatively infertile soils coincide with hydrological and management conditions which restrict the other two species[20]. If drier conditions do become more prevalent in these woodlands, then it is possible that it could be at a competitive disadvantage. It is, however, a persistent species with genets possibly surviving for over 100 years, so provided there is woodland cover, it might still persist in the southern part of its range. It may also be adversely affected by increased temperatures, as germination is high after long, cold winters[28], although its main means of spread is by vegetative reproduction[19].

Sanicle is also thought to be susceptible to summer drought[29] and to burial by beech litter[20]. A long-term study (1943–1981) of *Sanicula europaea* on permanent plots in a forest and a wooded meadow in eastern Sweden has shown considerable variation in flowering frequency, part of which seems to be caused by summer droughts suppressing flowering the following season[29,30]. Also, because of the large reproductive effort expended in flowering it tends not to flower in the following year[30]. The increased incidence of summer droughts that is predicted in southern England therefore suggests that this species could be particularly adversely affected. Although no persistent seed banks have been recorded, the sporadic appearance of seedlings suggests that they may exist, which would enable the population to recover after dry summers.

Conclusions

Woodlands in Britain face a dynamic future and one that could lead to changes in their occurrence and character. The exact nature of these changes is difficult to predict, but even now forestry needs to take into account the potential future climate changes, while those concerned with more natural woodlands need to be aware of the potential changes in habitat composition and species' distributions. Beech woodland is vulnerable to climate change because of its potential impact on the dominant overstorey species, although the other modelled species do not appear susceptible to its direct impacts. In southeast England, beech woodland could decline on some of the driest soils and other, more drought resistant species such as oak, may increase their competitive ability. Provided some form of woodland cover is maintained, then wood anemone and sanicle could be less susceptible to the indirect effects of climate change, but in southeast England there are several additional factors which could lead to their decline.

References

1. IPCC (2001). *Climate change 2001: impacts, adaptations and vulnerability. Summary for policymakers*. Intergovernmental Panel on Climate Change. Cambridge University Press, Cambridge.

2. HUNTLEY, B., BARTLEIN, P.J. and PRENTICE, I.C. (1989). Climatic control on the distribution and abundance of beech in Europe and North America. *Journal of Biogeography* **16**, 551–560.

3. HUNTLEY, B., BERRY, P.M., CRAMER, W. and McDONALD, A.P. (1995). Modelling present and potential future ranges of some European higher plants using climate response

surfaces. *Journal of Biogeography* **22**, 967–1001.

4. SMITH, S. and GILBERT, J. (2001). *National Inventory of Woodland and Trees – England*. Forestry Commission, Edinburgh.

5. HARRISON, P.A., BERRY, P.M. and DAWSON, T.P., eds (2001). *Climate change and nature conservation in Britain and Ireland: modelling natural resource responses to climate change (the MONARCH project)*. UKCIP Technical Report. UK Climate Impacts Programme, Oxford.

6. RODWELL, J.S. (1991). *British plant communities*, volume 1: *woodlands and scrub*. Cambridge University Press, Cambridge.

7. RACKHAM, O. (1980). *Ancient woodland*. Arnold, London.

8. HOSSELL, J.E., BRIGGS, B. and HEPBURN, I.R. (2000). *Climate change and nature conservation: a review of the impact of climate change on UK species and habitat conservation policy*. HMSO, DETR and MAFF, London.

9. BERRY, P.M., HARRISON, P.A., DAWSON, T.P. and PEARSON, R. (2001). Integrated impacts on biodiversity. In: *Regional climate impact studies in East Anglia and North West England*, eds I. Holman and P. Loveland. Final Report to MAFF, DETR and UKWIR. Soil Survey and Land Research Centre, Silsoe, 192–265.

10. HULME, M. and JENKINS, G.J. (1998). *Climate change scenarios for the United Kingdom*. UKCIP Technical Report No. 1. Climatic Research Unit, University of East Anglia, Norwich.

11. HUNTLEY, B. and WEBB, T. (1989). Migration: species' response to climatic variations caused by changes in the earth's orbit. *Journal of Biogeography* **16**, 5–19.

12. HUNTLEY, B.B. and BIRKS, H.J.B. (1983). *An atlas of past and present pollen maps for Europe 0–13 000 years ago*. Cambridge University Press, Cambridge.

13. PRENTICE, I.C., SYKES, M.T. and CRAMER, W. (1991). The possible dynamic response of northern forests to global warming. *Global Ecology and Biogeography Letters* **1**, 129–135.

14. PETERKEN, G.F. and JONES, E.W. (1989). Forty years of change in Lady Park wood: the young growth stands. *Journal of Ecology* **77**, 401–429.

15. PETERKEN, G.F. and MOUNTFORD, E.P. (1996). Effects of drought on beech in Lady Park Wood, an unmanaged mixed deciduous woodland. *Forestry* **69**, 125–136.

16. PETERKEN, G.F. and JONES, E.W. (1987). Forty years of change in Lady Park wood: the old growth stands. *Journal of Ecology* **75**, 477–512.

17. STRIBLEY, G.H. and ASHMORE, M.R. (2002). Quantitative changes in twig growth pattern of young woodland beech (*Fagus sylvatica* L.) in relation to climate and ozone pollution over 10 years. *Forest Ecology and Management*, in press.

18. HEATH, J. and KERSTIENS, G. (1997). Effects of elevated CO_2 on leaf gas exchange in beech and oak at two levels of nutrient supply: consequences for sensitivity to drought in beech. *Plant, Cell and Environment* **20**, 57–67.

19. SHIRREFFS, D.A. (1985). *Anemone nemorosa* L. *Journal of Ecology* **73**, 1005–1020.

20. GRIME, J.P., HODGSON, J.G. and HUNT, R. (1988). *Comparative plant ecology*. Unwin Hyman, London.

21. BERRY, P.M., VANHINSBERGH, D., VILES, H.A., HARRISON, P.A., PEARSON, R.G., FULLER, R., BUTT, N. and MILLER, F. (2001). Impacts on terrestrial environments. In: *Climate change and nature conservation in Britain and Ireland: modelling natural resource responses to climate change (the MONARCH project)*, eds P.A. Harrison, P.M. Berry and T.P. Dawson. UKCIP Technical Report. UK Climate Impacts Programme, Oxford.

22. BERRY, P.M. and BUTT, N. (2002). Climate change impacts on raised peatbogs: a case study of Thorne, Crowle, Goole and Hatfield Moors. Report to English Nature.

23. CESCATTI, A. and PIUTTI, E. (1998). Silvicultural alternatives, competition regime and sensitivity to climate in a European beech forest. *Forest Ecology and Management* **102**, 213–223.

24. HILTON, G. M. and PACKHAM, J. R. (1997). A sixteen-year record of regional and temporal variation in the fruiting of beech (*Fagus sylvatica* L.) in England (1980–1995). *Forestry* **70**, 7–16.

25. SYKES, M.T., PRENTICE, I.C. and CRAMER, W. (1996). A bioclimatic model for the potential distributions of north European tree species under present and future climates. *Journal of Biogeography* **23**, 203–234.

26. PATERSON, J. (2000). Modelling potential distribution changes of European tree species in response to climate change and the consequences for W12 *Fagus sylvatica–Mercuralis perennis* woodland in south east England. MSc dissertation. Oxford Forestry Institute, University of Oxford, Oxford.

27. DAWSON, T. P., BERRY, P. M. and KAMPA, E. (2001). Impacts on freshwater environments. In: *Climate change and nature conservation in Britain and Ireland: modelling natural resource responses to climate change (the MONARCH project)*, eds P.A. Harrison, P.M. Berry and T.P. Dawson. UKCIP Technical Report. UK Climate Impacts Programme, Oxford.

28. ERNST, W.H.O. (1983). Population biology and mineral nutrition of *Anemone nemorosa* with emphasis on its parasitic fungi. *Flora* **173**, 335–348.

29. INGHE, O. and TAMM, C.O. (1985). Survival and flowering of perennial herbs: IV. The behaviour of *Hepatica nobilis* and *Sanicula europaea* on permanent plots during 1943–1981. *Oikos* **45**, 400–420.

30. INGHE, O. and TAMM, C.O. (1988). Survival and flowering of perennial herbs: V. Patterns of flowering. *Oikos* **51**, 203–219.

13 Challenges Ahead: How Should the Forestry Sector Respond?

In November 2000 the Government published *Climate Change: The UK Programme*[1] which sets out the strategic approach that the Government and the devolved administrations will take to tackling climate change. Forestry is covered in both the main text and in the contributions from the devolved administrations. The summary to the Programme lists 'protection and enhancement of forests' among the policies to deliver mitigation of climate change. This chapter expands on some of the implications for forestry and the global concerns about climate change.

The climate is changing

Global change

There is little doubt that the global environment is changing and that these changes are already impacting on climate. The causes of change are not known with certainty but international strategies and policies derive from the mounting scientific evidence[2] that man-made emissions of 'greenhouse gases' are having a significant effect on the earth's climate. The consequences of change predicted by the world's scientists[1] include:

- dieback of tropical forests by the 2070s in northern Brazil and central southern Africa because of increased temperatures and decreasing rainfall
- a rise in sea level by over 40 centimetres by the 2080s, putting 80 million people at risk of flooding – principally in south and southeast Asia
- significant reductions in cereal crop yields affecting food supplies in Africa, the Middle East and India
- exposure of an additional 290 million people to the risk of malaria following increases in temperature and changes in rainfall patterns, with China and central Asia likely to see the greatest increase in risk.

Changes in the UK

Impacts in the UK are expected to be potentially less destructive but are likely to extend to all aspects of the environment, society and the economy. The predicted climate changes are covered in detail in Chapter 2, and continuing research aims to refine and improve these predictions. At present the 'headline' indications are for:

- a rise in average temperatures (possibly a further 3°C by 2100)
- increased rainfall (by as much as 10% over England and Wales and 20% over Scotland by the 2080s)
- changes in seasonal rainfall patterns leading to wetter winters and autumns and, possibly, to drier summers in the south
- an increase in 'extreme events'.

'Extreme events' include heavy rainstorms, leading to increased flood risk, and possibly more gales, although this prediction is more uncertain in view of the great natural variability in the occurrence of storms.

The changes in climate in the UK are likely to threaten some familiar landscapes, habitats and species. The agricultural community may need to adapt farming systems and crops to changing temperature and rainfall patterns. As described in Chapter 5, soil quality may deteriorate under pressure from increased winter precipitation, droughts and erosion. Chapter 12 and the recently published results of the MONARCH study[3] show how the areas suited to some semi-natural habitats and native species may change. Some of these changes could have extremely deleterious effects on biodiversity where suitable areas decrease or species are unable to move.

On a more positive note, climate change could allow expansion of some species and bring benefits to forestry, some forms of agriculture and tourism. The main benefit for forestry is expected to come from increases in tree growth rates as a result not only of increased temperature but also of the rise in carbon dioxide concentration which is believed to be driving much of climate change (see Chapter 9). All green plants use carbon dioxide as a raw material of photosynthesis to build cell walls, wood and fibre.

However, alongside the possible overall benefits to forest growth, climate change may bring some potentially serious problems – such as increased risks from exotic pests and storm damage[4] as outlined in Chapters 4 and 8. As recent research reported in Chapter 11 shows, use of the Ecological Site Classification model[5] suggests that changes in climate may cause some forest trees to become less suitable for timber production on sites where they are currently planted. This implies a need for adaptation of current forestry practice.

The global response to a changing environment

Rio and Kyoto

International concerns about man-made changes to the environment led directly to the Earth Summit held in Rio de Janeiro in 1992. Among many valuable outcomes was The United Nations Framework Convention on Climate Change (UNFCCC). In 1997, the countries that had signed the Convention agreed the Kyoto Protocol, which is now the document that dominates discussion of climate change. The purpose of the Protocol is to mitigate climate change by setting out internationally agreed measures by which the concentration of greenhouse gases in the atmosphere can be stabilised or reduced. The Protocol will impose legally binding commitments on the industrialised nations that ratify it to reduce emissions of greenhouse gases.

The Protocol introduces mechanisms through which countries may co-operate in achieving their targets for emission reduction. The most far reaching of these is 'emission trading' which allows countries that have achieved emission reductions in excess of their target to sell the excess to countries finding it more difficult to meet their obligations. Many developed countries propose to allow individual businesses to participate in emission trading to help achieve national targets. The UK government and business leaders are well advanced in developing a UK emissions trading scheme to utilise the Kyoto mechanisms.

International debate on the mitigation of climate change has not been confined to consideration of emission reduction. The Protocol also recognises 'sequestration' as an additional means of reducing atmospheric carbon dioxide concentration. Sequestration is the process of removing carbon dioxide from the atmosphere into a 'sink'. Vegetation and soils serve as sinks, the former through carbon dioxide accumulation by photosynthetic activity and the latter through build up of organic matter. Forests are the greatest terrestrial sink because the accumulation of carbon in biomass is long-lived and their soils accumulate large amounts of organic matter if they are undisturbed.

Developed countries with a commitment under the Protocol to reduce emissions can offset some of the emissions by forestry activities that increase the amount of carbon dioxide taken up – *carbon offsets*. The forestry activities named in the Protocol are afforestation and reforestation (net of deforestation). Other activities in *land use, land use change and forestry* are referred to in the Protocol but are so far undefined. It should be noted in particular that the management of harvested wood, which has a major impact on the longevity of the carbon store and hence on the value of sequestration, is not dealt with specifically by the Protocol. Moreover, the rules and accounting procedures by which credits for emission reduction or sequestration may be awarded and traded have yet to be decided.

The role of forests

Reservoirs, sinks and sources

There is intense debate in the international community about the weight given to sequestration as a means of mitigation. Sinks are vulnerable to conversion to sources of carbon dioxide. In the case of forests, fire, clear-felling, and dieback from drought, pests or disease can all lead to the carbon in trees (and sometimes in the soil as well) being converted back to carbon dioxide. The UK

Government takes the view that reduction of emissions should be the principal policy response, given the vulnerability and uncertainties associated with sinks.

Nevertheless, forests and forestry can assist (although perhaps temporarily) in mitigating climate change by serving both as stores of carbon and as sinks to absorb and accumulate more carbon. Whatever approach is taken to sequestration, preservation and enhancement of the global forest sink is a vital part of international policy and is recognised in the Kyoto Protocol. Additionally, forests can make a direct contribution towards the reduction of emissions by providing a renewable resource that may be used to substitute for fossil fuels and more energy-demanding materials.

Forest management

Management practices can influence the scale of all the benefits that we derive from multifunctional forestry and the contribution that it can make to the mitigation of climate change is no exception. The UN Food and Agriculture Organisation's (FAO) report on the state of the world's forests[6] recognises three categories of management in relation to carbon.

Conservation management

Existing stocks of carbon in forests can be maintained through forest protection, conservation, and sustainable harvesting.

Storage management

Activities that increase carbon storage in forests and forest products include increasing the forest area, increasing the forest carbon stored per unit of area through silvicultural measures (such as longer rotations, increased tree stocking densities and reduced impact logging), and extending the time over which harvested wood remains in use.

Substitution management

There are two forms of substitution:

- Substituting wood fuel from sustainably managed forests for fossil fuels produces a carbon dioxide benefit. Emissions from biomass combustion are offset by biomass growth, and depletion of the carbon store in fossil fuels is avoided.
- Substituting wood products for more energy-demanding products, such as steel and concrete, can reduce the carbon dioxide emissions from the product manufacturing industries.

The FAO report[6] notes that the impact of these management practices will vary considerably in terms of their timing, scale and permanence. For example, the carbon dioxide benefits of forest conservation measures may be cancelled out if the forest is eventually burned or over-harvested, or if biomass storage in one forest area results in over-cutting in another area. Some environmental groups have expressed concern that a greater dependence on plantation forestry, driven by a climate change agenda, could lead to the neglect and possible loss of natural forests as they become less valuable.

There are obvious trade-offs among the three types of forest management strategy. For example, substitution management may be an optimal strategy where biomass growth rates are high and where the biomass displaces other high-emission fuels or products. These management strategies are not mutually exclusive and can be used in combination. The FAO report also notes that, as fossil fuel combustion accounts for the majority of carbon dioxide emissions globally (and will continue to do so in the future), the primary response for reducing net carbon dioxide emissions will have to come from controlling the release of fossil fuel carbon.

The FAO has concluded[6] that *'the long-term contribution of forests for mitigating climate change will be to provide renewable materials and fuels that reduce reliance on fossil fuels, while still maintaining the role of forests as carbon reservoirs'*. Against this background, there may be opportunities within the forestry sector to reduce net carbon dioxide emissions through forest management practices which also have wider environmental benefits. For example, measures that reduce ground disturbance serve to protect soil and water resources as well as to reduce emissions of carbon dioxide from mineralisation of soil. Silvicultural systems that maintain tree cover and increase the biological diversity of the forest may also enhance the capacity and longevity of the carbon store.

How should the UK forestry sector respond?

Coping with change

Coping with change in the forestry sector is nothing new. At present it seems unlikely that climate change will impose a greater need for adaptability than any other changes that have taken place in recent years – for example, a much greater emphasis on the environmental and social functions of forests, falling timber prices, forest certification. While global atmospheric and climate changes are likely to alter the environment in which our trees grow, the magnitude of the changes and the speed with which they might happen are uncertain. We cannot even be sure whether, overall, the changes will be beneficial or detrimental. Adaptation strategies by the forestry sector need to be based on reliable information. We must therefore support research to reduce the uncertainties, and be prepared to act on its results. We should seize opportunities where forestry can contribute to national strategies (as in the provision of renewable energy), adopt 'no regrets' or 'low regrets' measures wherever we can, and co-ordinate actions with others outside our sector.

Research

The Government is collaborating with other countries in further research and contributes to the continuing work of the Intergovernmental Panel on Climate Change (IPCC). Sponsored by the World Meteorological Organisation and the United Nations Environment Programme, the IPCC organises the preparation of detailed scientific assessments covering all aspects of climate change. The Intergovernmental Panel on Climate Change has produced a special report on *'Land Use, Land Use Change and Forestry'* [7]. It has also published three major assessments of climate change in 1990, 1995 and 2001 [8-10].

Closer to home, research into the effects of climate change on forests is being carried out by universities, the Centre for Ecology and Hydrology, the Forestry Commission and others. The Forestry Commission's research programme includes:

- investigation of carbon sequestration by forests under different management regimes;
- means to predict the impact of environmental and climatic change on tree growth and condition;
- work to improve understanding of the impacts of forests on the environment, for example on soil and water resources.

Research on regional impacts across a range of sectors, including forestry, has been co-ordinated by the UK Climate Impacts Programme (UKCIP), which is sponsored by the Department for Environment, Food and Rural Affairs (DEFRA). As the lead UK department on climate change, DEFRA provides the principal interface between UK policy and research into all aspects of climate change.

Joined-up working

The forestry sector is used to working closely with others. 'Joined-up' approaches – not only within government – are even more important if we are to understand, respond to and mitigate climate change. Co-operation is already happening at the highest levels, as shown by the substantial international agreement achieved through the UN Framework Convention on Climate Change and the Kyoto Protocol.

The Forestry Commission and the forest industry need to continue to work together with other interests. The Forestry Commission is already working closely with DEFRA and with a range of other departments and agencies in the UK and the devolved administrations.

Forestry in the UK needs to be outward-looking and to consider the impacts that forests have on people in a changing global environment. The role of forestry in contributing to the Government's wider aims for sustainable development should not be underestimated. In its UK Strategy for Sustainable Development, *A Better Quality of Life*, published in 1999[11], the Government identified four objectives that need to be addressed in order to achieve sustainable development:

- social progress which recognises the needs of everyone
- effective protection of the environment
- prudent use of natural resources
- maintenance of high and stable levels of economic growth and employment.

Forestry can, and should, deliver on all these in a variety of ways.

Renewable energy

UK energy policy proposes that 5% of electricity requirements should be met from renewable sources of energy by the end of 2003, and 10% by 2010 (subject to the cost to consumers being reasonable). Regional renewable energy assessments should set the framework for a more strategic land use planning approach at regional level. This would provide the framework for decisions on individual renewable energy projects.

One of the most effective ways for forestry and agriculture to contribute to reductions in greenhouse gas emissions is through the production of biomass as a source of renewable energy. Although the burning of biomass produces carbon dioxide, it is recycled into further plant growth. The Government and devolved administrations are exploring ways of encouraging renewable energy generated from wood fuel, forest residues and energy crops. Currently, the most suitable energy crop for UK conditions is short-rotation willow coppice. It is technically ready for use, and the UK Climate Change Programme notes that 125 000 hectares of coppice for biofuel could deliver a significant part of the target to provide 10% of the UK's electricity supplies from renewables.

Under the Rural Development Plan for England, the Government introduced a new Energy Crops Scheme that will provide support for the establishment of short rotation coppice and for setting up short rotation coppice producer groups. The scheme will be accessed through the regional organisation of DEFRA and is being developed in partnership with the Forestry Commission. The Forestry Commission is already targeting grant support to stimulate plantings for project ARBRE in Yorkshire (the first wood-fuelled power station in Britain). One of the beneficial side-effects of project ARBRE has been an increased demand for forest residues and small dimension roundwood, which can help to finance woodland management.

The forestry sector needs to look carefully at the wood fuel opportunities in traditional forestry. As the UK Climate Change Programme recognises, wood is a versatile energy source that can be used in a wide range of situations, for example in domestic wood-burning stoves, industrial CHP plants and co-firing existing coal-fired stations. Novel technologies, such as gasification and pyrolysis, have been developed to utilise it as fuel. Sources may be whole trees, including small trees removed when woods are thinned, or branches, foliage and tops of trees felled for timber. Suitable material is potentially available from all parts of the UK. For example, a stable market for fuel wood would assist the sustainable management of currently undermanaged or derelict woods in the south of England and improve commercial conifer plantations in Scotland where timber production is set to double over the next 15–20 years.

The Government will work with a wide range of stakeholders to promote the utilisation of wood as fuel. The existing UK commitment to sustainable management of woodland will ensure that increased energy generation from wood has no effect on the overall carbon dioxide balance.

Carbon offset

A growing number of companies are showing interest in planting trees to help mitigate climate change. Such schemes have the potential to help the UK meet its climate change targets. They might also play a role in raising awareness among companies and individuals of their contribution to climate change, as well as offering them an attractive way of responding.

Nevertheless, the Government remains convinced that the UK's priority should be emission reductions rather than carbon sequestration because of the complexities and uncertainties involved with carbon sinks. For the time being at least, forestry projects are unlikely to be eligible under the UK emission trading scheme, though they may be included at a later stage. Rigorous long-term monitoring and verification of forestry projects would be crucial if they are to provide a credible source of tradable credits.

Under the Kyoto Protocol, the UK will receive allowances for woodland expansion by afforestation and reforestation. The contribution will be small, but important, because it flows from 'no regrets' policies. That is, we know we will get all the other benefits from forestry, and the carbon saving is 'icing on the cake'. In Scotland, the contribution of forestry will be considerably more significant than for the UK as a whole.

The UK has policies in place to protect and enhance forests and continues to support the planting of new woodlands. Under the UN Framework Convention on Climate Change the UK is committed to protect and enhance greenhouse gas sinks and reservoirs in general. *Climate Change: The UK Programme*[1] notes that this commitment should be interpreted widely and can include, for example, soil carbon stocks and the timber product pool. Because timber used in construction locks up carbon for very long periods, policies that encourage proper consideration of timber as an alternative to other materials can also maximise the value of the forest sink. Moreover, the energy characteristics of timber are extremely favourable compared to the high energy requirements for materials such as steel, concrete and plastics. Substitution of these products by timber can help to reduce actual emissions of carbon dioxide. We will promote tree planting and greater use of wood as a renewable material as ways in which everyone can contribute to mitigating climate change.

Forest planning

Our forest management planning methods already take account of change in the external environment. For example, current measures include assessments of the risk of wind damage which are then built into forest management and design plans[12]. Such measures can be modified to take account of new information and our forest management planning will increasingly need to take account of the potential impacts of climate change – on water supply and protection of threatened habitats, for example. These requirements emphasise the need for 'joined-up' approaches.

A sense of perspective

Climate change is a matter of global concern and there is wide international agreement that forests make an important contribution to storing and recycling carbon. Given the uncertainties about the full impacts of climate change it is important that we keep a sense of perspective in considering the response of the forestry sector. Nevertheless, the information and research results presented in this Bulletin are good reasons for forest managers and planners to take the implications of climate change seriously.

The European Union's forestry strategy, published in 1999[13], sets out a range of Community actions concerning forests and forestry. This states that *the role of forests as carbon sinks and reservoirs within the European Union can be best ensured through sustainable forest management and that the contribution to the European Union and Member States' climate change strategies, is in accordance with the Kyoto Protocol, and can best be achieved through the protection and enhancement of existing carbon stocks, the establishment of new carbon stocks and encouragement of the use of biomass and wood-based products*'. All of those are, of course, main elements of UK policy for the sustainable management of forests.

While our forests are very small in global terms, they do have a role in meeting a part of the Government's policies for managing net carbon dioxide emissions. And, although the UK's total emissions represent only a small proportion of the world's total greenhouse gas emissions, as a developed country our emissions per head of population are much higher than the global average. As the UK Climate Change Programme recognises, 'the burden of responsibility at the moment is on the developed countries to lead by example ...'.

We will not be practising single-purpose forestry – whether for carbon-fixing or any other purpose – at the expense of sustainable forest management as set out in the Government's *UK Forestry Standard*[14]. The underlying principles of multi-purpose forestry and sustainability become even more important as a survival strategy in responding to a changing world.

References

1. DETR (2000). *Climate change: the UK programme*. The Stationery Office, London.
2. IPCC (2001). *Climate change 2001: impacts, adaptations and vulnerability. Summary for policymakers*. Intergovernmental Panel on Climate Change. Cambridge University Press, Cambridge.
3. HARRISON, P.A., BERRY, P.M. and DAWSON, T.P., eds (2001). *Climate change and nature conservation in Britain and Ireland: modelling natural resource responses to climate change (the MONARCH project)*. UKCIP Technical Report. UK Climate Impacts Programme, Oxford.
4. BROADMEADOW, M.S.J. (2000). *Climate change – implications for UK forestry*. Forestry Commission Information Note 31. Forestry Commission, Edinburgh.
5. FORESTRY COMMISSION (2001). *Ecological site classification: A PC-based decision support system for British Forests*. Forestry Commission, Edinburgh.
6. FAO (1999). *State of the world's forests*, 3rd edn. Food and Agriculture Organisation, Rome.
7. IPCC (2000). *Land use, land use change and forestry*, eds R.T. Watson, I.R. Noble, B. Bolin, N.H. Ravindranath, D.J. Verardo and D.J. Dokken. Cambridge University Press, Cambridge.
8. IPCC (1990). *Climate change: the scientific assessment*, eds J.T. Houghton, G.J. Jenkins and J.J. Ephraums. Cambridge University Press, Cambridge.
9. IPCC (1995). *Climate change 1994: radiative forcing of climate change and an evaluation of*

the IPCC IS92 emission scenarios, eds J.T. Houghton, L.G. Meira Filho, J. Bruce, H. Lee, B.A. Callander, E. Haites, N. Harris and K. Maskell. Cambridge University Press, Cambridge.

10. IPCC (2001). *Climate change 2001: the scientific basis.* IPCC Third Assessment Report, WGI. IPCC, Geneva.

11. DETR (1999). *A better quality of life: a strategy for sustainable development for the United Kingdom.* The Stationery Office, London.

12. FORESTRY COMMISSION (2000). *ForestGALES: a PC-based wind risk model for British forests.* Forestry Commission, Edinburgh.

13. EU (1999). European forestry strategy. Council resolution of 15 December 1998 on a forestry Strategy for the European Union (1999/C 56/01).

14. FORESTRY COMMISSION (1998). *The UK forestry standard: the government's approach to sustainable forestry.* Forestry Commission, Edinburgh.

APPENDIX ONE

ICF Position Statement on Climate Change

'As we start this new century we know that, unless everyone fights to counteract the worst effects of climate change, people all over the world face more frequent severe weather conditions, rising sea levels and devastating floods, together with their growing economic and human costs.'

The Rt Hon John Prescott MP
Deputy Prime Minister
(UK Climate Change Programme Consultation, 2000)

Earlier this year, the Institute of Chartered Foresters held a National Conference on Climate Change and Trees. The Conference was addressed by the leading UK authorities on climate change. The Conference considered the latest trends and predictions for the UK; the implications of climate change on our soils and water and the balance of land use; the impacts on our native woodland and the flora and fauna; the impacts through storms, temperature extremes, and through the potential spread of new pests and diseases. The Conference looked at the impact of climate change on the growth of our trees; on the storage of carbon in trees and forests; and on the potential of wood as a source of renewable energy. The Conference heard from Government about its Climate Change Strategy, considered the role of forestry in carbon credit schemes and, finally, discussed ways in which the forestry sector should respond.

Conference findings

Some of the key information presented to the Conference is set out below. Delegates used the information to consider the wider implications of climate change on trees and forests in the UK. The Institute of Chartered Foresters has prepared a Position Statement based on the information presented and the discussion at the Conference (page 198).

Temperatures are rising

- Global temperatures rose by 5°C over the last 15 000 years, and by about 0.6°C over the 20th century. Average annual temperatures are predicted to rise by a further 3°C by 2100.
- In England, the 1990s experienced four out of five warmest years in a 340-year record, 1999 being the joint warmest year ever recorded.
- February to March warming is pronounced in the UK, increasing by 1.0–1.5°C over the last 100 years. Autumn temperatures have also risen markedly. Spring has advanced by at least two weeks over the last 50 years.

Rainfall patterns are changing

- In north Scotland annual precipitation is predicted to increase by 16% by 2080, with a summer increase of 5%.
- In Southeast England, annual precipitation is predicted to increase by 5% by 2080, but with a summer decrease of 16%.
- An increase in heavy rainfall events in winter is expected.

Carbon dioxide concentrations in the atmosphere are increasing. Atmospheric CO_2 concentrations were 280 parts per million (ppm) in the pre-industrial mid-18th century. They are 370 ppm now, with a concentration of 700 ppm predicted by 2100.

Implications and consequences

Soil, air and water

- Sea level is rising by 5 mm per year (and some predict catastrophic rises due to thermohaline collapse or collapse of the West Antarctic ice sheet).

- River floods and erosion events will increase.
- Drought induced clay shrinkage and subsidence damage will increase.
- Water resources will become more limited during the summer in the south and east.
- Higher temperatures may lead to poorer local air quality, especially in the summer.
- The risk of fires in the south will increase.

Ecology and ecophysiology

The impact of climate change on ecosystems and their constituent species are a matter of much conjecture but some examples give an indication of likely impacts and trends:

- Ecological zones will shift northward, but many woodland species have limited opportunity to respond due to habitat fragmentation. This is particularly critical in the UK as many species are on the edge of their ranges. A European study of 57 butterfly species over the 20th century has shown a general movement in ranges northwards and upwards. Changes in the distribution of the speckled wood butterfly have been slower than expected, probably due to woodland fragmentation.
- Flowering and emergence times are advancing and asynchrony of dependent species may be affected. Examples include insect availability for newly hatched birds and flower availability for nectar loving insects.
- The average growing season in Europe is extending, already by 10.8 days over the past 30 years.
- Improved over-winter survival is increasing the impact of deer. For example, at Monks Wood, dog's mercury cover has been reduced from over 30% to less than 1% as a result of grazing by muntjac deer.
- Changing rainfall patterns may be affecting species such as Capercaillie, whose chicks are vulnerable to spring rainfall.

Woodlands and trees

Climate change is beginning to manifest itself in tree health, species distribution and silvicultural suitability:

- Heat and drought damage will increase in the south and east, especially on beech, larch, hedgerow and urban trees.
- Top-dying of Norway spruce is increasing in England due, it is thought, to summer drought.
- Milder springs and autumns, ironically, may increase vulnerability to frost damage, particularly from autumn frosts in the south.
- Some models predict that substantial areas of the south and east will become too dry for beech.
- The zone of climatic suitability for native pinewoods will contract.
- The spread of some introduced woody species such as black cherry, downy oak and holm oak is likely to accelerate.

Pests and diseases

Climate change is likely to affect the relationship between pests, diseases and their hosts. Some pests and diseases may increase in impact directly due to climate change, for example:

- The dispersal potential of *Dendroctonus micans* (great spruce bark beetle) increases with temperature as flight temperature thresholds are more frequently exceeded.
- *Hylobius abietis* (pine weevil) could be favoured by climate warming.
- Enhanced over-winter survival of deer and grey squirrels will make population increase and range expansion more rapid.
- Some pests and diseases may increasingly exploit trees stressed by climate change, for example *Elatobium abietinum* (green spruce aphid) is predicted to increase in

impact as drought conditions increase the moisture stress that favours it. Infestation can lead to as much as a 20% yield reduction in spruce.

- Some existing minor pests may increase in impact due to climatic release from predators, for example spruce budworm is increasing in impact in parts of the USA due to climate change making conditions less suitable for parasitoids.
- Some non-indigenous pests may become a greater potential threat to the UK, for example pinewood nematode which is limited by mean summer temperature, gypsy moth and Asian longhorn beetle.
- Some impacts may increase as species choice responds to climate change, for example *Brunchorstia pinea* die-back may increase as the range of Corsican pine is expanded to substitute for declining Norway spruce.

Tree growth

Increasing atmospheric CO_2 concentrations is resulting in the 'CO_2 fertilisation effect'. An increase in atmospheric concentrations to 700 ppm could increase tree growth rates by 20% where not limited by consequent moisture stress.

Land use

Impacts on food markets and shifts in agricultural production could out-weigh direct impacts on forestry through shifts in optimal site types for major crop species, pressure on national and global food production capacity, and via land use subsidy systems.

The role of trees and forests in the UK policy framework

The United Nations Framework Convention on Climate Change and the 1997 International Kyoto Protocol are the basis for international co-operation on climate change. Additionally, the European Union's Forestry Strategy, published in 1999, considers the issue and states that '*the role of forests as carbon sinks and reservoirs within the European Union can be best ensured through sustainable forest management and that the contribution to the European Union and Member States' climate change strategies, in accordance with the Kyoto Protocol, can best be achieved through the protection and enhancement of existing carbon stocks, the establishment of new carbon stocks and encouragement of the use of biomass and wood-based products*'.

UK Government policy is to achieve a CO_2 emission reduction of 20% below 1990 levels by 2010. This goal will be achieved largely through cutting emissions from the burning of fossil fuels, but trees may have a role to play:

- In sequestering carbon.
- As a source of renewable energy.
- As a means of reducing energy use in urban areas.

The UK Government will introduce a Climate Change Levy in 2001, effectively taxing high CO_2 emission activities. In December 1999 the Government announced its intention to commit £30 million of levy revenue to energy crops over the life of the new Rural Development Regulation. This will contribute to the Government's target of meeting 10% of UK electricity demand from renewables by 2010.

Carbon sequestration

Forests play a significant role in moderating the net flux of greenhouse gases between the land and the atmosphere. They can serve in three ways, as:

- **Reservoirs:** by storing carbon in biomass and soils.
- **Sinks:** when the area or productivity is

increased, forests take up additional atmospheric CO_2.

- **Sources:** when the burning or decay of biomass and disturbance of forest soils result in emissions of greenhouse gases (global deforestation accounts for up to 20% of anthropogenic CO_2 emissions). Afforestation of peaty soils can lead to a net emission of CO_2 as improved soil aeration leads to peat oxidation.

Forest management practices can slow the accumulation of carbon dioxide in the atmosphere. The UN Food and Agriculture Organisation's (FAO) report *State of the World's Forests 1999*, groups these practices into three categories:

- **Conservation management:** retaining existing carbon reservoirs through forest conservation and sustainable harvesting. Increasing productivity on existing agricultural land can reduce the rate of deforestation and forest degradation and prevent associated CO_2 emissions.
- **Storage management:** developing sinks by increasing the forest area, increasing the forest carbon stored per unit of area through silvicultural measures (such as longer rotations, increased tree stocking densities and reduced impact logging), and extending the time over which harvested wood remains in use.
- **Substitution management:** there are two forms of substitution – substituting fuelwood from sustainably managed forests for fossil fuels, and substituting wood products for more energy-demanding products, such as steel, concrete and plastics.

It is generally agreed that in the UK, afforestation with the sole aim of carbon sequestration is not viable as a major mitigating measure (just one year of UK CO_2 emissions, if stored in forests, would occupy all of Devon and Cornwall!). However, increased woodland cover for social, conservation and economic reasons will also bring carbon sequestration benefits in the short and medium term.

The concept of carbon credits is gaining currency, whereby businesses offset the CO_2 they produce by engaging in CO_2 saving or sequestering activities, or by purchasing carbon credits. The concept may be attractive, but raises certain issues and problems in terms of:

- The permanence of sequestered carbon.
- Additionality: would it have happened anyway?
- Leakage: will more trees here result in fewer trees elsewhere?

The Government is currently considering whether such schemes should be permitted within a domestic carbon-trading scheme and, clearly, opportunity exists for foresters to engage with CO_2 producing enterprises which are keen to become involved with activities that contribute to the environment.

Energy crops

Wood fuel is as clean as natural gas and has low sulphur and oxides of nitrogen (NO_X) emissions. A large coal fired power station uses 3 kilowatt-hours (kW h) of fossil fuel energy to generate 1 kW h of electricity. The generation of 1 kW h of electricity from wood requires only 0.25 kW h of fossil fuel energy for both forest residues and short rotation coppice. Clearly, energy crops and use of wood residues have good potential to save carbon dioxide emissions when they substitute for fossil fuels. They are technically ready to be used in the UK with the most likely crops being short rotation willow or poplar coppice and the grass *Miscanthus*. It is estimated that 125 000 hectares could deliver a significant fraction of the 10% Government Renewables Obligation. The ARBRE eight-megawatt power station currently in commission in Yorkshire is the first large-scale facility to be entirely dependent on wood residues and energy coppice.

Urban trees

Climate warming will be particularly felt in cities where the 'urban heat island' effect increases temperatures compared to rural areas. Shade trees will take on an increasingly important role for pedestrians and for some types of building. Furthermore, as trees can demonstrably improve the micro-climate around buildings and reduce heating costs, they should increasingly become a consideration in efforts to improve energy use efficiency.

Storms, floods and subsidence are the UK's greatest natural insurance risks, and are likely to increase in severity and incidence. Trees and woodlands have the potential to mitigate the impact of flash floods, if combined with appropriate planning and management of flood plains and the upper reaches of vulnerable catchments. On the down side, climate warming and increased summer drought in the south may further increase the impact of trees on the subsidence of shrinkable clays.

How should the forestry profession respond?

Given the uncertainties about the future scale and impacts of climate change there is no definitive guidance on how forestry practices should be adapted to respond to climate change. The ICF 2000 National Conference identified some aspects and directions that need consideration by policy makers and by the profession.

Woodland conservation

The impacts of climate change on woodland species and ecosystems is uncertain. Fundamental questions on conservation policy and strategy need consideration:

- Nature conservation policy in the UK is largely based on the protection of designated sites. The Conference was convinced of the need to counterbalance this approach with a strengthening of countryside-wide strategies that allow species and ecosystems to adjust to climate change both in terms of geography and composition. The fundamental wisdom of the habitat network concept is further strengthened by climate change and should be applied on a variety of scales. The Conference was asked: '*Do we act as wildlife gardeners holding back the tide? Or do we accept change and define space in which it can take place?*'
- Climate change may force a reconsideration of policy towards species at the limit of their range. How much should be invested in trying to retain species for which the UK climate has become unsuitable, either due to underlying climate trends or due to the impact of extreme events?

Forest planning

- Professional foresters are accustomed to integrating site and climatic factors into forest planning processes. The tools to facilitate integration are becoming increasingly available such as, for example, Geographical Information Systems (GIS), ForestGALES (a probabilistic windthrow risk prediction tool) and Ecological Site Classification decision support systems.
- However, foresters must increasingly take into account predicted future climate in making long-term decisions about species choice and management systems. In the face of uncertainty over climate change, the precautionary principle suggests a continued diversification of the species and age structure of forests, where opportunity allows, to 'spread' the risk of direct climate change impacts and those that may come as

a result of the spread of new pests and diseases. In some circumstances, growing trees on short rotations may help to 'keep in step' with climate changes, in others, growing trees for longer may sequester more carbon. Increased temperatures may result in more reliable seeding allowing increased reliance on natural regeneration and continuous cover silvicultural systems.

Species choice and provenance

- The Conference identified situations where species choice may be influenced by climate change. An example of this is beech, which may no longer be suitable for sites in the southeast, if predictions of reduced rainfall are accurate.
- The Conference recommended against use of more southerly provenances of Sitka spruce to exploit climate warming, due to uncertainty over unseasonal frosts and extreme cold events.
- Introduced species with a narrow genetic base may be more vulnerable to climate change than naturally regenerated native species, as their ecological amplitude (ability of a population to tolerate a range of conditions) may be narrower.

Arboricultural and silvicultural practices

- Professional foresters and arborists are accustomed to growing trees on difficult sites, be they agriculturally marginal, in extreme wind climates, or in the urban environment. The Conference concluded that through use of best practice we can mitigate some of the impacts of climate trends such as increased wetness or drought on forestry and arboricultural practices, particularly as many of the changes are expected to fall within the natural variation of the UK climate.

Research

Climate change modelling and scenario testing are major international fields of research which are, on the whole, well funded. However, the implications of some of the climate change scenarios on forestry and woodland ecosystems are largely unresearched. The Conference identified the following priorities for research:

- Predicting the impact of climate change on pests and diseases, including the likely arrival of new pathogens, climatic release of existing low-impact pathogens, and the effects on predator, pest and host relationships which might influence the impact of pests and diseases. Contingency plans should be developed against the spread of new pests and diseases.
- The ability to model and predict the ecological requirements of woodland species is growing. However, this effort must be expanded into a greater number of declining plant and animal species, and the impact of climate change as well as habitat fragmentation incorporated into modelling efforts. Mitigation proposals must then be developed and action plans prepared for their implementation. The English Nature led MONARCH[a] project is an important step in the right direction, but a small step in comparison with the magnitude of the issue.
- The same modelling tools can be adapted to evaluate the risks of climatic release of introduced species in order that action on potentially pernicious species can be taken before they become difficult to control.
- Ecological Site Classification is becoming an important tool in ecologically based forestry. This tool should be developed to allow foresters to examine the likely impact of climate change on different tree species suitability.

[a]Modelling Natural Resource Responses to Climate Change.

- Information is needed on the likely contribution of CO_2 fertilisation to the productivity and economic sustainability of UK forests.
- Water resource management in the light of climate change will be a major area of research. The impacts and mitigating potential of trees, both where water resources are limited and where peak flows bring increased flooding risk, should form part of this consideration.

A more precise quantification is required of the potential contribution of trees to the improvement and protection of our towns and cities. This will help urban foresters to engage with planners to improve the functional effectiveness of trees in the urban environment.

The Institute of Chartered Foresters

POSITION STATEMENT ON CLIMATE CHANGE

The Institute of Chartered Foresters (ICF) has prepared this Position Statement following consideration of the papers presented at the Institute's National Conference 2000 on Climate Change and Trees:

1. The ICF recognises the fundamental impact that climate change is having, and is likely to have, on the global and UK environment.

2. The ICF believes that trees and forests have an important role to play in mitigating global climate change through:

   - Conservation of existing carbon stocks in forests.
   - Sequestration of atmospheric carbon through afforestation, as well as increasing carbon stocks in forest biomass and soils through sustainable forest management practices.
   - Substitution of wood in place of fossil fuels.
   - Substitution of wood in place of more energy intensive construction materials such as steel, concrete and plastics.

3. The ICF draws attention to the role that urban trees can serve in and around settlements in mitigating climate change impacts such as increased temperatures and peak river flows, as well as increasing energy use efficiency in certain types of building.

4. The ICF urges government conservation agencies and non-governmental organisations to review conservation policy and strategy in the light of climate change predictions for the UK. This may involve abandoning some species and accepting responsibilities for others displaced from elsewhere.

5. The ICF is concerned that climate change may increase the risk of new pests and diseases becoming problematic in the UK and recommends that, on the basis of sound research, contingency strategies are drawn up for species and areas perceived to be most at risk.

6. The ICF commends to research fund holders the research priorities set out in this document.

7. The ICF advises foresters and arborists to stay well informed of what is happening to our climate, and how this is likely to affect the biological and policy environment. In the light of this information, foresters and arborists are encouraged to:

   - Consider changes in management practices in response to climate trends and impacts.
   - Be aware of the likely impacts of climate change on woodland species and ecosystems.
   - Engage with other interests in ensuring that trees and forests play a full role in the UK in mitigating the damaging impacts of climate change.

Institute of Chartered Foresters
November 2000